Economics
for Health Care
Management

Matthew F

Classificat

Economics for Health Care Management

ANN CLEWER AND DAVID PERKINS

UNIVERSITY OF KENT AT CANTERBURY

PRENTICE HALL

LONDON ■ NEW YORK ■ TORONTO ■ SYDNEY ■ TOKYO ■ SINGAPORE

MADRID ■ MEXICO CITY ■ MUNICH ■ PARIS

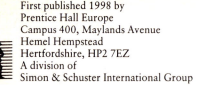

First published 1998 by
Prentice Hall Europe
Campus 400, Maylands Avenue
Hemel Hempstead
Hertfordshire, HP2 7EZ
A division of
Simon & Schuster International Group

Typeset in 9½/12pt Sabon by Hands Fotoset, Ratby, Leicestershire

Printed and bound in Great Britain by
Redwood Books, Trowbridge, Wiltshire

Library of Congress Cataloging-in-Publication Data

Available from the publisher

British Library Cataloguing in Publication Data

A catalogue record for this book is available from
the British Library

ISBN 0-13-209461-4

1 2 3 4 5   02 01 00 99 98

Contents

Introduction   xi

1. The basic economic questions   1
    Introduction   1
    1.1 Health care and health   5
        What is health?   6
        The costs of poor health   6
    1.2 Demand for health care   7
    1.3 Production of health   7
    1.4 Requirements of health services   8
        Economy   8
        Effectiveness   8
        Efficiency   8
        Value for money   9
        Equity   9
        Ethical issues   10
    1.5 Health care and economics   10
    1.6 Economics and management   12
    References   12
    Questions for consideration   13

2. Basic economic concepts   15
    Introduction   15
    2.1 Scarcity and choice   16
    2.2 Opportunity cost   17
    2.3 Economic choices   17
        How are decisions to be made?   18
        The best use of resources   21

2.4 Conclusion   23
References   23
Questions for consideration   24

3.   Efficiency   25
Introduction   25
3.1 Aspects of efficiency   26
     Productive efficiency   26
     Technical efficiency   26
     Effectiveness and efficiency   27
     Allocative efficiency   29
     Social efficiency   29
     Distribution of output   29
3.2 Efficiency and externalities   31
3.3 Efficiency in health care systems   32
3.4 Measuring efficiency in the NHS   34
3.5 Value for money and efficiency   36
3.6 Summary of efficiency measures   36
Appendix: Calculation of measures of bed utilization   37
References   39
Questions for consideration   40

4.   Introduction to demand and supply analysis   42
Introduction   42
4.1 Demand   43
     Types of products   43
     Assumptions about consumers   43
     Factors determining demand   44
4.2 Supply   49
     Factors determining supply   50
4.3 Demand and supply in health care   52
4.4 Elasticity   53
     Price elasticity of demand   54
     Factors affecting the value of the price elasticity of demand   55
     Price elasticity and revenue   56
References   58
Questions for consideration   58

5.   The determination of price   60
Introduction   60
5.1 The determination of price   60
5.2 The effect of price restrictions   62
     Effect of a maximum price   62
     Effect of a minimum price   65

5.3 The effect of changes in the conditions of demand and supply   65
5.4 The price mechanism and the allocation of resources   67
5.5 The determination of prices and the price mechanism in health care   68
References   69
Questions for consideration   69

6. The economic analysis of production   71
Introduction   71
6.1 The production function   71
     Examples of the use of production function analysis in health care   72
     Example of the use of production functions in social care   72
     Average and marginal product   73
     The short run in economic analysis   73
     The law of diminishing marginal returns   74
     The long run in economic analysis   76
     Substitutability of inputs   76
     Varying the skill-mix   79
6.2 Returns to scale   80
6.3 Measurement of output in health care   81
     Average and marginal product   82
     Returns to scale   83
     Substitution of inputs   83
References   84
Questions for consideration   84

7. The economic analysis of costs   85
Introduction   85
7.1 The classification of costs   85
     Fixed costs   85
     Variable costs   86
     Semi-variable costs   86
7.2 Direct and indirect costs   87
7.3 Allocation of indirect costs   87
7.4 Total, average and marginal cost   88
7.5 Short-run cost curves   89
     The total cost curve   89
     Total fixed costs and marginal cost   89
     The average cost curves   91
     Average cost and marginal cost   91
7.6 Marginal cost and decision-making   94
     Costs and pricing   97
7.7 Long-run costs   99
     Economies of scale   99
     The long-run average cost curve   100

	Economies of scope	102
7.8	Other cost concepts	103
	Sunk costs	103
	Incremental costs	103
	Historical costs	103
7.9	Estimating cost functions	104
	References	104
	Questions for consideration	105

8. Marginal analysis   107

	Introduction	107
8.1	Marginal analysis and efficiency	108
8.2	Marginal analysis and revenue maximization	111
	Total, average and marginal revenue	111
8.3	Marginal analysis and employment	112
8.4	Marginal analysis and profit maximization	114
8.5	Marginal analysis and maximization of output subject to a minimum profit constraint	114
8.6	Marginal analysis and isoquants	116
	The marginal rate of technical substitution (MRTS)	116
8.7	Marginal analysis and the optimal combination of outputs	117
	Summary of chapter results	119
	References	119

9. Market structures   120

	Introduction	120
9.1	Market structures	121
	Buyers and sellers	121
	Product	121
	Information	122
	Barriers to entry and exit	122
9.2	Types of market structure	123
	Perfect competition	123
	Monopoly	124
	Monopolistic competition	125
	Monopsony	125
	Bilateral monopoly	126
	Oligopoly	127
9.3	Quasi-markets	127
	Efficiency	127
	Responsiveness	127
	Choice	128
	Equity	128
9.4	Market failure	128

	Market structure	128
	Information problems	131
	Transaction costs and uncertainty	132
	Objectives	133
	Externalities	133
	Mobility of factors of production	133
9.5	Markets and hierarchies	133
9.6	Transaction cost economics	134
	The nature of transaction costs	134
	The assumptions of transaction cost economics	134
	Dimensions of transactions	135
	Market or organization?	135
9.7	Contracts	136
	Types of contract	136
	Forms of contract in the health service	137
	Features of types of contract	138
	References	139
	Questions for consideration	140

10. The firm and its objectives 142

	Introduction	142
10.1	Alternatives to profit maximization as an objective of the firm	143
10.2	Hospital objectives	144
10.3	Other health care providers	147
	References	149

11. Measurement and valuation in health care 150

	Introduction	150
11.1	Health status measurement	151
11.2	Scales of measurement	151
	Ordinal scales	152
	Cardinal scales	152
	Measures of health status	153
11.3	Health profiles	154
	Nottingham health profile	154
11.4	Valuation in health care	155
11.5	Attempts to identify shared values	156
	Quality-adjusted life years	156
11.6	Matrix of illness state ratings	157
	Making decisions about treatment	160
	Common values	161
	References	162
	Questions for consideration	163

12. Financial analysis and economic appraisal   166

Introduction   166

12.1   Decision rules in financial analysis   167

    Net present value   167

    The net benefit investment ratio   168

    The internal rate of return   168

    The benefit–cost ratio   169

12.2   Economic appraisal   169

    Types of analysis   170

12.3   Why not leave it to the market?   170

    Social efficiency   171

    Measuring benefits in money terms   172

    Time preference and discounting   173

    Risk and uncertainty   174

    Aggregation and equity   176

12.4   The stages of economic appraisal   176

    The choice of a project   177

References   181

Questions for consideration   181

13. Financing health care   182

Introduction   182

13.1   Patterns of health service financing   183

13.2   National patterns of health care   186

    Tax finance   186

    Compulsory social insurance   186

    Private insurance-based schemes   188

13.3   Financing patterns and the key economic questions   189

    What services should be provided?   189

    How should goods and services be provided?   190

    Who should receive goods and services   191

13.4   Key objectives of health care reform   192

    Cost control   192

    Equity   193

    Provider efficiency   194

Appendix: Health financing   195

    Levels of health expenditure   195

    Increasing health expenditure/cost control comparisons   195

References   196

Review exercises   198

Index   199

Introduction

This book explores the contribution that the discipline of managerial economics can make to the management of health services. According to Mansfield (1993), managerial economics 'attempts to bridge the gap between the purely analytical problems that intrigue many economic theorists and the day-to-day decisions that managers must face'. Hirschey and Pappas (1995) add, 'Managerial economics also helps managers to recognise how economic forces affect organisations and describes the economic consequences of managerial behaviour.'

The scope of this book is rather different from that of the many excellent texts on health economics, for example, *Economics, Medicine and Health Care* (1992) and *Key Issues in Health Economics* (1994), both by Mooney. Mooney himself defines health economics as 'the discipline of economics applied to the topic of health'. Clearly the study of managerial economics in a health services context cannot be carried out independently of the study of health economics. However, the emphasis of the book will be on managerial economics with particular reference to problems encountered in the management of health care.

The discipline of economics, whatever its field of application, deals with the use of scarce resources to satisfy human wants and needs. Whether in the public sector or in the private sector, organizations have to be managed and decisions have to be made about how best to use the resources available. This applies to the delivery of health care as well as to the production of cars or chocolate biscuits. However, what differentiates health care from other fields where managerial economics is applied are the very personal and often urgent needs the service meets. We are often dealing with pain and suffering, with life-and-death decisions, and access to the service is often considered to be a basic human right irrespective of ability to pay.

In traditional managerial economics, it is implicitly assumed that the output of the enterprise is of merchantable quality, in other words, that it works. Consumers have rights; they can return faulty goods and demand refunds. Manufacturers of substandard goods receive adverse publicity from newspapers and consumer groups. Given the incentive for producers to sell products that are fit for their purpose, much of managerial economics focuses on the production process itself, and on the demand for the product.

In health care it is the case that many treatments are unproven. Lewis (1993) and Coulter *et al.* (1993) point out that diagnostic dilatation and curettage (D and C) operations on young women, although quite commonly carried out, are of unproven value. There is a lack of evaluation studies of many common treatments. In addition, even when the results of studies are available, there are problems with both the dissemination of the results (Haines and Jones, 1994) and the extent to which clinicians are willing to change their preferred treatment regimes. In the UK the Department of Health is encouraging the move towards evidence-based medicine, where decisions about medical interventions will be more firmly based on research evidence about their effectiveness (Appleby *et al.*, 1995)

Also in health care, it is not the consumer who demands the treatment, but the doctor, acting as the agent of the patient. This agency relationship is not exclusive to health care but it does raise special problems in demand and resource allocation studies.

In this book we consider the nature of health and health care and the special problems associated with measuring output and efficiency. We introduce the basic tools of managerial economics – demand and supply analysis, the theory of production and costs, and the analysis of market behaviour, competitive behaviour and contracting. We examine methods of assessing health status and of carrying out economic appraisals of health programmes and projects. Finally, we examine the way health care is financed in different countries and the implications for the way in which the services are distributed to members of the population.

References

Appleby, J., Walsh, K. and Ham, C. (1995) *Acting on the Evidence: A Review of Clinical Effectiveness, Sources of Information, Dissemination and Implementation*, NAHAT, Birmingham.

Coulter, A., Klassen, A., MacKenzie, I. Z. and McPherson, K. (1993) 'Diagnostic Dilatation and Curettage: Is It Used Appropriately? *British Medical Journal*, 306, pp. 236–9.

Haines, A. and Jones, R. (1994) 'Implementing Findings of Research', *British Medical Journal*, 308, pp. 1488–92.

Hirschey, M. and Pappas, J. L. (1995) *Fundamentals of Managerial Economics* (5th edn), Dryden Press, Forth Worth, London.

Lewis, B. (1993) 'Diagnostic Dilatation and Curettage in Young Women', *British Medical Journal*, 306, pp. 225–6.

Mansfield E. (1993) *Managerial Economics* (2nd edn), Norton, New York.

Mooney, G. (1992) *Economics, Medicine and Health Care* (2nd edn), Harvester Wheatsheaf, Hemel Hempstead.

Mooney, G. (1994) *Key Issues in Health Economics*, Harvester Wheatsheaf, Hemel Hempstead.

CHAPTER ONE

The basic economic questions

Objectives

■ To show how economic concepts and techniques assist in the understanding and resolution of critical problems in the delivery of health services.

■ To introduce the key economic questions which have to be addressed by all enterprises whether private or public.

■ To introduce some of the special problems which arise due to the particular character of health and health care.

Introduction

We begin this chapter by introducing two case studies. The first is based on the UK National Health Service, a public service funded from general taxation, structured as an 'internal market' where provider units such as hospitals compete to provide services to purchasers such as GPs and health authorities. The second is based on the US health care industry, which is largely a private sector system where health insurance companies pay the bills for insured patients and the government provides some safety-net services for those who cannot obtain or cannot afford health insurance.

The UK National Health Service used to be organized as a hierarchy. Activities concerned with both purchasing and providing health care were planned and coordinated within the organization. The internal or 'quasi-market' introduced in 1989 (*Working for Patients*, CM555) separates the functions of purchasers and providers with the aim of introducing greater incentives for efficiency and greater choice for patients with less government intervention. Nevertheless, total funding for the NHS is determined by the government out of taxation revenue, and most of the NHS services remain free at the point of use. The quasi-markets are highly regulated with strict guidelines about range and quality of services and about pricing. The election of a new Labour government in May 1997 means that the system is likely to be altered again but as yet no clear indication has been given as to the precise nature of the change.

In the USA, markets for health care services are less highly regulated. The distribution of the output of the economy between health care and other goods and services is largely determined by market forces. As will be seen in the case studies below, both these types of market organization appear to give rise to problems.

In this chapter we discuss some of the problems suggested by the case studies and the extent to which the study of economics might be able to shed some light on them. We examine the nature of health and its relationship to health care systems. We briefly discuss the role of economics in the analysis of health care systems and finally the way in which the study of economics might be of use to managers in health care systems.

Case study 1.1 ■ No operations before April

Daily News, 14 November

Hospital chiefs have announced that there will be no routine surgery in Barchester hospital until next April because the budget for this financial year has been spent. The hospital will make an exception for patients from GP fundholders who are able to pay for their patients from their practice funds.

Mike Barnes representing 'Unison', the NHS workers' union, has accused the hospital of spending money on managers and administration rather than patients. He blames the introduction of the 'internal market' for the fact that the hospital will keep beds empty and close wards because it does not have the funds to treat patients on the waiting list.

Bill Jones, the local MP, has written to the Minister complaining that many patients will now have to wait for 3 months for treatment while the patients of fundholders are able to jump queues as a matter of course.

A hospital spokesman admitted that the facts of the case as reported were basically correct but claimed that the cause was that the hospital had been more efficient than in the past and had completed all its contracts for the year in just nine months' work. While it was unable to treat patients for whom there was no budget, it would also be irresponsible not to treat the patients of fundholders where the funds were available, given that there were empty beds.

At a press conference the Chief Executive Officer assured the public that the standstill did not apply to those who suffered from life threatening conditions or to those whose conditions would seriously deteriorate if forced to wait an additional three months. She did accept that the situation was far from acceptable and that a few patients might suffer some discomfort and inconvenience because of the delay.

Discussion

This article raises a great many questions, at least some of which may be amenable to economic analysis, as we shall see later in this book. The first and most obvious set of (related) questions is:

1. Have managers failed to plan and budget accurately for the financial year?
2. Are the hospital's costs higher than those of its major competitors for comparable activities?
3. Has the hospital obtained fewer contracts than its major competitors?
4. What are the economic and financial consequences of having expensive facilities lying unused?
5. Can this situation, of having unused facilities while there are waiting lists for treatments, be predicted using traditional economic models of market behaviour?

On a broader canvas we might ask:

6. What are the consequences and costs of this situation for patients?
7. Is the NHS underfunded?
8. Is it fair that GP fundholder patients should continue to be treated while others have their treatments postponed?

The first five questions are concerned with the demand for and supply of services, the way the services are being planned and organized, the characteristics of the market in which the hospital is operating, the efficiency or otherwise of resource use and the pricing and marketing of the services. These topics can be addressed using the ideas and techniques of managerial economics and we shall be examining them in detail (in later chapters).

Questions 6, 7 and 8 are questions which can be answered only by using value-judgements. They are outside the scope of conventional or **positive** economics which does not tackle problems which require interpersonal comparisons of welfare (Buchanan, 1959). Positive economics attempts to establish cause and effect in a scientific manner. Hypotheses are formulated and these are then checked against observed facts.

By contrast, **normative** economics is concerned with establishing the means by which socially desirable outcomes can be achieved. It is prescriptive. It suggests what 'ought' to be. Questions about whether the distribution of incomes and output is equitable are normative since there is no universal agreement about what is fair. Questions such as question 6 about health consequences for patients are also normative because they require interpersonal comparisons of health status and the measurement of health status requires value-judgements.

It could be argued that all economic questions about the allocation of resources in health care are normative, since the final outcome is generally some change in the health status of the patients. Nevertheless, managers operating the service on a day-to-day basis are more likely to concentrate on intermediate and easily measurable outputs such as the number of patients treated and will therefore treat such questions as problems of positive economics. This problem, of whether questions about resource allocation in health care are normative or positive, may lie at the root of some of the conflicts between health service managers and clinicians.

Questions 7 and 8 are clearly normative. For example, the question of whether the service is underfunded or not requires us to consider what the level of funding **ought** to be, bearing in mind that if more public funds are devoted to health care there will be less available for education and other public services. Similarly, a question such as question 8 which asks 'Is it fair that . . .' requires us to make judgements about what is fair and what is not.

> 'Fairness', like 'needs' is in the eye of the beholder. If all are to have 'fair shares', someone or some group of people must decide what shares are fair – and they must be able to impose their decisions on others. (Friedman, M. and Friedman, R., 1980)

Nevertheless, one of the basic principles of the NHS and of many other public health care systems is that treatment should be provided on the basis of need rather than on the basis that funds are available, and that equity should be one of the objectives of the service. This type of issue would not be central to most treatments of managerial economics but in health care it is an important issue and we shall consider it later. The topic of equity in health care has been given extensive consideration by Mooney (1992, 1994).

Case study 1.2 ■ The health of America

Hillary Clinton's plan to reform the US health care system is now history. It can be consigned to the archives which house many previous attempts to deal with an expensive system which fails to provide adequate services for a large proportion of the population.

The United States spends a massive 14% of its considerable Gross Domestic Product on health care. Health care spending per head is the highest in the world. Yet life expectancy in the USA is lower than that of Greece and Spain, and the infant mortality rate higher in the USA than in the UK. What is more, the variation in health levels between citizens in the US is higher than in many other developed countries. Although hard evidence is difficult to come by, anecdotal evidence suggests that in the poorest parts of the United States, infant mortality rates approach third world levels.

Those who can afford it receive probably the best level of health care in the world. The private health care and insurance markets are full of firms competing for the most attractive patients, those who have high incomes and good general health. These firms have attempted to cherry-pick or cream-skim by insuring the potentially least-cost clients, avoiding the middle aged, poor and sick and leaving 37 million uninsured and perhaps a similar number underinsured.

Since insurance companies pick up the bills, and fee-for-service doctors who advise on treatment are also the suppliers of care, the incentive to overtreat those covered by insurance is high. In many cases employers pay for health insurance for their employees. In such a situation there is little incentive for patients or doctors to consider cost-containment.

The Clinton health plan would have introduced health purchasing alliances to increase buyer power and force suppliers to lower prices. There was a suggestion that drug companies would have their prices controlled. Lower costs would have allowed provision of universal coverage for all citizens. The plan failed since it cost so much to buy the support of powerful competing interest groups, and those groups finally sank the scheme. The more well-to-do Americans value their freedom of choice and feared any scheme which suggested that their freedom might be curtailed. Doctors, insurance companies, pharmaceutical companies and private hospitals were opposed to any system of regulation which might interfere with their ability to make high profits.

It is not surprising that the Clintons could not devise a scheme which would satisfy such a range of powerful interests. On reflection, it required a world war and a bankrupt voluntary hospital system for the creation of the UK NHS and that has not been without its own particular problems. 'Socialized medicine' is viewed with horror by many on the other side of the Atlantic, but in terms of cost control and outcomes it appears to have much to recommend it.

Discussion

The first case study was very much concerned with the process of providing hospital care. The second study is concerned with the American health care system as a whole. Whereas the UK health care system is largely publicly funded with a small private health care sector, the US health system is largely privately organized, funded from private health insurance schemes and has limited public safety-net provision.

Questions that come to mind at this point are:

1. The USA spends a great deal more per capita on health care than the UK and yet life expectancy is lower in the USA and the infant mortality rate is higher. Why is this? Is the private market failing to allocate resources efficiently?
2. In private sector health care markets, as in the USA, which organizations or individuals have the most economic power? What are the implications of this?
3. How do we judge which system is better?

In managerial economics we analyse the competitive environment and the effect of market forces on pricing, wages and salaries, output and efficiency. We look at managerial objectives in for-profit and not-for-profit hospitals and discuss the effects of different objectives and incentive structures on economic behaviour. This analysis will help us to answer questions 1 and 2.

The overall outcomes in the USA appear to be no better than in the UK and inequality is greater. There will be some people who enjoy much better access to services and quality of amenities in the US than in the UK. Whether the UK system is better than the US system is therefore a normative question – it depends on your point of view. Nevertheless, we can use economic analysis to throw light on the effects of different types of funding mechanisms and market structures on prices and output.

1.1 ■ Health care and health

Health care systems provide services, but what exactly are these services intended to produce? Presumably the purpose of health care is to produce an improvement in health, the maintenance of good health and/or a reduction in suffering. That being the case, we need to address the question of the nature of 'health'.

What is health?

Although health care services can be bought and sold, health cannot. It is not tradeable. Health is difficult to define and even more difficult to measure. To be in a state of good health is to be not just alive, but capable of enjoying life to the full. Twaddle (1974) puts forward a possible definition of perfect health from a social point of view: 'a state in which an individual's capacities for taste and role performance are maximised'. According to the World Health Organization (WHO), good health is 'a state of complete physical and mental well-being and not merely the absence of disease or infirmity'. These are ambitious definitions which suggest that good health is the result of more than just an efficient and effective health service, a point to which we will return below (see Hanslukwa, 1985).

The definition of health adopted by governments may well have implications for the range of services offered by their national health services. Which department, if any, will take responsibility for the care of people permanently disabled by strokes or those rendered frail by age?

There are not just different degrees of ill-health; there are different dimensions. Pain, mental impairment and physical disability are all aspects of ill-health. Governments, managers and clinicians may view their health service as a sickness service in which illness is any state which has been diagnosed as such by a health service professional. Once treatment has been applied and the specific illness cured, then, in the words of Trillian in *The Hitch Hiker's Guide to the Galaxy*, 'we have normality. . . . Anything you still can't cope with is therefore your own problem' (Adams, 1979). But the definitions of health given at the beginning of this section suggest that good health is much more than just the absence of illness.

The costs of poor health

Poor health in an individual imposes costs on the individual in terms of reduced ability to enjoy life, to earn a living or to work effectively. Improved health thus allows the individual to lead a more fulfilling and more productive life.

Poor health in an individual will have an impact on and may pose threats to others. For example:

1. A person with an infectious disease may infect others . AIDS is a case in point.
2. The family of a breadwinner in poor health may suffer the consequences of reduced income, a poorer diet, less good housing.
3. Family members may have to devote time and resources to caring for the sick person and in addition may be unable to take paid employment.
4. The employer of a workforce in poor health may suffer reduced productivity and hence incur higher average costs.
5. More people in poor health pose extra costs on taxpayers if the health service is funded through taxation. This may become an increasing problem as the ratio of the retired to the working population, sometimes called the dependency ratio, increases.

6. The knowledge that some members of the population are in poor health may cause distress to other healthier members.

Improved health care services thus provide benefits to society as a whole if they result in improved health, as well as providing benefits to the individual. In addition, the process of providing health care may have significant effects on the well-being of an individual, the carers and their families (Mooney, 1994). Authors such as McKeown (1976) have argued that the role of medicine in improving the health status of the population has been exaggerated and that factors such as housing, education, dict, hygiene and standard of living have had a more significant impact on levels of health than what we conventionally think of as health services.

1.2 ■ Demand for health care

The demand for health care services will depend on the demand for health and on the perception of the link between health care and health. One complication of trying to model or predict this demand is that individuals value apparently equal health states differently. Damaged knee ligaments may cause two individuals the same degree of pain, but, as Mooney (1992) points out, will probably have worse implications for a professional footballer than for a health economist. The demand for health care will also vary according to the age structure of the population.

1.3 ■ Production of health

Contributions to health are made by many agencies apart from health care services. A model relating health outcome to health inputs was introduced by Grossman (1972), who included housing, education, employment status and nutrition as inputs alongside health care. It is assumed that the individual seeks to maximize life-time utility which is a function of, among other things, the number of healthy days in different time periods up to the individual's death.

Thus, health care is only one input into the production of health. It is worth noting that most health care is carried out by families within the home using simple measures and over-the-counter medicines rather than by the formal health care system.

Of course health care systems may produce outputs other than health. As noted above, they may produce comfort, in that the patient's experiences during the process of being treated are possibly as important as the outcome. They may provide security, in the sense that although no one wants to be run over by the proverbial bus, it is reassuring to know that if the worst happened, the country has a well-equipped, efficient and effective health service for dealing with emergencies. It is also reassuring to know that the nearest Accident and Emergency unit is not far away!

We all have an interest in health care, the systems with which it is paid for, produced, managed and made available to consumers/patients. Whether privately insured or dependent upon public services we seek a comprehensive service for examination and diagnosis, care and cure should we require it. Additionally we would like to be protected from infectious diseases which might hurt ourselves or our children. We expect there to be effective public and environmental health services which will protect us from infectious diseases or from ill-health caused by the behaviour of individuals or enterprises through failures in hygiene or activities which pollute.

Managers, health professionals, and politicians have an interest in the services for which they work or for which they claim an electoral mandate. We therefore have a diverse and sometimes conflicting set of interests between those who pay for health services, those who provide them, those who shape them through strategic and operational management, and those who would like to benefit from them if necessary. We, as stakeholders, have the following related (and sometimes conflicting) requirements of our health service.

1.4 ■ Requirements of health services

Economy

We would like the services to be inexpensive. As taxpayers, insurance premium payers, or simply customers who pay directly for the services we receive, we would like the price to be low. We know that 'there is no such thing as a free lunch' and that somebody always pays either directly or indirectly. Managers, clinicians, politicians and consumers are increasingly paying attention to the cost of services, cutting out waste and eliminating services which confer no benefit upon recipients. Nevertheless, there are certain basic thresholds below which we would not want to see levels of care fall.

Effectiveness

We expect the service to be effective. We want each procedure to produce perceptible health gains (or reductions in suffering). Where we have an effective procedure we want it to be provided (and do not want to have to wait for it). The evidence-based medicine movement shows how this requirement is beginning to influence health care providers (Frater, 1996).

Efficiency

We expect our services to be efficient. If we can achieve the same outcome with different procedures we would rather the least expensive procedure is used, enabling us to provide more care per pound or to spend the money in a different way. Similarly, if we can deliver an equally effective service in different ways then we would want to choose the least expensive. Note that efficiency differs from economy, in that to measure efficiency we require some reliable measure of the benefits provided by the treatments.

An increase in the number of patients treated at no extra cost does not necessarily imply greater efficiency. If treatments are less effective and outcomes are worse, the service may be making a less efficient use of its resources. We will be examining the concept of efficiency in much greater detail in Chapter 3.

Value for money

These three requirements, economy, effectiveness and efficiency, come under the heading of 'value for money' (VFM). Organizations in the private sector might have the maximization of profits as their main objective, but in the UK public sector the financial objective of public sector organizations is to deliver 'value for money' (see Glynn, Perkins and Stewart, 1996; National Audit Office, 1984). It is worth noting that the value-for-money criteria proposed by the National Audit Office, known as the '3 Es', can be interpreted as being different aspects of efficiency (see Chapter 3).

In the UK NHS, and in many other health care systems, there is a fourth requirement:

Equity

Many of us would also like the services we pay for or provide to be distributed fairly. We would like patients with similar needs to receive similar services, equitable treatment for citizens of different ethnic backgrounds, and equal opportunities whether you live in Westminster or Wigan.

Equity does not mean the same as equality. Equality implies receiving equal shares of some good or service, whereas equity implies some broader concept of fairness. Mooney (1994) suggests three broad ways of defining equity in health care:

1. Equality of health status attained.
2. Equality of use of health care (for equal need).
3. Equality of access to health care (for equal need).

It is clear that these definitions may conflict in the sense that, for example, in order to achieve greater equality of health status, it may be necessary to ensure that some individuals make greater use of health care services than others. If resources are limited, equality of health status may only be achievable at a low level (Mooney, 1987).

Much discussion of equity issues centres on horizontal equity – the principle of equal treatment for equal need. However, the issue of vertical equity, where the problem is the decision about provision of unequal treatment for unequal need, is more difficult to resolve but equally important to the process of decision-making about resource allocation.

In addition, the objective of equity (however defined) may conflict with the other objectives. For example, economy and efficiency will suggest that the provision of certain treatments is better done in a few large specialist centres. However, this may lead to inequality of access since those on low incomes or of limited mobility may find that they have difficulty attending the centres because of the long distance they have to travel and the cost involved. This is a situation in which the technique of economic appraisal of the options would be appropriate.

Ethical issues

A detailed discussion of medical ethics is outside the scope of this book. However, they constrain the behaviour of doctors and other health care professionals and may put them into conflict with those who manage resources. An example of the importance of medical ethics is the way the agency relationship between doctor and patient functions.

In most purchasing situations the consumer is assumed to be able to make a fully informed decision. However, when it comes to health care, the consumer is generally ill-informed. The consumer, the **principal**, consults the well-informed doctor, the **agent,** for advice. In the perfect agency relationship, the consumer would then make a fully informed decision about treatment, and this would be the same as the one the doctor would have made. In practice, the doctor may also take the responsibility of making the decision for the patient. The doctor may, in many cases, also supply the health care that has been recommended.

The economic theory of agency would suggest that in this situation the doctor could manipulate the situation for financial gain. For example, if the doctor was paid on a fee-for-service basis, there would be a clear financial advantage for the doctor to suggest that the patient has more tests and treatments than is really required. Or if the doctor is a fundholder whose practice is allowed to keep any surpluses, there is a clear incentive to give as little treatment as possible, and to try to avoid taking potentially expensive patients in the first place. The patient is protected from these abuses by the doctor's ethical and professional codes of conduct. The problem of agency in health care is discussed in detail in Mooney (1992) and in McGuire, Henderson and Mooney (1988). Other ethical issues are raised in Chapter 11.

1.5 ■ Health care and economics

Economics is the study of the way in which choices are made about how best to use scarce resources to satisfy human wants. Because resources are scarce, not all needs can be met. Objectives conflict and choices must be made about which needs are met immediately, which are met eventually, and which are not met at all.

The application of economics to health and health care raises particular difficulties not found when considering, for example, the car market. As noted above, health is difficult to define and measure, the benefits of health care are often difficult to assess and not restricted to just the patient, and many (but not all) would argue that individuals have a right to health care irrespective of their ability to pay for it. Certainly in the UK there appears to be a greater concern with equity of provision than there is in the USA.

The methods by which health care is financed vary greatly from country to country. So too do the methods by which production and delivery of services are organized. But all health care systems face the same basic economic questions:

1. Which goods and services to produce?
   How many resources should be allocated to the different specialties? Should cosmetic surgery or infertility treatment be provided at public expense?
2. How to produce the goods and services?
   Will the mentally ill be cared for in small community-based units or in large hospitals? What proportion of surgical procedures will be carried out on a day-care basis?
3. Who receives the goods and services?
   Should the state provide health services only for the poor? When funds are scarce, will preference be given to patients of fundholding practitioners?

Whatever the methods of finance, organization and delivery, health care systems throughout the developed world have been facing the same problems of ever-increasing demand and rising costs. This increasing pressure on resources has had many sources, which include:

1. Medical advances, such as organ transplants and gene therapy, have provided new treatments and therefore created greater expectations and new needs.
2. As life expectancy increases, more resources are required for medical treatments and continuing care for the elderly.
3. Changes in family structure in the developed world mean that it is ever more likely that the elderly will not be cared for by their families.
4. Populations in developed countries have higher expectations about levels of health and have demanded more and better health care.

In a private market health care system, shortages are easily resolved. The poor cannot afford the high prices and go without or rely on whatever basic safety net the state provides. In a state system funded by national insurance or taxation, some form of rationing is inevitable (although it may not be *called* rationing). As the first case study illustrated, in many cases the rationing of non-urgent care may be done on an apparently arbitrary basis.

Faced with the problem of spiralling costs, many countries have changed or are in the process of changing their methods of financing and/or organizing their health services. In the UK, significant changes have taken place in the last few years in the organization of the National Health Service (NHS). An 'internal market' has taken the place of the previous bureaucracy. Public and private sector providers compete with each other to supply services to purchasers, the rationale being that competition will cut costs (economy) and increase efficiency. (Critics suggest that effectiveness and equity are being compromised by the new system.) Similar elements of competition between providers have been introduced in the Netherlands. These changes are producing new problems and new challenges for clinicians and managers.

Supporters of markets argue that a market system, although resulting in a more unequal distribution, is nevertheless likely to lead to a larger overall output (Enthoven 1985, 1991). It is better, they say, to have an unequal slice of a large cake than an equal slice of a smaller cake. In the second case study, it appears that the private market system has led to the US health care 'cake' being divided very unequally indeed; the poor are left with the 'crumbs' and statistics suggest that their health suffers greatly as a result. But does the fault lie with the market system itself?

1.6 ■ Economics and management

Within a health service or health-related organization, people whose job description includes the word 'manager' are responsible for the running of many different types of departments, sections or units. Some managers are responsible for the day-to-day running of a section. Others, more senior, may be more concerned with long-term planning. However, they all face the same problem: how best to use the scarce resources at their disposal to achieve an objective, or a set of objectives. Choices must be made. A decision to use resources for one purpose means that they are not available for some other purpose. These days, managers are required to be accountable; they have to be able to provide justification for their decisions. In our first case study, management and clinical decision-makers had exhausted the budget in the first nine months of the year, and managers were heavily criticized as a result.

The problem of making the best use of scarce resources is, as outlined above, the problem with which economics is mainly concerned. Many of the models and techniques of traditional managerial economics can be used to describe and analyse problems in a health care context and these models and techniques form the main subject-matter of this book.

In the remainder of the book, we will consider the basic economic questions in more detail, examine the theory of how markets allocate resources and look at the problems of market failure. We will examine the variation in types of market organization and regulation, from the US loosely regulated, free market insurance-based system to the UK taxation-financed tightly regulated quasi-market system. We will cover the economics of production, short- and long-run costs, rules for the efficient use of resources, market structures, how to measure and value health status, techniques of financial and economic appraisal and, finally, methods of financing health care.

References

Adams, D. (1979) *The Hitch Hiker's Guide to the Galaxy*, Heinemann, London.
Ahmed, P., Coelho, G. and Kolker, A. (1979) *Towards a New Definition of Health: Psychosocial Dimension*, Plenum Press, New York.
Audit Commission (1983) *The Audit Commission Code of Practice*, HMSO, London.
Buchanan, J.M. (1959) 'Positive Economics, Welfare Economics and Political Economy', *Journal of Law and Economics*, 2, pp. 124–38.

Enthoven, A. C. (1985) *Reflections on the Management of the NHS: An American Look at Incentives to Efficiency in Health Service Management in the UK*, Nuffield Provincial Hospitals Trust, London.

Enthoven, A. C. (1991) 'Market Forces and Health Care Costs', *Journal of the American Medical Association*, pp. 2751–2.

Frater, A. (1996) 'Measuring Clinical Effectiveness', in *Managing Health Care: Achieving Value for Money*, Glynn, Perkins and Stewart (eds), Saunders, London.

Friedman, M. and Friedman, R. (1980) *Free to Choose*, Penguin, Harmondsworth.

Glynn, J. J., Perkins, D. A. and Stewart, S. (1996) *Managing Health Care: Achieving Value for Money*, Saunders, London.

Grossman, M. (1972), *The Demand for Health: A Theoretical and Empirical Investigation*, National Bureau of Economic Research, Occasional Paper No. 119, Columbia University Press, New York.

Hanslukwa, H. E. (1985) 'Measuring the Health of Populations', *Social Science and Medicine*, 20, pp. 1207–24.

McGuire, A., Henderson, J. and Mooney, G. (1988) *The Economics of Health Care: An Introductory Text*, Routledge, London.

McKeown, T. (1976) *The Role of Medicine*, Nuffield Provincial Hospitals Trust, London.

'Managing for Health Gain', *Health Services Management*, June 1993.

Maarssen, A. and Janssen, R. (1994) 'Reforming Health Care in the Netherlands', *Health Services Management*, January 1994.

May, A. (1994) 'Equity in the Balance', *Health Service Journal*, 29 September 1994.

Mooney, G. (1987) 'What Does Equity in Health Mean?' *World Health Statistics Quarterly*, 40, pp. 296–303.

Mooney, G. (1992) *Economics, Medicine and Health Care* (2nd edn), Harvester Wheatsheaf, Hemel Hempstead.

Mooney, G. (1994) *Key Issues in Health Economics*, Harvester Wheatsheaf, Hemel Hempstead.

National Audit Office (1984) *A Framework for Value for Money Audits*, HMSO, London.

'Out of the Moral Comfort Zone', *Health Services Management*, July/August 1994.

Twaddle, A. C. (1974) 'The Concept of Health Status', *Social Science and Medicine*, 8.

Questions for consideration

1. Decide whether each of the following statements is positive or normative:
   (a) Older patients generally need a longer stay in hospital after operations than younger patients because they are slower to recover.
   (b) Patients can reduce their waiting time for operations by paying to go privately.
   (c) Patients with successful kidney transplants have a better quality of life than those on renal dialysis.
   (d) Cosmetic surgery should not be provided on the NHS.
   (e) The demand for health care should not be analysed in the same way as the demand for holidays.
   (f) There are too many managers in the NHS.
2. The following statements were quoted in *The Times*, 4 August 1994. How do you think each

statement should be interpreted? What are the implications for the allocation of resources in the health service?

> 'There is an ethical need to regard the life of every NHS patient as being of equal value' (Sir Patrick Nairne, former permanent secretary at the Department of Health).
>
> 'There is a need to ensure that within the NHS care for patients is provided equitably' (Professor Sir Leslie Turnbull, president of the Royal College of Physicians).

3. Consider the following case study, which is based on newspaper reports in 1997. What issues of equity are highlighted here?

Case study 1.3

Two women with advanced breast cancer, and being looked after by the same consultant, are receiving very different treatment on the NHS. The consultant wants to treat both women with Taxol, a treatment often used for patients for whom other treatments have failed. Clinical trials have shown that the drug can extend life. One of the women will receive the drug free because her health authority has agreed to pay. The other woman, who lives in a different area, will have to pay £10,000 for the drug because her health authority will not pay, believing that spending on other aspects of cancer care will be more beneficial for patients overall.

CHAPTER TWO

Basic economic concepts

Objectives

- To show how the basic economic questions relate to hard choices which have to be made every day by patients, clinicians, managers and politicians.

- To illustrate various approaches to difficult decisions about the content of health care, the pattern of services, and the distribution of those services in conditions of scarcity.

- To introduce some of the issues in the theory and practice of rationing in health care.

Introduction

For purchasers and providers in public health services a critical feature of everyday life is that there are never sufficient resources to meet legitimate needs, and sometimes not enough to meet serious needs. For instance, patients in London attending an Accident and Emergency Centre and requiring inpatient admission for investigation or treatment will frequently require transfer to another hospital because there are no available beds in the hospital concerned. Similarly, doctors deciding whether to discharge a patient will need to take into account the clinical and social needs of the patient but also the alternative demands being made upon a bed by patients whose needs may be considered more urgent.

The purpose of this chapter is to show that many of the fundamental questions with which patients, clinicians, managers and politicians are concerned are basic economic questions. These questions are at the heart of the hard decisions which have to be made every day and which underpin important plans about the future pattern of services and use of resources.

2.1 ■ Scarcity and choice

The fundamental problem faced by consumers and providers is that while human wants are unlimited, the supply of resources available to satisfy those wants is finite. This means that choices must be made by consumers, or their representatives, about which services to buy out of their limited incomes, and by producers about which goods and services to supply with their limited resources. This dilemma is difficult enough without considering the need for consumers to plan for possible needs in the future and for providers to plan so that they can meet those needs when they arise.

The resources available for producing goods and services are generally classified into three categories: **land**, which refers to all natural resources such as farmland, urban land, oil, minerals and water; **labour**, a measure of the amount of human resources and expertise available to be used in the production of goods and services; and **capital**, goods such as buildings and equipment used in the process of production. In addition, economists talk of **human capital**, which relates to labour skills. If a health authority or a hospital sends staff on a training programme, the aim is to increase the stock of human capital available for the production of goods and services.

There is a fourth factor of production, generally associated with private sector activities. This factor is called **entrepreneurship,** and it essentially refers to the skills and talents needed to make a success of creating and running a business. Entrepreneurs see new opportunities and take risks by using resources to bring new products to the market place. If they are successful they will make profits; if unsuccessful they will make losses.

The new public management implies a shift from administration to management by which is meant a move from the implementation and interpretation of predetermined rules and instructions to a more entrepreneurial or active management style (Gray and Jenkins, 1995; Glynn and Perkins, 1995) The strategist has a somewhat broader, though compatible, view of resources which contributes to the so-called RBV or resource-based view of the firm (Hamel and Prahalad, 1994).

Resources are available to varying extents and at different costs. It cannot be assumed that they will be available for purchase when they are needed so consumers and providers need to plan ahead with some care. For instance, the director of a hospital will want to be clear about whether it will be possible to recruit paediatric nurses in the next five years and whether s/he should contribute to a training programme to secure that supply. The same hospital director might want to extend the hospital site and will be interested in the availability and price of land and the views of the appropriate planning authorities to such a development.

While the hospital budget may be healthy, it may be that these basic resources are not available for purchase, are very expensive because they are in short supply, or can only be made available in two or three years' time. Managers must combine the scarce resources at their disposal in order to achieve an objective or a set of objectives, but every choice they make involves a sacrifice – the sacrifice of the opportunity to use the resources for some other purpose.

2.2 ■ Opportunity cost

Hard choices involve employing a limited resource so that it is used to achieve the best possible result. For instance, using a skilled surgeon for a routine operation might not be the best use of that resource if the surgeon can be used for a more complex activity. Using an expensive acute hospital bed for an elderly patient may not be the best use of that bed if there is a less expensive bed in a nursing home which can be used instead with no detriment to the patient. Using a resource for one purpose usually means that it is not available for another purpose.

Economists refer to this as the **opportunity cost.** The opportunity cost of using scarce resources in one way is measured by the loss incurred by not using those resources for some other purpose. For example, given a limited budget, the decision to increase resources devoted to orthopaedic surgery may mean that fewer resources can be given to maternity services. The cost is therefore those maternity services which cannot be provided because the money has been spent in another way. More contentiously, the opportunity cost of introducing a hospital computerized accounting system might be that the operating theatres cannot be refurbished within the particular time period covered by the budget.

More formally, we define the opportunity cost of using resources in one way as the highest-valued alternative that must be sacrificed. In cost-benefit studies, examples of which are discussed later in the book, the opportunity cost of using a hospital building for one specialty is measured by the highest-valued alternative use to which the buildings could be put. This raises questions to which we shall return, not least the questions of valuation. How can it be decided that one activity is of greater value than another?

2.3 ■ Economic choices

The basic problems to be solved by any society are:

1. What goods and services should be produced (and how much of each)?
2. How are they to be produced?
3. To whom should the goods be allocated?

These are questions that clinicians, managers, politicians and consumers have to face. Since resources are always limited, decisions have to be made about how many hip replacements to carry out, how many cataract operations, whether drugs or surgery should be used to treat certain conditions, and, of course, which patients should be treated first. It may be the case that some treatments are not provided at all. Each stakeholder will have to balance their own particular interests with the broader objective to provide the best possible pattern of services within the available resources.

Within the public sector, a fourth and important question is:

How are decisions to be made?

As we discussed in Chapter 1, the UK and Dutch governments have taken the view that an internal market mechanism within a public sector service is the best framework in which these decisions should be made since it provides a series of incentives for efficiency and effectiveness. However, whatever the overall framework, decisions about how best to use the given resources have to be made. We shall see in Chapters 8 and 12 that the economic techniques of marginal analysis and economic appraisal can be of great assistance in determining the optimal pattern of resource use.

Case study 2.1 ■ What to produce

Rationing health care the Oregon way

The majority of American citizens are covered by private health insurance schemes, often paid for by the employer. However, a significant number of the poorer members of the population do not have insurance cover and seek medical care under the Medicaid scheme, a government scheme financed by federal and state taxation. (There is another government scheme, Medicare, which is for those over 65 years of age, disabled people and those on renal dialysis.)

Administrators in the state of Oregon, faced with declining federal funds for its Medicaid programme and an increasing number of uninsured citizens, took a decision to limit the range of treatments covered by Medicaid in order to make basic health care more widely available to the uninsured.

Six hundred and eighty-eight treatments were ranked in order of their benefit–cost ratio. Estimates of health improvements produced by different treatments were obtained from doctors and a telephone survey of residents was used to obtain views on how valuable the population considered the health improvements to be. In addition there were open meetings to assess public opinion.

The Oregon legislature decided to fund the top ranked 568 of the 688 treatments considered. Procedures that would be covered included treatments for severe head injuries, diabetes and brain cancer, obstetric care and appendix removal. Procedures not covered included treatments for benign skin cancers, liver transplants for liver cancer sufferers and surgery to remove benign tumours of the digestive system.

It is estimated that as a result of the explicit rationing, Medicaid can be made available to 360,000 uninsured people, as against 240,000 covered at present.

Discussion

Like most other administrators of health care budgets, administrators in Oregon face the problem of a shortage of funds. Use of these resources to provide one service means that the opportunity to use them to provide other services is forgone. By consulting doctors and residents, the economic question 'what goods and services should be produced?' has been resolved in an apparently democratic fashion. Essentially, the state has decided not to provide those services with the lowest perceived benefit–cost ratio. Although consulting the public may appear to be a democratic way of resolving allocation problems, in health care it may not be appropriate. The general public may have insufficient knowledge of the degree of distress and pain caused by some medical conditions, and may hold prejudices in favour of treatment of, for example, children rather than the elderly.

The decisions about which services to provide also have implications for the third economic question 'To whom should the goods be allocated?' On one hand, 50% more people can now be treated than before. On the other hand, some people who might have expected to be treated now find that their condition is no longer covered by Medicaid. There are gainers and losers. The allocation of resources is different – but is it better? How would you decide? What criteria would you use?

Case study 2.2 ▓ How to produce

The production of health gain

Recently, the term 'health gain' has been gaining prominence in discussions of health management and health policy. Health gain simply means an improvement in health (Hunter, 1995). In the private sector, firms combine scarce resources in order to add value to their inputs. Similarly, we can view the job of managers and clinicians in hospitals as being to combine scarce resources in order to produce health gain in the patients treated. District Health Authorities, who purchase services on behalf of the resident population, will be concerned with trying to produce health gain in that population.

The question arises of how to use the scarce resources in order to produce the maximum possible health gain. There are problems here. The first and most obvious is how health gain can be measured. There are a variety of different indicators of the general health of the population such as life expectancy, infant mortality rates and death rates from heart disease and cancer in different age groups. Hospital league tables are being produced to compare death rates after various treatments. Measures such as quality-adjusted life years (QALYs) (Rosser and Kind, 1978) attempt to assess treatment benefits by looking at both the extra years of life given by a treatment and the quality of that life. However, there in no universally accepted index of health gain.

The second problem is that some measures intended to produce health gain take a long time to work. Educating the population to improve their diet by cutting down on fat and increasing their intake of vegetables may well reduce the incidence of heart disease, but the effect may not be noticeable for twenty years.

A third problem is that the health gain of an individual or a group of individuals has to be assessed in the context of the community as a whole. A family will be most concerned about the health gain of their sick child, a GP will be concerned about the health gain of her patients, a trust hospital will be concerned about the health gain across all specialties and the government will be concerned about the health gain of the community. The interests of these groups may well come into conflict. The sad fact is that for some individuals, a very large amount of money would be required to produce even a small health gain. In some cases, no matter what expensive medical intervention is tried, the patient will most probably die. The money could produce a greater health gain if it was used for other purposes.

> Given a limited budget, choices have to be made about how to use the scarce resources of the health service to produce the maximum possible health gain. Would shifting some resources from breast cancer screening to screening for cardiovascular disease produce an increase in health gain?

Discussion

The argument here is about how to use scarce resources to produce the maximum possible health gain. The issue of opportunity cost arises again, as it does in all economic analysis. If resources are used for one purpose, then they cannot be used for some other purpose. Are they being allocated in such a way as to produce the maximum health gain?

Although this particular case study focused on the problem of how to produce health gain, decisions about this also have impacts on the other economic questions. Which goods and services should be produced in order to produce the maximum health gain? Which individuals should receive the goods and services if health gain is to be maximized?

Case study 2.3 ■ How is the output distributed?

Ageism in medicine

Professor John Grimley Evans, of the Department of Clinical Geratology at Oxford University, has argued that the NHS is ageist in the sense that elderly people are denied treatments that could be effective, enabling significant improvements in health status or functional abilities.

He points to evidence of treatment for coronary symptoms and to earlier evidence about admission to renal dialysis programmes to suggest that in some cases doctors respond to limited resources by excluding elderly patients from programmes which might provide them with positive benefits. He argues that old people are expected to do badly in comparison with those from younger age groups and consequently when poor progress is due to poor treatment, nobody notices.

Economic arguments might point to different conclusions. How do we measure the benefit of coronary surgery to an individual of 50 and to one of 80? Effective surgery for the elderly patient might prevent several years of vastly expensive nursing care. The individual of 50 who requires such surgery may be in very poor health and may gain comparatively little benefit. It appears that age is not, or should not be, the only criterion.

Professor Grimley Evans uses the interesting analogy of the RAC. The member whose car has broken down expects prompt and expert service whether he is driving a 1970 Ford Fiesta with a broken axle or a 1996 BMW with a puncture.

We can ask the question as to whether utilitarian considerations should be the only issue to be taken into account when resources are scarce.

Discussion

Given a limited budget, if resources are used to treat an elderly person, perhaps using coronary angioplasty, then the resources are not there to treat some other (younger?)

person. Have some doctors decided that the opportunity cost of treating the elderly in this way is too high? The problem may be that although many elderly people do gain some benefit from the treatments, they do not benefit as much as a younger person would. We do not know the grounds on which the decision is made not to treat elderly patients. It is an important question. How have the benefits been assessed and measured?

How should decisions about who to treat be made? According to Professor Evans, some doctors are simply prejudiced against the elderly. Resources are not being allocated to the treatments of those who could benefit. The technique of economic appraisal, which we will examine in Chapter 12, can be used to aid decision-making in this difficult area.

Do citizens have any rights when it comes to the distribution of health care resources? In a private insurance system the nature of the insurance contract specifies rights and obligations. In social insurance things are not so simple.

The best use of resources

These case studies have illustrated the basic economic questions and each of them has also raised an important issue: What is the **best** way to allocate the resources? The question of how best to use resources to achieve an objective, which might be treating the maximum number of patients, or producing the maximum possible health gain, is really about the **efficient** use of resources.

The word 'efficiency' is often heard these days in discussions about the use of health service resources. It tends to be associated with cost-cutting measures, but there is more to the concept of efficiency than simply cutting back on resource use. It is one of the most important concepts in economics and it is the subject of Chapter 3.

If the distribution of health care resources is to be other than haphazard and inequitable, than it has to be based on some clear pattern of values. A recent attempt to further this debate is described in the following case study.

Case study 2.4 ▦ **Health care rationing**

While politicians speak the language of health priorities or Citizen's Charter Standards, there are few members of the health care professions, or indeed of the general public who deny the need to ration health care resources. They may feel that rationing through market mechanisms is preferable to deliberate decisions to give or withhold treatment but none the less scarcity of resources implies some measure of rationing. The heart of the debate centres on who should make such decisions, who should make policies that promote some services and reduce others, and on what basis should such decisions be made.

Ann Bowling (1996) describes the first study of a national random sample of respondents to identify their priorities for health services and the attitudes which underpin them. Twelve treatments were identified and respondents were asked to rank them in priority order. This exercise resulted in the following rank order:

Higher ranked
1. Treatment for children with life-threatening illnesses.
2. Special care and pain relief for people who are dying.

Lower ranked
11. Treatment for infertility.
12. Treatment for people aged over 75 with life-threatening illnesses.

Respondents made a clear distinction between treatments for children with life-threatening illnesses and treatments for over 75s with life-threatening illnesses, ranking the children first and elderly last. They ranked in second place palliative care for the dying which in the UK is likely to be made up substantially of the elderly for whom aggressive treatment is a low priority.

The survey ranked preventive services of proven value highly (3) and health promotion services designed to help people lead more healthy lives as of less value (8).

Participants were asked about their attitudes to health care priorities and produced some interesting findings: high cost technologies should be available to all regardless of age; quality of life should be considered in determining whether to employ life-saving technology; and rationing decisions should lie with doctors rather than managers, politicians, health authorities, or government ministers. Rationing decisions should take into account the views of the public and surveys such as this were an appropriate way of assessing that opinion.

Discussion

Pressure on resources arises from an ageing population, new technological developments and increasing public expectations about the availability and quality of treatments. Many treatments are uncertain or unproven, particularly if they have not been subjected to the gold standard of the random controlled clinical trial. No single individual has a monopoly of information about treatment outcome probabilities or the costs and relative benefits of alternative treatments. How should rationing questions be addressed, who should make decisions to ration resources, and how might ideas from health economics inform our thinking?

This case raises issues that relate to each of the three economic questions:

1. What to produce?
2. How to produce?
3. How to distribute?

First, it is clear that infertility services are seen as a low priority. This view may change after the Spring 1996 series of TV programmes on Professor Winston's infertility services at the Hammersmith Hospital in London. Secondly, the public felt that the elderly should not necessarily be the subject of aggressive therapies but rather be given the opportunity of palliative care which emphasizes quality of life considerations. And thirdly, it was thought that high-technology medicine should be available regardless of age where it could achieve a worthwhile benefit in terms of length and quality of life. Additionally, children should have a very high priority in the allocation of curative and high technology services.

2.4 ▓ Conclusion

This chapter has introduced three key management problems using the language and concepts of health economics:

1. What goods and services should be produced and in what quantities?
2. How should they be produced?
3. To whom should they be distributed and on what grounds?

We have pointed to the question of opportunity cost recognizing that the use of resources in one service precludes the use of those same resources in another service and that the opportunity cost is the value of the most valuable service which is forgone.

We have pointed to the issue of health gain as a widely discussed aspiration of purchasers and providers in health care.

We have raised questions about the allocation of services and procedures under conditions of scarcity pointing to the utilitarian basis of much health thinking but recognizing the limits of this approach.

References

Bowling, A. (1996) 'Health Care Rationing: The Public's Debate', *British Medical Journal*, 312, pp. 670–4.

Carruthers, I. (1996), 'Purchasing for Impact in the NHS', in Glynn, J. J., Perkins, D. A. and Stewart, S. (eds), *Managing Health Care: Achieving Value for Money*, Saunders, London.

Glynn, J. J. and Perkins, D. A. (1995) *Managing Health Care: Challenges for the 1990s*, Saunders, London.

Gowland, D. and Paterson, A. (1993) *Microeconomic Analysis*, Harvester Wheatsheaf, Hemel Hempstead.

Gray, A. G. and Jenkins, W. I. (1995) 'Public Management and the National Health Service' in Glynn and Perkins (eds), *Managing Health Care: Challenges for the 1990s*, Saunders, London.

Grimley Evans, J. (1993) 'Health Care Rationing and Elderly People', pp. 43–52 in M. Tunbridge (ed.), *Rationing of Health Care in Medicine*, London, Royal College of Physicians.

Hamel, G. and Prahalad, C.K. (1994), *Competing for the Future*, Harvard University Press, Boston, MA.

Hunter, D. (1995) 'Creating Health Service Strategy', in Glynn and Perkins (eds), *Managing Health Care: Challenges for the 1990s*, Saunders, London.

McGuire, A., Henderson, J. and Mooney, G. (1988) *The Economics of Health Care: An Introductory Text*, Routledge and Kegan Paul, London.

'Managing for Health Gain', *Health Services Management*, June 1993.

Office of Health Economics (1993) *The Impact of Unemployment on Health*.

Rosser, R.M. and Kind, P. (1978) 'A Scale of Valuation of States of Illness: Is There a Social Consensus?', *International Journal of Epidemiology*, 7, pp. 347–58.

Questions for consideration

1. Consider the case study below:
   (a) What examples of opportunity cost can you find in this article?
   (b) Use this article to explain and to illustrate the three economic questions that any economic system must address.
   (c) How are these decisions made in the NHS? How does the decision-making procedure compare with that proposed in Oregon? What problems does the system face in trying to address these economic questions?

Case study 2.5 ■ Cosmetic surgery

Should cosmetic surgery be available on the NHS? Those who think it should, point out that in many cases it can transform the lives of young people, give them confidence and improve their quality of life. After all, no less a body than the World Health Organization has defined health care as a service that should aim to deliver a sense of complete physical and mental well-being. They also point out that much cosmetic surgery is reconstructive after treatment for cancer. In addition, the resources used for cosmetic surgery cannot necessarily be transferred smoothly and costlessly to other areas of treatment.

Those against cosmetic surgery on the NHS make the point that resources are scarce and that advances in medical knowledge are increasing the gap between what might be desirable and what is actually affordable. Informal rationing already takes place, with some GPs being prepared to refer patients for treatment and others not. There should be a system for deciding priorities nationally. Do we really want to make people with cancer wait for treatment by using scarce resources for cosmetic surgery?

---

2. What are the implications of the following studies for government policy on health? What other information would be useful?

   (a) A report by the Office of Health Economics (1993) about the impact of unemployment on health concludes that unemployment causes a deterioration in mental health and is very probably also associated with physical ill-health. There is evidence that the unemployed and their families make greater use of NHS facilities than the employed.
   (b) A study by Richard Wilkinson, published in the *British Medical Journal* in 1992, reports that European countries which redistributed income from rich to poor between 1975 and 1985 had greater gains in life expectancy than those that did not. He estimated that people in Britain would live two years longer if the gap between the rich and the poor was reduced to that prevailing in the countries where income is most equally distributed.

CHAPTER THREE

Efficiency

'When *I* use a word,' Humpty Dumpty said in a rather scornful tone, 'it means just what I choose it to mean – neither more nor less.'

Lewis Carroll, *Through the Looking-Glass*, Chapter 6.

Objectives

- To introduce the concept of efficiency, distinguishing between the common usage of the term and the rather more useful approach of economics.

- To distinguish effectiveness and efficiency and show how they are related.

- To examine various approaches to measuring efficiency, demonstrating their strengths and weaknesses.

Introduction

Efficiency is a word we hear a great deal about these days. The introduction of the internal markets in health care is supposed to provide the incentive to make services more 'efficient'. The problem is that there appear to be many definitions and interpretations of the word 'efficiency', each depending on the context. When numbers of hospital beds are reduced, when nurses are replaced by care assistants, when local hospitals are closed and services concentrated at larger regional centres, it is all done in the pursuit of efficiency. Small wonder then, that the general public often equate efficiency with cost-cutting and reduction of services.

Even textbooks and professional handbooks are not entirely in agreement in their definitions of different aspects of efficiency. In this chapter we examine in detail these aspects, their relationship to the 'value-for-money' criterion and discuss the implications for managers. It will be seen that efficiency is a far more complex concept than is commonly realized. As will be shown below, it is very important to be clear about whether it is the **quantities** or the **values** of inputs and outputs which are being measured.

3.1 ■ Aspects of efficiency

Productive efficiency

An enterprise will attain productive efficiency if it produces its quantity of output with the minimum possible quantities of inputs, or, equivalently, produces the maximum quantity of output with given quantities of inputs. This implies that the amount of waste is minimized. In a hospital setting, if output is being measured in some crude way such as 'number of patients treated', it will imply high levels of bed occupancy, short lengths of stay and high patient throughput.

In production and operations management, effective capacity is defined to be the rate of output the enterprise is capable of achieving given process limitations such as maintenance (Evans *et al.*, 1990). Efficiency is then measured as the ratio of actual output to effective capacity. Efficiency in this context clearly means productive efficiency.

It is important to note that generally in production there may be many different productively efficient ways of producing the same quantity of output, each with different combinations of quantities of inputs. For example, keyhole surgery requires different amounts of theatre time and equipment from conventional surgery, but both methods can be used to treat identical gall bladder conditions. As long as each is done with the least possible amounts of inputs and the least possible waste, they will both be productively efficient methods.

This type of efficiency is sometimes called technological efficiency, and some authors refer to it as technical efficiency, which is a cause of some confusion, as many other authors have a different definition of technical efficiency.

Technical efficiency

McGuire, Henderson and Mooney (1988), along with many others, define technical efficiency to mean the production of a given **quantity** of output with the **least cost combination** (the minimum **value** of inputs). This is the definition we will use in this text. It implies that of all the productively efficient methods of production, the cheapest method has been chosen. This type of efficiency is also known as cost efficiency (Heather, 1994) and operational efficiency (Donaldson and Gerard, 1993).

It is important to note that if relative input prices change, the technically (or cost or operationally) efficient method of production may change also. For example, if capital assets become more expensive compared to labour, the enterprise may well turn to more labour intensive methods of production in the longer run. The introduction in the NHS reforms of the requirement that hospital trusts should earn a 6% return on their net relevant assets was intended to make hospitals stop using their capital assets as a 'free' good. It was thought that this had encouraged the use of expensive capital intensive treatments and an excessive demand for capital resources.

Case study 3.1

According to a report in *The Guardian* on 30 September 1993, the Audit Commission found evidence of widespread inefficiency in hospitals. Examples cited included the following:

1. To change a light bulb took six NHS workers 20 minutes and required an administrative process involving 17 separate steps.
2. To X-ray a patient involved ten staff and took 127 minutes, with 104 minutes devoted to administration and only 23 minutes to taking, developing and reading the X-ray.

Discussion

The implication of the Audit Commission's findings is that, in some hospitals at least, there is productive inefficiency. Simple procedures are being made unnecessarily bureaucratic and thus take more staff time and, presumably, cost more than they should. If administrative costs could be cut, then more money would be released for patient care.

Effectiveness and efficiency

So far, we have considered output as though it was something that could be counted, like cars or washing machines. In health care systems, outputs are often measured in terms of 'number of treatments provided' or 'number of in-patient days'. However, these are only *intermediate outputs*. They do not tell us how the patients fared. Did they all benefit from the treatments? Were there any serious side-effects?

In health care, output should include some measure of the improvement in health (or the relief of suffering) in those patients treated. It is helpful to distinguish between the intermediate outputs, such as the number of patients treated, and *outcomes* – the benefits for the patients and possibly their significant others. *Effectiveness* is concerned with the degree to which outputs (treatments) produce improved outcomes for the patients.

In health care the issue of **effectiveness** is of crucial importance when considering efficiency. For example, it is now widely thought that the use of grommets as a treatment for children with 'glue ear' produces little or no lasting benefit. A hospital unit may supply many such operations in an apparently cost-efficient manner but since the operations are not benefiting the patients, the resources used are actually being wasted.

Case study 3.2 ▓ The clinical effectiveness initiative

The 1990s has seen a major development in the ideas of 'Evidence Based Medicine' supported by the Department of Health who believe that there is an unacceptable level of variation in practice between the best clinical teams and the rest. This variation is thought to result in ineffective treatments, poor outcomes for patients, wasted resources, and in some cases avoidable deaths.

The Department of Health has promoted a clinical effectiveness initiative which aims to ensure that the best scientific evidence is collected, interpreted and disseminated in practical ways so that clinicians can adjust their activities to reflect best practice. New centres have been created to promote this work including the Cochrane Centre in Oxford, the UK Outcomes Clearing House in Leeds and the NHS Centre for Reviews and Dissemination in York. Together with the publication of clinical review series and the establishment of new journals there is an unprecedented commitment to evidence-based medicine which suggests that the scientific evaluation of medical and surgical practice is well and truly on the agenda.

Common medical practices which are now the subject of intense scrutiny include:

- ■ Hip replacements: one in five operations has to be repeated.
- ■ D & C: research suggests it rarely provides any benefit to the patient.
- ■ Grommets: relief from deafness in children is often only temporary.
- ■ X rays: are often carried out for no clinical reason.
- ■ Keyhole surgery: safety fears.
- ■ Heart surgery: operations to relieve angina have to be repeated in an unacceptably large percentage of cases.

(For a detailed review of these issues see A. Frater (1996) 'Measuring Clinical Effectiveness' in Glynn, Perkins and Stewart (eds), *Managing Health Care: Achieving Value for Money*, Saunders, London.)

Discussion

The point here is that it does not matter how (technically) efficiently the services mentioned in the case study appear to be provided. Managers may be ensuring that technically efficient procedures are being followed. Nevertheless, if the procedures are not effective the resources are being wasted.

A treatment is effective if it achieves its objectives without causing serious side effects. Thus, the procedure for treating a broken leg would normally be regarded as effective if the patient is returned gradually to full functioning capacity in a period of months. By contrast, it is generally accepted that there is no effective treatment for the common cold, although it is possible to control the symptoms to some extent.

When we move from the individual to the community level, the issue of definition of effectiveness becomes more complex. For example, vaccination against measles may be effective for an individual. The immunity of other individuals will also prevent the infection of those who cannot be vaccinated because of contra-indications, but epidemics cannot be prevented unless a high proportion of the susceptible population is vaccinated. *Impact* is the term used to describe the collective effect of services on populations. Vaccination against infectious diseases such as measles is effective for the individual but will have little impact on the community if the take-up rate is low.

At the service level, assessment of effectiveness is hampered by lack of information and by the fact that patient outcomes may vary between hospitals or departments simply because the case-mix is different. We will return to the complex issue of measurement of effectiveness in Chapter 11.

Allocative efficiency

Allocative efficiency occurs when, given the existing distribution of income, it is not possible to reallocate resources to make one person better off (in terms of their satisfaction obtained from the goods they consume) without making at least one other person worse off. This situation is known as 'Pareto-optimality', a concept first introduced by the Italian economist, Wilfred Pareto. In effect there is no more scope for so-called efficiency savings and managers have to 'rob Peter to pay Paul'. Note that in this case it is the **value** of output which is being considered, rather than its quantity.

Clearly, definitions of efficiency are related. If productive or technical inefficiency exists, the scope exists to produce extra output by using the existing resources more efficiently. This extra output can be used to make some people better off without making anyone else worse off. If resources are being used to supply ineffective treatments, then output can be increased by using the resources to supply effective treatments instead, without anyone being worse off. Allocative efficiency **implies** productive and technical efficiency.

Social efficiency

It is important to realize that a situation in which allocative or Pareto efficiency has been attained is not necessarily a desirable one. In a society with a very unequal distribution of income, it might not be possible to improve the situation of the poor without increasing taxation of the rich. Thus the poor could be made better off, but only by making the rich worse off. Nevertheless, such a step might be considered socially just and desirable in a society concerned about equity.

It is very difficult to introduce changes in tax or welfare systems without having some losers; a change is considered to be **socially efficient** if the total benefits to the gainers outweigh the total losses of the losers. Whether the change actually takes place or not will depend on the political power of the different interest groups.

Distribution of output

Note that allocative efficiency implies not only efficiency in production but also efficiency in distribution. In a free market economy, individuals can trade with each other in order to obtain the goods and services they value most highly given their budget limitations. In health care the equivalent situation is that if output is measured by the health gain of those treated, the most efficient use of resources will be achieved if the treatments are allocated to those who will benefit most from them.

Thus the way in which treatments are allocated will have implications for some measures of efficiency. In a social care context, Davies (1987) has defined measures of efficiency related to the distribution of services including 'horizontal target efficiency' – the proportion of those needing the service who actually receive it – and 'vertical target efficiency' – the extent to which services go to those who need them rather than to those who do not.

A diagram may help to clarify these definitions (see Figure 3.1). Suppose the population, represented by the entire rectangle, can be divided into those who need the service or treatment, the shaded portion B , and those who do not, the unshaded portion A. The oval represents the way in which the treatments have been distributed. The section C represents the number of treatments going to those who do not need them. The section D represents the number of treatments going to those who do need them.

Then vertical target efficiency can be measured by the ratio D/(C + D) and horizontal target efficiency can be measured by the ratio D/B. If better eligibility criteria were developed, the oval could be shifted further to the right so that proportionately fewer non-needy individuals received the service. It would be possible to increase vertical target efficiency to 100%. In that case all the services available would be going to those who needed them. However, even with 100% vertical target efficiency, horizontal target efficiency could be less than 100% if there are insufficient funds to supply the services to all who need them.

In many cases, the degree of need will vary from case to case. Davies (1987) also defines 'output mix efficiency' – 'the degree to which the mix of outputs produced corresponds to the relative valuation of the outputs'. Assuming that it is possible to measure and value health status and health gain in a reliable and valid manner, output mix efficiency corresponds to correctly allocating services with the greatest priority going to those who will benefit the most.

A major problem is that the measurement and valuation of health status is controversial and laden with value-judgements. Managers may not have the tools at their disposal to carry out this assessment of the 'output' of their organization. But without some attempt to measure patient outcomes, it is very difficult to assess the true efficiency of health care services. The issue of measurement and valuation of health status is covered in Chapter 11.

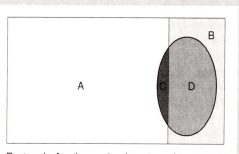

Rectangle A = those who do not need treatment.
Rectangle B = those who do need treatment.
Oval = those receiving treatment.
Vertical target efficiency = D/(C + D).
Horizontal target efficiency = D/B.

Figure 3.1
Vertical and horizontal
target efficiency

3.2 ■ Efficiency and externalities

Another important issue is the range of costs and benefits to be considered when assessing efficiency. An enterprise will consider its own costs of production when making decisions but it may also be imposing costs on others, such as pollution or heavy traffic, which it does not take into account. These costs are known as **externalities** or **spillover effects**.

A change in the production process may appear to be efficient from the firm's point of view in that it reduces the firm's private costs of production, but if this process creates more pollution and other external costs then it may not be efficient from the point of view of society as a whole. For example, a decision by a hospital to shorten patients' lengths of stay may result in extra work and costs for community nurses and doctors. A decision to discharge patients with only two days' rather than one week's supply of drugs will simply transfer the cost to the general practitioner. Costs which were internal are now borne by someone else.

Not all externalities are harmful. Vaccination is an example of an activity which provides an external benefit. When a parent has a child vaccinated against whooping cough, for example, not only is that child protected against the disease, but also all those children who might have caught the disease from that child had he or she not been vaccinated. This provides a strong economic argument for generous public compensation for those very few children who have had severe adverse reactions to the whooping cough vaccine.

Where there are external benefits, it is likely that a market system will provide less than would be desirable from the point of view of the community as a whole. This is because, as the benefits are external, there is no mechanism for those receiving the benefit actually to pay for it. In the vaccination example above, those who benefit by not catching the disease from the vaccinated children have no way of paying them for this benefit.

Another example is the provision of 'option' benefits (McGuire *et al.*, 1988). Option benefits are benefits that an individual receives from the provision of facilities he or she may never use. As noted earlier, most of us receive some reassurance from knowing that there are well-equipped accident and emergency departments within easy reach should the worst happen. Health managers only record income from actual usage; no payment is directly received from all those people who do not want to have to use the facilities but who derive considerable comfort from knowing the facilities are there. Thus casualty departments may be closed on 'economic' grounds, depriving many people of their option benefits. Managers become aware of this when the public protest.

The existence of external costs and benefits means that a market system may not achieve a socially efficient allocation of resources even if managers are running health care facilities in cost-efficient ways. There may well be a tendency to provide too little of certain types of service where external benefits exist.

> ### Case study 3.3 ■ Intensive care beds
>
> Consider the case of intensive care beds. These facilities are expensive to provide, requiring teams of trained nurses as well as costly equipment. As with all services, surplus 'production'

cannot be stored. Insufficient capacity means that emergency cases have to be turned away. Managers are using more sophisticated and detailed measures of the costs of treating the patients admitted to their establishments. However, no consideration is given to other costs, such as the costs incurred by and on behalf of patients who are turned away because there is no spare capacity.

In the case of patients turned away from intensive therapy units (ITUs), several sources of external costs can be identified:

■ An increased risk of death or permanent injury for the severely ill patient who is refused a bed.
■ There may be pressure in ITUs to remove severely ill patients prematurely to general wards, thus increasing the risk of death or injury to the patient as well as increasing workloads of staff on those wards.
■ There may be increased pressure on ITUs in other hospitals, forcing them to turn away patients, thus increasing the costs for those patients.

These costs may be difficult to measure but they do exist and their existence suggests a less than efficient allocation of resources will be arrived at if the provision of these facilities is left entirely to the market system. The provision of extra beds will reduce external costs, but since the costs are external, there is little or no incentive for managers to try to reduce them.

Discussion

This is an illustration of a general problem in service industries. Surplus capacity in one time period cannot be stored for future use. There are statistical methods for calculating, based on past data, the minimum capacity necessary to keep the probability of demand exceeding the available supply to some low level. However, the lower the probability of turning people away, the higher the probability that there will be surplus capacity at other times – and surplus capacity generates no revenue.

3.3 ■ Efficiency in health care systems

The main purpose of the introduction of internal markets in the Netherlands and in the UK NHS was to try to increase cost efficiency (Walsh,1995). The hope was that competition between providers and the new system of capital charging would lead to less waste and to cost reductions, thus enabling a greater level of output to be produced with the same amount of resources. The view of the UK government was that sufficient resources were already available to the NHS, but that the considerable inefficiencies of the system meant that output was well below its potential level.

Both purchasers and providers are interested in questions of efficiency. The provider is particularly interested in questions of cost efficiency. An efficient hospital will hope to win new contracts and to keep the contracts it already has. The purchaser wants to contract with cost-efficient hospitals but also has to take account of equity. It will be particularly sensitive to the criticism that it is trying to appear efficient by maximizing the number of routine treatments at the expense of what may be very expensive treatments.

Some problems will arise for providers which we will deal with later. Do the provider hospitals face the same levels of costs for their staff, buildings and other essential resources? Does a London hospital face higher costs than a hospital in Yorkshire and are these accounted for in the resource allocation and contracting processes? Is the mix and complexity of cases seen by different hospitals similar and do these hospitals have similar access to the equipment and resources required to treat patients efficiently?

Managers in provider units are likely to focus on cost efficiency; trying to find ways of reducing the costs without reducing activity levels, or increasing activity levels without significantly increasing costs. Measures of capacity utilization will be examined to see how intensively the available resources are being used. In a hospital, common measures of capacity utilization are:

▇ *Length of stay:* the average number of days a patient spends in hospital.
▇ *Occupancy rate:* the average percentage of the available capacity occupied each day.
▇ *Throughput rate:* the number of patients treated per unit of capacity (for example, per bed) in the time period under consideration.
▇ *Turnover interval:* the average time that beds are empty between patients.

These measures are clearly related to one another. For example, if the turnover interval stays the same, then reducing length of stay will increase throughput. Given values for any two measures, it is always possible to calculate the other two. The precise relationships between the four measures are shown in the appendix at the end of the chapter.

Case study 3.4 ▇ Bed utilization

According to the Audit Commission's report, *Lying in Wait*, published in 1992, measures of utilization in hospitals in England and Wales have altered considerably in recent years.

All acute specialties

	1974	1988–9
No. of patients treated	4.1 million	5.0 million
No. of beds	158,000	123,000
Throughput/bed/year	26	41
Length of stay (days)	10.2	6.7
Turnover interval (empty bed-days between patients)	3.9	2.3

Discussion

These figures certainly suggest that some of the resources of the NHS are being used more intensively. What they do not tell us is how effectively the resources are being used in terms of patient outcomes. Also, we do not (in this table) have any figures for staffing levels or length of waiting lists. Thus we cannot say unequivocally that the NHS has become more efficient on the basis of these figures alone.

With a fixed amount of capacity, the cost of treating additional patients will depend on how this is achieved. For example, additional patients could be treated by shortening lengths of stay or by increasing occupancy rates. It might appear at first glance to be cost efficient to choose the cheaper method, particularly if performance is assessed by measuring the number of patients treated.

However, trying to measure efficiency simply by the counting the increase in the number of patients treated, or by examining the intensity of capacity utilization is inappropriate because it focuses on **processes** rather than **outcomes**. A hospital may be able treat more patients by shortening length of stay, but if early discharge leads to more readmissions, this may be inefficient. As noted above, if many of the treatments are ineffective, then the hospital is not using resources efficiently. Thus any discussion of efficiency in health care should include some consideration of the effectiveness of treatments and measurement of patient outcomes. In addition, if costs are simply being **shifted** on to someone else (GP, social services) then this may not be efficient from the point of view of the community as a whole (Pollitt,1990, 1993)

3.4 ■ Measuring efficiency in the NHS

We would say that the NHS had achieved technical efficiency in any particular time period if, with a given set of resources, it produced the maximum possible output. But how do we measure the output of the NHS?

Ideally we would like to have some measure of the improvement in health of the patients treated such as *health gain*. However, health is difficult to define and measure. As noted above, there is a tendency in health care to use more readily available measures of intermediate output, such as the number of patients treated. Hospital 'league tables' have been introduced, in which hospitals are compared on various measures such as waiting times in out-patient clinics and for operations, but again these are concerned with the process of receiving treatment rather than the outcomes of those treatments. It has been suggested that death rates should also be included but these would obviously require considerable standardization for case-mix and severity to have any meaningful use.

The Department of Health's measure of efficiency is based on changes in activity levels; it is the change in activity between one year and the next divided by the change in real spending over the same time period. If activity increases by 3%, for example, while real costs rise by only 1%, then this would, according to the Department of Health, suggest an improvement in efficiency.

Activity is measured by an index called the cost-weighted activity index (CWAI). Changes in amounts of different activities are weighted by the shares of the activities in total health service spending. The activity with the highest weight in the index is 'ordinary admissions/day cases CCEs (completed consultant episodes)', a measure which has been widely criticized because of the scope for double counting of patients who see more than one consultant or who are moved from one ward to another.

The CWAI has also been criticized because of the inaccuracy of the raw data used to construct it, the possibility that it may induce providers to concentrate on services with a high weight, its emphasis on treatment rather than prevention and the lack of any measure of quality of care. The index tells us nothing about **outcomes**. According to Appleby *et al.* (1993) the activities and weights are:

Activity	Weight
Ordinary admissions/day cases CCEs: all specialties	0.69
Outpatient and AandE attendances: all specialties	0.13
Day care attendances: learning disabilities, mental illness, geriatrics	0.02
Community contacts: district nursing, health visiting, community mental health and psychiatric nursing	0.14
Ambulance journeys	0.02

Source: John Appleby and Val Little, 'Health and Efficiency', *Health Service Journal*, 6 May 1993.

However, it is clear from the preceding discussion that the CWAI is **not** a true measure of efficiency. It measures activity. It does not consider outcomes at all.

Case study 3.5   Counting consultant episodes

When it is reported that the number of consultant episodes has increased, can we assume that therefore the health and welfare of the population has increased? Not necessarily. An obvious point is that an increase in activity might be the result of more individuals becoming ill.

But an increase in the number of consultant episodes does not necessarily mean an increase in the number of patients treated, according to Seng *et al.* (1993), who studied the records of patients admitted to a major provider hospital between April and July 1992. They estimated that 28% of completed consultant episodes (CCEs) 'would not generally be regarded as multiple episodes of care'.

They gave the following examples of treatments of individual patients which were then recorded as multiple CCEs:

1. Requests for advice from professional colleagues in other specialties.
2. Move of the patient from one part of the hospital to another.
3. Transfers to other departments for investigations.
4. Patients admitted repeatedly for a series of planned treatments.

Discussion

The number of completed consultant episodes is given a relatively high weight in the CWAI. The suggestion here is that hospitals may be deliberately finding ways to increase the figures to improve their efficiency rating. The problem is that comparisons over time and between hospitals will be distorted as not all will follow exactly the same practices.

This illustrates the problem of measuring performance by attaching weights to different aspects of activity. It is to be expected that all those being assessed will try to achieve a good score by producing the highest figures they can on activities with the highest weight. The results of this may not be those that the policy-makers had intended.

3.5 ▓ Value for money and efficiency

In the 1980s the UK government Financial Management Initiative spelled out the government's determination to reduce costs and increase efficiency in public services. The search was on for 'value for money', defined by the National Audit Office as comprising three elements (as noted in Chapter 1). These are:

▓ *Economy*: minimizing the cost of resources used, having regard to the appropriate quality.
▓ *Efficiency*: the relationship between the output of goods and the resources used to produce them. How far is maximum output achieved for a given input, or minimum input used for a given output?
▓ *Effectiveness*: the relationship between the intended results and the actual results of projects. How successfully do outputs of goods and services or other results achieve policy objectives?

It is easy to see, from the definitions earlier in the chapter, that 'economy' has much in common with the concept of technical efficiency and that 'efficiency' sounds very like productive efficiency. A cost-efficient allocation of resources would certainly satisfy the first two conditions if intermediate outputs were being considered.

'Effectiveness' in this context refers both to the extent to which intermediate outputs such as the number of treatments actually result in health gain for the patients, and also to the extent to which targets or policy objectives are being realized. Both vertical target efficiency and horizontal target efficiency are relevant measures here. The higher these measures are, the more effective the programme, in the value-for-money framework.

3.6 ▓ Summary of efficiency measures

Productive efficiency

Producing the maximum quantity of output with a given quantity of inputs, or, equivalently, producing a given quantity of output with the minimum quantity of inputs. Sometimes called technological efficiency. Occasionally (and confusingly) referred to as technical efficiency.

Technical efficiency

The more usual definition is the production of the maximum quantity of output for a given value of a set of inputs or the production of a given quantity of output produced with the least cost set of inputs. Sometimes called cost efficiency or operational efficiency.

Allocative (Pareto) efficiency

Considers the distribution of output. An allocation of resources such that it is not possible, by reallocating resources, to make one individual better off without making at least one other individual worse off. External costs and benefits must be included. Implies cost efficiency but the resulting distribution of outputs could be inequitable. In this definition of efficiency it is the value of output which is considered as well as the value of inputs.

Social efficiency

A change in the allocation of resources is considered to be socially efficient if the total benefits of those who gain outweigh the total losses of those who lose. Again it is the values of outputs and inputs that are considered. Note that it is the costs and benefits to society that are relevant here.

Horizontal target efficiency

The proportion of those needing the service who actually receive it.

Vertical target efficiency

The proportion of services supplied that go to those who need them (rather than to those who do not).

Appendix ■ Calculation of measures of bed utilization

The four measures of bed utilization are:

1. Occupancy rate (OCC).
2. Throughput (TPT).
3. Length of stay (LOS).
4. Turnover interval (TIN).

The definitions were provided in this chapter.

It is possible, given any two of the measures, to calculate the values of the other two. The formulae which follow are based on those in Appendix B of an excellent book by Christopher Day on the use of basic statistics in the health service, *From Figures to Facts* (1985).

Note that in the formulae, DAYS refers to the number of days in the period under consideration. For example, DAYS = 365 if the period under consideration is a year.

1. Occupancy rate (OCC)

$$OCC = \frac{100 \times LOS}{LOS + TIN} = \frac{100 \times LOS \times TPT}{DAYS}$$

$$= \frac{100 \times 1 - TIN \times TPT}{DAYS}$$

2. Throughput

$$TPT = \frac{DAYS}{LOS + TIN} = \frac{DAYS \times OCC}{100 \times LOS}$$

$$= \frac{DAYS \times (100 - OCC)}{100 \times TIN}$$

3. Length of stay

$$LOS = \frac{DAYS - TIN}{TPT} = \frac{TIN \times OCC}{100 - OCC}$$

$$= \frac{DAYS \times OCC}{100 \times TPT}$$

4. Turnover interval

$$TIN = \frac{DAYS - LOS}{TPT} = \frac{100 \times LOS - LOS}{OCC}$$

$$= \frac{DAYS \times (100 - OCC)}{100 - TPT}$$

Using these formulae, we can calculate the axes and gridlines for the Barber-Johnson diagram (see Figure 3.2), which can be used to show all four measures of bed utilization at the same time. The horizontal axis measures turnover interval, while the vertical axis measures length of stay. Using the relationships given above, the positions of the gridlines for occupancy (lines radiating from the origin) and throughput (the third side of the triangle formed with the other two sides being the two axes) can be derived. Measures for any particular hospital or unit can then be marked on the diagram and changes over time can be monitored visually. For more detail see Day (1985).

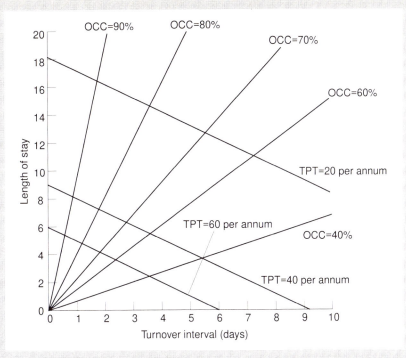

Figure 3.2 Barber–Johnson diagram.
All four measures of bed use at any one time can now be illustrated by one single point on the diagram. Changes over time can be monitored. The more intensively the beds are being used, the closer the point illustrating the measures of bed use will move towards the bottom left-hand corner of the diagram where the vertical and horizontal axes meet.
Note: The lines represent occupancy rates and throughput were derived from the formulae for length of stay with those particular values inserted. Lines representing other values for occupancy rates and throughput can be derived in the same way.

References

Appleby, J. and Little, V. (1993) 'Health and Efficiency', *Health Service Journal*, 6 May.

Appleby, J., Sheldon, T. and Clarke, A. (1993) 'Run for your Money', *Health Service Journal*, 3 June.

'Bulb-changing Operation Sheds Light on Hospital Inefficiency', *The Guardian*, 30 September 1993.

Davies, B. P. (1987) 'Allocation of Services in England: Facts and Myths about the Equity and Efficiency of Social Care Agencies', *Rev. Epidem. et Sante Publ.*, 35, pp. 349–58.

Day, C. (1985) *From Figures to Facts*, King's Fund (on behalf of the NHS/DHSS Health Services Information Steering Group).

Donaldson, C. and Gerard, K. (1993) *Economics of Health care Financing: The Visible Hand*, Macmillan, Basingstoke and London.

Evans, J. R., Anderson, D. R., Sweeney, D. J. and Williams, T. A. (1990) *Applied Production and Operations Management* (3rd edn), West Publishing Company, St Paul, New York, Los Angeles, San Francisco.

Heather, K. (1994) *Modern Applied Economics*, Harvester Wheatsheaf, Hemel Hempstead.

McGuire, A., Henderson, J. and Mooney, G. (1988) *The Economics of Health Care: An Introductory Text*, Routledge and Kegan Paul, London.

National Audit Office (1984) *A Framework for Value for Money Audits*, HMSO, London.

National Audit Office (1992) *Lying in Wait: The Use of Medical Beds in Acute Hospitals*, HMSO, London.

Pollitt, C. (1990) *Managerialism and the Public Services*, Blackwells, Oxford.

Pollitt, C. (1993) 'Running Hospitals' in Maidment, R. and Thompson, G. (eds), *Managing the United Kingdom: An Introduction to its Political Economy and Public Policy*, Sage Publications, London (published in association with The Open University).

Roberts, C. *et al.* (1996) 'The Wasted Millions', *Health Service Journal*, 10 October.

Seng, C., Lessof, L. and McKee, M. (1993) 'Who's on the Fiddle', *Health Service Journal*, 7 January.

Walsh, K. (1995) *Public Services and Market Mechanisms: Competition Contracting and the New Public Management*, Macmillan, Basingstoke.

Questions for consideration

1. Read the following case study and comment on the definitions and measures of efficiency that would be appropriate.

Case study 3.6

According to a report by Tony Sheldon in the *Health Service Journal* in November 1996, efficiency measures have left the Dutch health service with a 'quality gap'. Apparently the Dutch health service has been under pressure to increase efficiency. The growth in health care costs has been limited to only 1.3% per annum for the last two years, whereas the growth over the previous decade was equivalent to 2.3% per annum.

Now a report has been published by Professor Arie van der Zwan and economists at Nijenrode University which suggests that the pressure for efficiency has had the effect of reducing quality. They cite the following examples:

1. A psychiatric hospital which now offers two courses at mealtimes rather than three courses.
2. A rise in the number of nursing home beds in dormitories of five or six beds rather than in single or twin-bedded rooms.
3. A sharp increase in waiting times for treatment.

2. Queue jumping is to be outlawed. The Secretary of State for Health refused to permit 'queue jumping' for medical or surgical beds by the patients of GP fundholders. He agreed with the representatives of NHS consultants to discuss the detail of procedures to ensure that admission to hospital was based solely on the priority of clinical need. Consultants claimed to have evidence that patients were being admitted on the basis of the payment mechanism ahead of

those whose clinical needs were more urgent. Hospital managers argued that since the health authorities had used up their funds for the financial year, the beds would remain empty unless filled by patients from GP fundholders, and that having empty beds was inefficient.

Is it possible for the clinicians to argue their case on efficiency as well as equity grounds?

3. What type(s) of inefficiency does the following case study illustrate?

Case study 3.7

A study by Professor Colin Roberts and colleagues, described in an article 'The Wasted Millions' in the *Health Service Journal* in October 1995, reported the results of an analysis of the purchasing practice of eight health commissions.

Professor Roberts and his colleagues were highly critical of the block contract, where a total cost is paid for a package of services without specifying the price per service or the volume of service, for purchasing community and non-acute hospital services.

They identified five categories of what they call 'ill-founded spending'. These were:

1. 'Inappropriate' expenditure on services which in their view should have been bought by agencies other than the NHS.
2. 'Blind' expenditure where imprecisely specified services are purchased.
3. 'Premature' expenditure where a service is paid for before its effectiveness has been demonstrated.
4. 'Straight over-buying' where a higher volume than necessary of effective service is purchased.
5. 'Over-paying' where the item-of-service payments are excessively high compared with prices elsewhere both outside and inside the health sector.

Professor Roberts and his colleagues suggest that over 20% of spending came into these categories. Given the size of purchasers' budgets, this represents a great deal of wasted money. They also point to the wide variations in prices paid by different commissioners for the same service.

---

4. Consider the following comparative statistics on bed utilization over one year (365 days) for three hospitals.

	Bed occupancy (%)	Turnover interval (days)
Hospital A	80	3
Hospital B	80	2
Hospital C	80	1

For each hospital, calculate length of stay and throughput. Comment on your results.

CHAPTER FOUR

Introduction to demand and supply analysis

Objectives

■ To introduce the economic techniques of demand and supply analysis.

■ To show the factors which influence patterns of demand, supply and prices of health services.

■ To illustrate the dynamic relationship of demand, supply and price pointing out how they are influenced by changes in relevant environments.

Introduction

The economic techniques of demand and supply analysis are very important and useful tools. They can be used to examine many problems and issues facing the health services and to predict the effects of changes in demand and supply conditions. The important concept of elasticity allows us to estimate the magnitude of such changes.

4.1 ■ Demand

Economists define demand as the desire to purchase a good or service *backed by the necessary purchasing power*. In economics, demand does *not* mean 'want' or 'need'. The poor and underprivileged have many needs but they have no purchasing power; they cannot *demand* the goods they need. Demand is a flow over time – two kilos of sugar per week, for example, or twenty gallons of petrol per month. An increase in demand means a permanent increase in the rate of flow – from two kilos of sugar per week to three kilos per week or from twenty gallons to thirty gallons of petrol per month. The demand for hip replacements may rise from 5,000 per year to 6,000 per year as the average age of the population increases, assuming funds are there to pay for the extra services.

Types of products

Consumer goods are goods which are purchased by the consumer usually for the satisfaction (utility) that they yield either directly or in the form of a flow of services. The consumption of food yields satisfaction directly (usually) whereas a television provides viewing services over a period of time. However, some goods purchased by consumers do not fall into this category. For example, consumers do not get satisfaction directly from the purchase of petrol. They buy petrol because it is necessary in order to run their cars. In economists' jargon, the purchase of petrol is a 'distress' purchase. In the same way, a visit to the dentist may be physically uncomfortable and cause apprehension for some, but it is seen as a necessary purchase for the relief of toothache.

Producer goods or investment goods are goods not required for direct consumption but are used in the manufacture of other products for final consumption. Thus the demand for these goods depends on the demand for the goods and services they help produce. The demand for these goods is a 'derived demand'. As noted in Chapter 1, all health care services can be viewed as inputs into the production of health. Regular visits to the dentist may be undertaken in order to produce healthier teeth and gums in the future. In that sense, the patient is investing in dental care now in order to produce healthier teeth in the future.

Hospital buildings, X-ray equipment and laparoscopes are inputs into the production of health care services. The demand for them will depend on the demand for health care services, which in turn depends on individuals' and society's demand for health. The demand for staff is also a derived demand, depending on the demand for health care. Remember that demand in economics has to be backed up by purchasing power. The total demand for health care in a country will depend on, among other things, how much individuals and the state are willing to pay. Unmet need does not count as demand if there is no willingness or ability to pay.

Merit goods are those goods which are believed by society to provide benefits not just to the individual who consumes them but to society as a whole. Left to themselves, many people might consume less than the optimum from society's point of view because they may incorrectly value the benefits to themselves and to others, or because they may have insufficient income. As was pointed out in Chapter 1, improved health in an individual benefits not just him or herself but the family, friends, employers and even taxpayers.

Many argue that it is economically beneficial for society if merit goods are subsidized or even provided free. In the UK, health and education are viewed as merit goods and they are provided free at the point of use by the state. The state does not *have* to organize the production of the merit goods itself; it could allow private provision but subsidize the good, perhaps by the issue of vouchers to the population.

Assumptions about consumers

1. Consumers are assumed to be **rational**. If two goods are similar in all aspects apart from price, the consumer will prefer the cheaper one. If the consumer prefers A to B and B to C, then A will be preferred to C.

2. Consumers gain satisfaction or **utility** from the goods they consume. The more units of a product the consumer already has, the lower will be the extra satisfaction or **marginal utility** gained from an extra unit. For example, if the consumer already has purchased and eaten one hamburger, another hamburger may provide some extra satisfaction. However, a third hamburger will probably add less satisfaction than the second. This phenomenon is known as diminishing marginal utility.
3. Consumers aim to maximize their total satisfaction or **utility** from the goods they consume. It can be shown that in order to maximize their total utility, consumers should allocate their expenditure such that for each product the marginal utility per pound or dollar (satisfaction per pound or dollar gained from the last unit consumed) is equal across all products purchased.

    This is because if the marginal utility per pound gained from product A was higher than it was for product B, then the consumer could increase total utility by taking a pound away from the expenditure on product B and allocating it to product A.

Consider the following (contrived) example. We measure a consumer's satisfaction in units called utils. Products A and B cost the same amount, £20 per unit. Given the consumer's present pattern of expenditure, the marginal utility obtained from one extra unit of A is 5 utils (cost £4 per util) whereas the marginal utility obtained from an extra unit of B is 2 utils (cost £10 per util) . The consumer's total utility would increase if he or she gave up one unit of B – loss 2 utils and used the £20 to buy an extra unit of A – gain 5 utils. Net gain equals 3 utils. Only if the satisfaction gained from the last unit of each product consumed costs the same per util will it be impossible to increase total utility by rearranging purchases.

Factors determining demand

The price of the commodity

For most goods it is reasonable to assume that demand will vary inversely with the price of the good; in other words, the higher the price, the less will be demanded. This assumption follows from the assumption of diminishing marginal utility. If the consumer's extra utility declines with each extra unit purchased, then the consumer will only buy more if the price falls. This relationship between the demand curve and the consumer's marginal utility means that the demand curve can also be thought of as the *marginal private benefit* curve. This distinguishes it from the *marginal social benefit* curve; where there are external benefits, the marginal benefit to society will exceed the marginal benefit to the consumer.

Thus we draw a downward sloping demand curve, shown in Figure 4.1. This diagram illustrates the relationship between the quantity demanded and the price, assuming that all other factors affecting demand are held constant. Note that the variable 'price' is measured on the vertical axis. At the high price p_1 a relatively small quantity q_1 is demanded, whereas at the lower price p_2 a larger quantity q_2 is demanded.

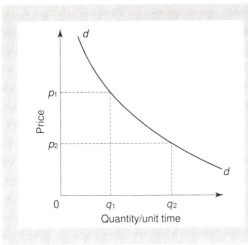

Figure 4.1 The demand curve. There is an inverse relationship between price and demand. When the price is high, demand is low. When the price falls, demand increases.

| Case study 4.1 ■ Demand and price |

The introduction of charges for eye tests in the UK had the dual effect of reducing the demand for such tests and raising revenue towards the cost of the service. The number of NHS eye tests fell by 52% between 1987 and 1992 after the introduction of charges, from just under 14 million to about 6.5 million. The number of private tests has increased but not by enough to cover the fall. The UK Government is estimated to have saved about £61 million, although there may be extra costs if more cases of diabetes and glaucoma go undetected in the early stages.

Discussion

The introduction of charges affects those not entitled to free tests. When the price goes up from zero, demand falls considerably. When eye tests were free, the quantity demanded would have been illustrated by a point on the horizontal axis on a demand curve diagram corresponding to a zero price. The quantity demanded would be affected by other factors such as the cost of spectacles, the opportunity cost of an individual's time and perhaps supply constraints, evidence for which would be long waiting lists for tests. The situation would be similar to that illustrated in Figure 5.5 in the next chapter.

Income

The quantities of goods and services that an individual is able to buy are constrained by his or her available income. This is also true of a purchaser in the NHS. If the purchaser's budget increases, then more of a service can be purchased at any given price. The effect of an increase in income on demand is shown in Figure 4.2. At any given price the quantity demanded is greater than before, thus the demand curve shifts from d_1d_1 to d_2d_2.

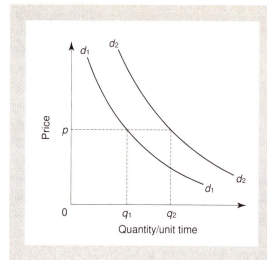

Figure 4.2 The demand curve and the effect of an increase in income. If incomes increase, consumers can afford to buy more at existing prices. Demand will increase even though the price is unaltered.

However, there is a class of products for which demand might fall as income increases. These goods are known as inferior goods. They are goods which a consumer buys because he cannot afford the better quality product. It used to be the case that margarine was an inferior good. Consumers preferred butter but butter was more expensive. As incomes increased, consumers bought more butter and less margarine. This is no longer the case, thanks to changing attitudes to diet and health, and a very successful marketing campaign by producers of margarine.

Dental implants are a very successful but expensive form of treatment; at present cost considerations may limit patients to the inferior (but adequate) alternative treatments. The drug Imigran has been found to be extremely effective in treating and preventing severe cases of migraine. However, it is extremely expensive compared with other forms of treatment. Therefore it is likely that given a limited budget, practitioners would prescribe Imigran for only the severest cases, prescribing other less expensive forms of treatment for the rest. However, if the budget was not limited, perhaps Imigran would be prescribed more frequently.

Case study 4.2 ▮ Demand and income

During the recession of the early 1990s, companies were less profitable and personal incomes fell. As a result of the reduction in income, the demand for private health insurance fell. The demand curve shifted to the left. At the original prices, fewer policies were being demanded.

Discussion

The situation can be illustrated by a diagram similar to that in Figure 4.2, except in this case the demand curve shifts inwards. Of course, the insurance companies will respond to the fall in demand. We will examine the likely consequences of this in Chapter 5.

Prices of other goods

The demand for a good is affected by changes in the prices of other goods. The demand curve will shift, but the direction and amount of the shift will depend on the nature of the good whose price has changed.

Substitutes are goods with similar characteristics and which may be bought as alternatives to one another. For example, there may be more than one type of treatment available for a particular illness. If they are equally effective, decisions may well be made on the basis of price (and, possibly, of convenience). If Treatment A's price increases, other things being equal, then the demand for it will fall and the demand for the alternative (and equally effective) Treatment B will increase (see Figures 4.3a and b). Note that the price increase and subsequent fall in demand for Treatment A are illustrated by a movement along the demand curve, whereas the increase in demand for Treatment B is shown by a shift of its demand curve to the right.

Complements are goods which are generally used together so that increased consumption of one implies increased consumption of the other. Examples are cars and petrol, computers and software or heart bypass operations and intensive care unit beds. If the price of one good rises, thus depressing the demand for the good, we would expect the demand for its complements to decrease. Figures 4.4a and b show the demand curves for

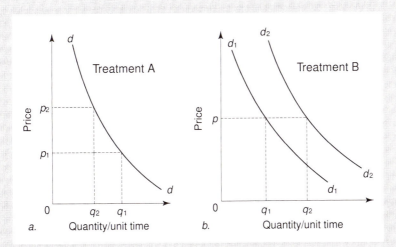

Figure 4.3 The demand curve: substitutes.
When the price of a good changes, the demand curves for its substitutes will shift. If the price rises, the substitute demand curve will shift to the right because more of it will be demanded. If the price falls, the substitute demand curve will shift to the left because less of it will be demanded.

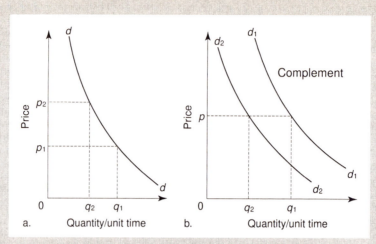

Figure 4.4 The demand curve: complements.
When the price of a good changes, the demand curves for its complements will shift.
If the price rises, the complement demand curve will shift to the left because less will
be demanded. If the price falls, the complement demand curve will shift to the right
because more will be demanded.

the good and its complement. Note again that when the price of the good rises, causing the demand to decrease, this is illustrated by a movement along the demand curve while the fall in demand for the complement is illustrated by a shift of its demand curve to the left.

In health care, many services are complementary in nature. An increased number of operations will be associated with an increased demand for hospital beds and associated 'hotel' services, drugs, nursing staff and consumables such as sterile gloves. An increase in the number of day surgery cases at a large provider hospital may cause an increase in demand for community nurses and GP services as aftercare is delivered at the patient's home.

Case study 4.3 ■ Substitutes

The introduction of the NHS internal market saw a reduction in the number of patients being referred from the home counties to London hospitals. Local purchasers in these areas placed contracts with their local hospitals thus substituting one set of hospital providers for another. The change was encouraged by the lower prices offered by some local hospitals. The demand for cheaper local services increased (a movement along the demand curve) while the demand curves for services at London hospitals shifted to the left.

Another form of substitution occurs if GP fundholders decide to treat diabetes patients within their practices rather than through the more traditional hospital outpatient departments. The demand curve for the hospital services will shift to the left.

Discussion

The extent to which services or personnel may be substituted for one another in health care will depend on factors such as the available technology and the rules which limit the scope of activities of different types of medical staff. For example, nurses may now take a limited role in prescribing drugs. Thus they may now substitute for doctors in certain situations.

Tastes

Changing tastes and preferences can cause demand curves to shift over time. While much development in health care is based on research evidence, it is often the case that such evidence is not unambiguous. Changes in the pattern of treatment may follow fashions of 'informed opinion'. Many years ago, tonsillectomy was a treatment very commonly given to children; now it is not.

Population size and structure

As the population size and/or its structure alters, there will be corresponding shifts in the demand curves for many goods and services. A falling number of births will mean reduced demand for baby clothes and equipment; then demand for midwives and obstetric beds will fall. An increasing number of people aged over 70 will mean increased demand for geriatric beds, residential home places, wheelchairs and walking frames; whether there will be an increased demand (from the economist's point of view) will depend on the families' and society's ability and willingness to pay.

There will be a *need* for more effective treatments for Alzheimer's Disease; whether this will be translated into demand will depend on the willingness of the government to fund research and development and on the willingness of purchasers to pay for such treatments. A new drug, Aricept, is said to be effective in slowing the progress of the disease in those patients in the early stages. However, the drug is expected to cost £1,000 per patient per year and it is estimated that about 200,000 sufferers could potentially benefit. If they all received the treatment it would take up a large percentage of the total NHS drugs budget.

4.2 ■ Supply

The market supply of a good is the total amount offered for sale by producers. Economists generally assume that producers are aiming to maximize their profits but other goals, such as revenue, market share or output maximization, are possible. Supply is a flow over time and it is determined by the price of a good and a number of other factors which will be discussed below.

Factors determining supply

Price

It is expected that the quantity of a good that will be supplied to the market is directly related to the price of the good, other things being equal. If the market price increases, more will be supplied. It is reasonable to assume that suppliers will be willing to supply more if a higher price is being offered. In addition, extra units of inputs may well be available only at higher prices. Unit costs of production may rise as output increases, so a higher price is necessary to induce the supplier to supply more. (This last point is explained in more detail in Chapter 7.) Thus the market supply curve has the shape illustrated in Figure 4.5.

At the low price p_1, only a small quantity q_1 will be supplied to the market whereas at the higher price p_2 a larger quantity q_2 will be supplied, other factors being held constant. In the private health care market we might reasonably expect to find an upward sloping supply curve for cosmetic procedures such as face-lifts.

Prices of other goods

If the price of good A increases relative to that of good B then it is likely that some resources will be attracted from the production of good B to the production of good A because good A is now relatively more profitable to produce. Thus the supply curve for good B will shift to the left. This is illustrated in Figure 4.6a and b.

Note that the increase in supply of good A is shown by a movement along the curve whereas the decrease in supply of good B is shown by a shift of the curve. Some suppliers will supply less; others will stop providing service B altogether, preferring to concentrate

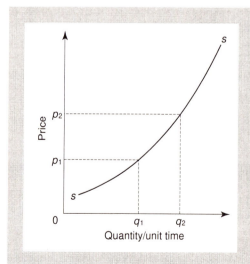

Figure 4.5 The supply curve. The amount that suppliers wish to supply is positively related to the price (other things being equal). The higher the price, the more suppliers wish to supply.

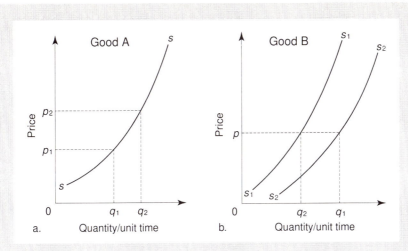

Figure 4.6 The supply curve: substitute products.
When the price of a good changes, the supply curves for other products will shift. If the price falls, the product will be less profitable to produce (other things being equal). Suppliers may shift resources into the production of the more profitable products. The supply curves for these other products will shift to the right.

on services where margins are better. For example, if the price of places in nursing homes falls, owners may choose to supply places to the fitter elderly people whose need of nursing care is not very great.

Cost of factors of production

If, other things being equal, the cost of producing a good increases, then at any given price its production becomes less profitable than before. Thus we would expect the supply curve to shift to the left. Similarly, if a technological breakthrough or a fall in input prices means that the good can be produced at a lower unit cost, then at any particular price the production of the good is more profitable than before. Thus we would expect the supply curve to shift to the right as shown in Figure 4.7.

At price p_1 a quantity q_1 is supplied to the market. After a fall in unit costs the supply curve shifts to the right. Now a larger quantity q_2 is supplied to the market. For example, if private hospital costs fall, private health insurance policies would be more profitable for insurance companies at existing prices. They would wish to supply more. New technology makes it possible for the supply of certain services to be increased, perhaps by reducing costs or use of other inputs. New surgical procedures which lead to a reduced length of stay might lead to an increase in supply, especially if previously supply had been constrained by lack of bed availability. In each of these cases, the supply curve would shift to the right, other things being equal.

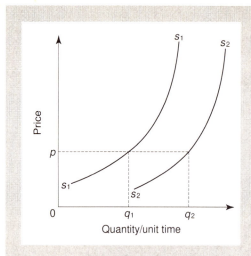

Figure 4.7 Effect of a fall in input prices. A fall in input prices will cause the supply curve to shift to the right. The product is now more profitable to supply. New technology which cuts production costs will also cause the supply curve to shift to the right. At the original selling price, a greater quantity will be supplied.

4.3 ■ Demand and supply in health care

Demand and supply decisions take place in a markets which are subject to various forms of regulation. One of the most important forms of regulation in the UK is the distinction between generalist and specialist medical services. Specialist medical staff, whether self-employed or working for public or private enterprises, are not permitted to treat patients without a letter of referral from a general medical practitioner, except in cases of urgency. Thus, unlike the USA, a patient with recurring headaches cannot self-refer to a neurologist but must first visit a GP as NHS or private patient. The GP will act as agent and gatekeeper, making referral to a specialist if deemed appropriate. Thus in the UK the patient's access, regardless of financial eligibility, requires clinical legitimization by a GP, unlike the situation in France where patients are able to approach a specialist directly if they wish, although they still need referral to a hospital specialist.

It follows that in the UK the patient does not have the right to purchase specialist care in the same way that a pools winner might purchase a Rolls Royce. GPs are able to separate those with serious problems from those with trivial complaints. It also follows that the translation of needs into demands is not necessarily straightforward and involves factors other than financial eligibility.

Suppliers will want to know about how the agents such as health authorities and GP fundholders who purchase on behalf of patients are planning future purchases as well as the underlying patterns of sickness of individuals and communities. Clearly an ageing population will imply increasing needs for certain forms of social and chronic care. Whether these needs can be translated into demands for services is another matter.

Demand

As we saw in the early part of the chapter, the theory of demand assumes that consumers are rational and that they aim to maximize their total utility. It is also the case in most developed economies that consumers are protected by law. Suppliers are not allowed to make misleading claims about their products. Goods must be fit for the purpose for which they are sold. Consumers have access to a wide range of information about various products through reports from magazines and consumers' organizations.

This is far from being the case in formal health care systems. As noted in Chapter 1, purchases are made on the consumer's behalf by a GP, a specialist or government agency. It is not always entirely clear what the objectives of the purchasers are. If the aim is to maximize total benefits or health gain, then expenditure should be allocated in such a way that the marginal benefit per pound is equal for each of the services purchased. Where a purchasing organization is buying services on behalf of a group of patients, it has to be assumed that the purchaser has sufficient information about the client group to make rational purchasing decisions.

How are the benefits of treatments to be assessed and valued? There is in many cases a lack of information about the effectiveness of treatments. Effectiveness itself depends in part on accurate diagnosis, a process which is subject to some margin of error. In addition, there is much uncertainty about the outcomes of some treatments. Although a consumer would not buy a car which only had a 75% chance of working on any particular occasion, some health care treatments have even less chance of being successful.

Large purchasing organizations often place block contracts with providers for entire groups of services, rather than for individual treatments. The volume and the price per item of service are not specified (although this type of contract is being discouraged by the NHS Management Executive). The purchaser is therefore unaware of prices of different services. Thus the purchaser needs to be aware of new procedures and changes in clinical practice across a range of specialties. This process is costly in itself; the costs may outweigh the benefits.

Demand may be variable in the sense that it is not spread evenly throughout the year. Some patients may be more susceptible to accidents or disease during the winter and some diseases appear infrequently in the form of epidemics. Demand for elective services, as the term suggests, may be predictable and stable, permitting careful planning and management.

Supply

We shall have to leave much of the formal discussion of supply until after we have covered the theory of the firm. In many health care systems, supply is highly regulated and does not respond to market forces in the same way as the supply of consumer goods would be expected to do. The way in which the supply of health care services is financed and organized is discussed in Chapter 13.

4.4 ■ Elasticity

The purpose of this section is to introduce the important concept of elasticity, the responsiveness of demand and supply to changes in price, income and any of the other factors which affect demand or supply. As well as knowing the direction in which demand or supply will change in response to changing conditions it is useful to have some measure of how much the quantity demanded or supplied will change. In economics we use a measure of responsiveness called elasticity.

The concept of elasticity is useful in handling managerial questions such as 'Will an increase in price result in an increase in the amount spent on the product' or 'How much will sales increase if we reduce our prices by 5%?'

Price elasticity of demand

The price elasticity of demand, denoted by E_p, measures the responsiveness of demand to changes in price. It is defined as the proportionate change in the quantity demanded divided by the proportionate change in the price, i.e.

$$E_p = \frac{\text{percentage change in quantity demanded}}{\text{percentage change in price}}$$

Example

If when the price of a good increases from 20 to 21, an increase of 5%, the quantity demanded falls from 200 units to 180 units, a fall of 10%, then the value of E_p is given by

$$E_p = \frac{-10}{5} = -2$$

Note that the price elasticity of demand is negative, because when the price increases the quantity demanded falls and vice versa; in other words, price and quantity move in opposite directions.

If the absolute value (ignoring the sign) of E_p is less than 1, then demand is said to be inelastic with respect to price; the proportionate change in the quantity demanded is less in absolute terms than the proportionate change in the price. Demand is not very responsive to price changes. This tends to be the case for necessities and goods for which there are no close substitutes.

If the absolute value of E_p is exactly equal to 1, demand is said to be unit-elastic. The proportionate change in the quantity demanded is in absolute terms exactly equal to the proportionate change in the price. If the absolute value of E_p is greater than 1 then demand is said to be price-elastic. The proportionate change in the quantity demanded in absolute terms is greater than the proportionate change in the price. Demand is very responsive to price changes. If there are many substitutes for a product, the demand for it may well be responsive to price changes. If the price rises, purchasers will seek supplies elsewhere.

Factors affecting the value of the price elasticity of demand

Four main factors determine the value of the price elasticity of demand. These are:

1. **The number of substitutes**
   If there are many close substitutes for the product, and if the price rises, consumers are likely to switch to alternative suppliers. Demand will tend to be very responsive to price changes.
2. **Whether the product is a luxury or a necessity**
   If the product is not a necessity, consumers may choose to go without if the price rises. Thus demand for luxuries tends to be more price-elastic than the demand for necessities.
3. **The proportion of income spent on the product**
   If the amount spent on the product is only a very small amount of the total budget, then consumers are unlikely to be very sensitive to price changes. Demand will tend to be price-inelastic. If, however, the product is expensive and absorbs a large proportion of the consumer's income, then a price rise may reduce demand considerably.
4. **The time period involved**
   It often takes time for consumers to rearrange their spending plans. A price change may have little effect on demand in the short run but have a much greater effect on demand in the long run. Thus, the longer the time period, the more price-elastic the demand for the product.

Case study 4.4

Drug companies are frequently criticized for the high prices they charge for new drugs. When a new drug is developed and given approval, the company usually has a patent which prevents other companies from producing and marketing the drug for a number of years. During this period, the producer of the drug is able to charge a very high price because there are no substitutes. If the drug is effective and the only one of its kind, then the price-elasticity of demand will be very low. The drug companies argue that for every successful drug, many hundreds have to be abandoned in the research stage and therefore high prices are necessary to cover the huge research and development costs.

This is the case with the very successful anti-ulcer drug Zantac, produced by Glaxo Wellcome. It has produced huge profits for the company from its large worldwide sales but the drug is expensive (about £28 for a month's supply in the UK). Now the end of the patent period is approaching. It is not surprising that the company is applying for an extension of the patent period. Once substitute products can be produced by other companies, the price elasticity of demand will increase and the price is likely to fall considerably.

Discussion

The effect of the entry of new competitors once the patent has expired would be expected to have two effects on the demand curve for Zantac. The demand curve would shift to the left as less would be demanded at each possible price. In addition, the section of the demand curve corresponding to possible price-quantity combinations would become less steep. When the curve is less steep, any price change has a larger effect on the quantity demanded; the demand for the drug has become more price-elastic.

Price elasticity and revenue

Revenue is equal to the quantity sold times the price at which the product was sold, i.e.

Revenue = price × quantity

For example, if 100 units of a product are sold at a price of £5 each, the total revenue will be equal to £5 × 100 = £500. If there is a price change, the direction in which revenue changes will depend on the value of the price elasticity of demand for the product, as shown in the table below.

Effect of price changes on revenue

Price elasticity	Price change	Revenue change
Inelastic	Fall	Fall
	Rise	Rise

because the percentage change in the quantity demanded is less than the percentage change in the price (but in the opposite direction).

Unitary	Fall	Unchanged
	Rise	Unchanged

because the percentage change in the quantity demanded is the same as the percentage change in the price (but in the opposite direction).

Elastic	Fall	Rise
	Rise	Fall

because the percentage change in the quantity demanded is greater than the percentage change in the price (but in the opposite direction).

Thus if a company attempted to increase its revenue by raising its price, it would be successful only if the demand for its product was inelastic.

In a health care market where hospitals were free to set the prices of their services at the price they thought the market would bear, the prices of services for which the demand was price-inelastic would include a greater markup on cost than the prices for which the demand was price-elastic.

Cross-price elasticity of demand

This measures the responsiveness of demand for one good or service to changes in the price of another good or service. The cross-price elasticity of demand for good A relative to the price of B is calculated using the formula:

$$E_{px} = \frac{\text{percentage change in demand for good A}}{\text{percentage change in the price of good B}}$$

It would be relevant in cases where providers produce several services for which the demand is related. Changing the price of one of the services would affect not just the demand for that service but also demands for the other services.

If the services A and B are complementary the cross-price elasticity of demand will be negative because if the price of B goes up the demand for B will fall *and so will the demand for A*. If services A and B are substitutes, the cross-price elasticity will be positive because if the price of B goes up, the demand for B will fall *and the demand for A will rise*.

Income elasticity of demand

This measures the responsiveness of demand to changes in income. It is calculated by the formula:

$$E_I = \frac{\text{percentage change in quantity demanded}}{\text{percentage change in income}}$$

For most goods and services we would expect this measure to be positive: if income rises we would expect the demand for the product to increase. However, this is a category of goods for which the income elasticity of demand is negative: the inferior goods described in the section on demand. Staple foods tend to come into this category. Poor people buy a lot of bread and potatoes. As incomes increase they buy less bread and potatoes, and more foodstuffs such as meat.

Goods for which the income elasticity is positive are called **normal** goods. Those for which the income elasticity is between zero and one have demands which are not very sensitive to changes in income. As income rises and falls over the business cycle, the demand for these products tends to fluctuate less than income. Basic clothing is a product with a low but positive income elasticity of demand. The demand for private health care in the UK also falls into this category. The demand is said to be **income-inelastic.**

Those for which the income elasticity is greater than one have demands which are very sensitive to rises and falls in income. As national income fluctuates over the business cycle the demand for these products tends to fluctuate more. Profits on these products can be badly hit in an economic recession. Luxury cars and face-lifts are products with a high income elasticity of demand. The demand for these products is said to be **income-elastic.**

Price elasticity of supply

The price elasticity of supply measures the responsiveness of supply to price changes. It is defined to be:

$$E_s = \frac{\text{proportionate change in quantity supplied}}{\text{proportionate change in price}}$$

We would expect the price elasticity of supply to be positive. As with demand, an elasticity value greater than 1 indicates that supply is responsive to price changes (elastic), whereas a value less than 1 indicates that supply is not very responsive to price changes (inelastic).

Factors affecting the value of the price elasticity of supply

1. The ease with which factors of production can be transferred to or from existing uses.
2. The cost and availability of additional factors of production.
3. The time period involved.

The last point, the time period involved, is very important in determining the price elasticity of supply. Remember that supply is a flow; to increase the production rate may involve increasing hospital size, the amount of equipment in use and the labour force. All these things take time and so it is the case that the supply of many services is inelastic in the short run. It takes many years to train doctors; thus the supply of doctors is inelastic in the short run but more elastic in the long run.

Thus, if there is a sudden increase in the demand for a service or a resource, if supply is inelastic in the short run it is likely that the price will rise, if it is free to move.

Other elasticities

Elasticity is a measure of how responsive one variable is to changes in another variable. The elasticity of X with respect to Y is calculated by

$$E = \frac{\text{Percentage change in } X}{\text{Percentage change in } Y}$$

Thus we can calculate the advertising elasticity of demand, a measure of how responsive demand is to advertising spending, or the elasticity of revenue with respect to occupancy, for example.

References

Gowland, D. and Paterson, A. (1993) *Microeconomic Analysis*, Harvester Wheatsheaf, Hemel Hempstead.
McGuire, A., Henderson, J. and Mooney, G. (1988) *The Economics of Health Care: An Introductory Text*, Routledge and Kegan Paul, London.

Questions for consideration

1. An insurance company has recently announced a new offer to subscribers of private treatment at NHS hospitals at low premiums without any loss of benefits. Recent studies have shown that

health insurers are demanding more services from the NHS as prices at independent hospitals have risen sharply. At the same time the number of NHS pay beds has increased greatly over the past few years.

Use diagrams to show the effect of the changes described above on the demand for

(a) private health insurance,

(b) private health care services,

(c) pay beds at NHS hospitals and

(d) services at independent private hospitals.

2. Minimal access surgery (MAS) is an example of new technology and techniques affecting the supply of certain services. However, at the moment the overall effect is far from clear. On the one hand it generally results in a shorter stay in hospital, less pain and less scarring for the patient. On the other hand, the technique requires trained and skilled surgeons, requires more expensive equipment and each operation takes longer. As MAS is more widely used, discuss the possible effects on

(a) the supply curve for gall bladder operations which can be done either using conventional surgery or the new technique,

(b) the demand for trained surgeons, and

(c) the demand for hospital beds.

3. Real elasticities (with the effect of price inflation removed) of total health expenditure with respect to Gross Domestic product (a close relative of national income) over the period 1960–85 have been estimated for the OECD countries. Some results are shown below.

Australia	1.0	Austria	0.9
Sweden	3.0	UK	2.2
USA	2.3		

Source: Schrieber and Poullier (1987), quoted in Culyer et al. (eds) Competition in Health Care. Interpret these figures and comment on the differences between the values for the different countries.

4. In 1993 BUPA, a health insurance company, responded to the loss of revenue caused by a fall in demand by raising its premiums. What does this strategy suggest about the company's estimate of the price elasticity of demand for its product?

5. In 1992 20 new companies entered the UK health insurance market and the market share of BUPA, the dominant firm, fell to 50% (it had been about 70% in earlier years).

(a) Show the effect of the new entrants on the total supply curve for health insurance.

(b) What effect would you expect the entry of 20 new firms to have on the price elasticity of demand for BUPA's policies?

CHAPTER FIVE

The determination of price

Objectives

- ▓ To show how price is determined in market and quasi-market situations.

- ▓ To show how the price of health care services impacts on the behaviour of health care providers, customers and consumers.

- ▓ To show the effects of setting prices at different levels on incentives of providers and the patterns of competition.

- ▓ To show the impact of changes in input prices and broader changes in technological and regulatory environments.

Introduction

In Chapter 4, we introduced the concepts of demand and supply, and discussed the properties of demand and supply curves. We looked at the way demand and supply curves might alter in response to changes in factors such as income, prices of other products, technology, tastes and population structure. In this chapter we examine the way in which the market price of a product is determined by the interaction of demand and supply. We analyse the effects of price restrictions and of changes in the conditions of demand and supply on the market price of a product, with examples drawn from the field of health care.

5.1 ▓ The determination of price

The market price is determined by the interaction of the market demand for the commodity and the market supply of the commodity. If we superimpose the market demand curve and the market supply curve as in Figure 5.1, we can see that there is only one price

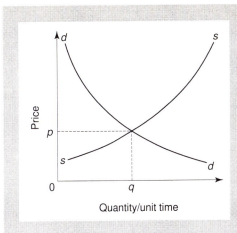

Figure 5.1 The determination of price (1). The price of a product is determined by the interaction of demand and supply.

at which the amount that purchasers wish to buy is exactly equal to the amount that suppliers are willing to supply. It is given by the price level at which the two curves intersect. This price is known as the equilibrium or market clearing price and the corresponding quantity is known as the equilibrium quantity.

The mechanism by which equilibrium is established in a market may be analysed by considering what would happen if the initial price prevailing in the market is either higher or lower than the equilibrium price. First, consider what would happen if the initial price was above the equilibrium as in Figure 5.2. At the high price p_1, the quantity demanded is q_1 but the quantity producers are willing to supply is much greater at q_2. There is excess supply at this price. Suppliers will have to lower their prices to get rid of their surplus stocks and the price will tend to fall.

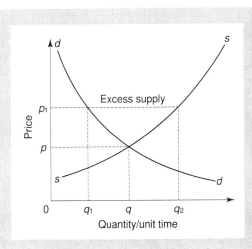

Figure 5.2 The determination of price (2). If the price is above the equilibrium price, suppliers will lower their prices to sell the surplus stock.

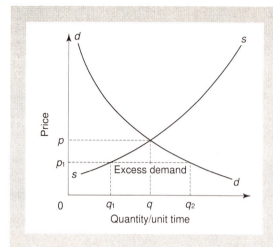

Figure 5.3 The determination of price (3).
If the price is below the equilibrium price, demand will exceed supply. Competition for the scarce good will put upward pressure on prices.

Now consider what would happen if the initial price was too low, as illustrated in Figure 5.3. This time, at the low price p_1 suppliers would be willing to supply only q_1 to the market whereas purchasers would wish to buy the much larger quantity q_2. This time we have excess demand in the market. Competition between purchasers for the scarce good will drive the price up. Once equilibrium is achieved there is no tendency to move away from it as long as the conditions of demand and supply do not change.

Note that in the real world the movement towards equilibrium may not take place smoothly and promptly. Faced with excess supply and unsold stocks of goods, suppliers may be reluctant to cut prices initially, preferring to increase advertising or to offer non-price inducements to purchasers

Nevertheless, if the excess supply persists, competition between suppliers will drive prices down, assuming prices are free to move.

5.2 ▓ The effect of price restrictions

The previous analysis assumes that prices are free to move towards equilibrium, but what happens if they are not?

Effect of a maximum price

Suppose the government sets a maximum price for a good or service, and that this maximum price is below the equilibrium price. Because the price is low, demand will be high. However, at that low price there will be little incentive for suppliers to supply the market. There will be excess demand (the distance AB in Figure 5.4). However, prices are unable to rise and so the excess demand persists. There will be queues, rationing of the

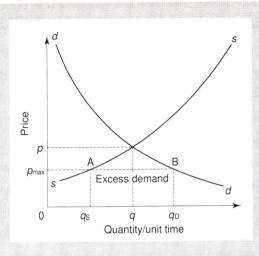

Figure 5.4 The determination of price (4).
When the maximum price is fixed below the equilibrium price, there will be persistent excess demand, since the price cannot rise.

product and possibly the emergence of some sort of black market. (Note that if the maximum price is above the market clearing price, the market will clear.)

Case study 5.1 ▨ The National Health Service

In the UK, the health service is financed from taxation and free for services such as GP consultations and hospital out-patient and in-patient services at the point of delivery. The supply is constrained by the availability of public funds. Because the service is free, demand exceeds supply as shown in Figure 5.5.

The price cannot rise to clear the market so the excess demand persists. There are queues and sometimes long waiting times at GP surgeries, there are waiting lists for hospital treatment and treatments, especially for non-urgent problems, are rationed. The alternative is to seek treatment privately.

Contrast this with the situation in the USA where the health services are mostly provided privately with most people being covered by health insurance, paid for either by themselves or by their employers. Here a third party, the insurance company, is paying for the treatment. The patient may have to pay a small proportion of the price, but most of the fees are paid by someone else.

The effect of this system is shown in Figure 5.6, which shows the demand and supply curves for health services.

In the absence of third party payments, the market would clear at a price of p_e and a quantity of q_e. However, the consumer only pays the low price p_1 and so the demand is at the high level q_1. In order to supply the large amount demanded, the price actually paid for the services has to rise to p_2. Thus much more than the market clearing quantity is supplied, at a price much higher than the market clearing price. Consumers only pay p_1, insurance companies pay the difference $(p_2 - p_1)$. Thus the system of third party payments leads to high prices and a large proportion of the country's resources being devoted to health care services.

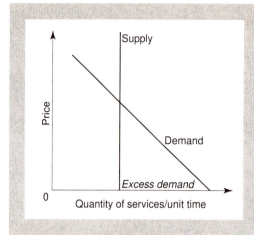

Figure 5.5 Demand and supply in the NHS.

Because the service is free, there is excess demand for NHS services.

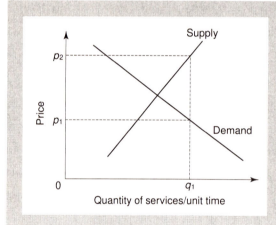

Figure 5.6 Effect of third party payments.

Because consumers pay a low price p_1, they demand the large quantity q. The third parties have to pay p_2 to the suppliers to bring forth that level of supply.

Discussion

In the UK everyone is entitled to treatment and the majority of services are free at the point of use. The drawbacks of the system are that some treatments may be rationed and there may be long waiting lists for others. In addition, some patients might be inclined to ask for unnecessary consultations and visits.

In the USA private insurance-based system not everyone can get insurance. In addition, because of the high prices which result from the system of third-party payments, insurance premiums are high. For employers, paying health insurance premiums for their employees adds significantly to costs and ultimately results in higher prices for consumers of a wide range of goods and services.

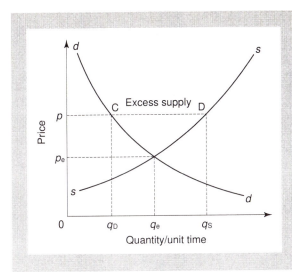

Figure 5.7 The determination of price (5).

When the minimum allowed price is above the equilibrium price, there will be persistent excess supply, since the price cannot fall.

Effect of a minimum price

Now suppose that a minimum price is set for a product or service, or for labour, and that this minimum price is above the market clearing price. The high price encourages suppliers to supply but demand is low. This time there is excess supply (the distance CD in Figure 5.7). The suppliers have 'priced themselves out of the market'. Because the price cannot fall excess supply will exist. The market is unable to clear. Of course, if the suppliers were in a position to create extra demand (supplier-induced demand), the demand curve would shift to the right and the excess supply would disappear.

5.3 ■ The effect of changes in the conditions of demand and supply

A change in any of the factors affecting demand or supply, other than the price of the commodity, will cause one or other, or perhaps both the demand and supply curves to shift. Our earlier discussion enables us to predict the likely effects on the equilibrium price and quantity.

For example, suppose that there is a general increase in incomes of purchasers. The demand curve will shift to the right as shown in Figure 5.8. Because this is a change in the conditions of demand, the supply curve does not shift. The old equilibrium price was p_1 and the equilibrium quantity was q_1. When the demand curve shifts to the right, there is now excess demand (the distance AB) at the old price p_1. This excess demand causes the price to rise until a new equilibrium is reached at the higher price p_2 and quantity q_2. Note that the increase in the quantity supplied has been caused by the increase in the price and is simply a movement along the unchanged supply curve.

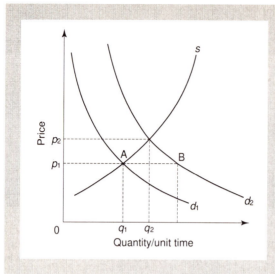

Figure 5.8 The determination of price (6).
When the demand curve shifts to the right, there is excess demand at the original price. The price will rise.

Case study 5.2

UK private nursing home operators faced a fall in profits in 1996 because of falling occupancy rates. Although the outlook in this sector is good, given the expected increase in the proportion of elderly people in the population, in the short run problems have been caused by cuts in local authority budgets which means that the demand for places has fallen. In addition, there is a move towards providing home care rather than nursing home care wherever possible. At present there is overcapacity in the nursing home market and as a result of this many of the larger companies are merging and/or taking over smaller companies.

Discussion

The situation is exactly that represented by Figure 5.9. The demand curve for nursing home places has shifted to the left because purchasers' incomes have fallen and because there is increased demand for the cheaper substitute product, home care (partly because of a change in tastes but also because of the pressure on local authority budgets). As a result, there is evidence of excess supply in the form of lower occupancy rates, in other words, empty beds. Economic theory would suggest that prices should fall. Instead, it seems that the excess places are going to be removed by consolidation of the sector.

Now consider the situation which arises when a technological advance reduces the cost of production. The supply curve will shift to the right, as shown in Figure 5.10. Note that this is a change in the conditions of supply and thus the demand curve is unchanged. At the old equilibrium price p_1 there is now excess supply (the distance CD). The excess supply will drive prices down until a new equilibrium is reached at price p_2 and

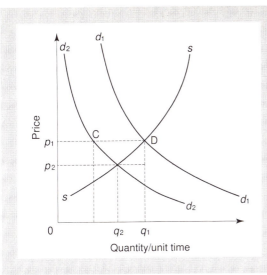

Figure 5.9 The determination of price (7).
When the demand curve shifts to the left there is excess supply at the original price. The price will fall.

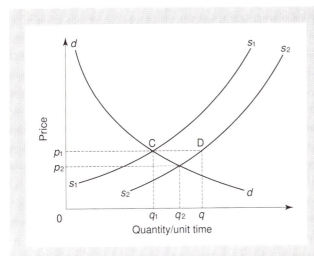

Figure 5.10 The determination of price (8).
When the supply curve shifts to the right, there is excess supply at the original price. Competition between suppliers drives prices down.

quantity q_2. Note that the increased demand has come about because the price has fallen; there has been a movement along the unchanged demand curve.

5.4 ■ The price mechanism and the allocation of resources

In a free market economy where there is no interference in the operation of supply and demand, the allocation decisions of what to produce, how to produce and for whom to produce are made through the price mechanism. As we have seen, the establishment of an equilibrium price through the interaction of supply and demand determines the quantity produced and, through their willingness to pay at that price, the distribution of the product to purchasers. With the same process taking place in all markets, the decision of what to produce and the distribution of the products are achieved through the determination of relative prices in the different markets.

Where resources are scarce their prices will be high and producers and purchasers will use less of them; where they are abundant their prices will be low and producers and purchasers will use more of them. If there is an increase in the demand for a commodity, the excess demand will cause the price to increase, leading suppliers to wish to supply more of the commodity. Resources will be attracted into the production of goods and services which are in great demand and away from the production of goods and services where the demand is falling.

Thus the price mechanism appears to cause resources to be allocated in response to purchaser demand. It is the 'invisible hand' which guides the working of the market economy. If purchasers are trying to maximize patient benefits subject to their limited budgets and providers produce using the 'least-cost' combination of inputs, then resources will be allocated efficiently under this system as long as all markets are competitive and there are no market imperfections or failures. These last points will be discussed in more detail in Chapter 9 on market structures.

5.5 ▓ The determination of prices and the price mechanism in health care

In a market system, if prices are free to move then the prices of services will be determined by the forces of demand and supply; markets will clear. There will be no excess supply or excess demand. Note that this does not mean that there will be no unmet need. As we pointed out in Chapter 4, need is only translated into demand if it is backed up by the necessary purchasing power. However, in health care prices are frequently subject to some form of regulation by governments. Where a resource is in short supply, or where the supplier is able to restrict supplies, the price will be high. Price restrictions may be seen to be in the public interest.

Doctors can only practise if they are licensed by their professional organizations. Thus these organizations have control over entry into the profession. The demand for doctors' services in developed countries is high. A restricted supply coupled with a high demand will lead to a high price for doctors' services as shown in Figure 5.11.

Of course, if the government is the only employer of doctors' services, it will have the market power to impose a maximum wage. Shortages may develop, if some doctors seek employment in other countries which pay higher salaries. It was noted that in the USA in 1986, where there is competition between institutions for doctors and pay is not nationally determined, doctors' salaries were 5.12 times average earnings, whereas in the UK, where doctors' salaries are nationally determined and the main employer is the NHS, doctors' salaries were 2.39 times average earnings (Leigh, 1992).

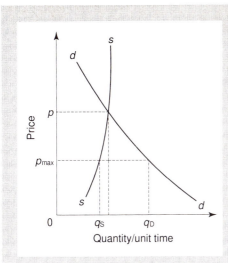

Figure 5.11 The determination of price (9). A combination of restricted supply and high demand will lead to a high price, p. If the government introduces a maximum price, demand will exceed supply. There will be shortages.

In the UK National Health Service internal market, provider units have been instructed to set the price for each service equal to its average cost. Guidelines for the calculation of these average costs have also been issued. Thus, if there is a shortage of a particular service, the excess demand should not lead to higher prices. Thus prices cannot act as signals to providers to encourage them into areas where there are shortages, as they would in markets in the private sector of the economy. Instead, agreements about quantities are struck between purchasers and providers. If there is a shortage of a service, the purchaser will negotiate with providers in order to induce them to supply more.

References

Gowland, D. and Paterson, A. (1993) *Microeconomic Analysis*, Harvester Wheatsheaf, Hemel Hempstead.

Leigh, J. Paul (1992) 'International Comparisons of Physicians' Salaries', *International Journal of Health Services*, **22** (2), pp. 217–20.

McGuire, A., Henderson, J. and Mooney, G. (1988) *The Economics of Health Care: An Introductory Text*, Routledge and Kegan Paul, London.

Questions for consideration

1. Use economic analysis and appropriate diagrams to examine the effects of the following measures on the price and quantity of private sector health services.
   (a) A large and well-publicized increase in National Health Service waiting lists.
   (b) A significant increase in rates of pay for all medical personnel.

2. If all health services were supplied privately through a free market system, how would a change in the age structure of the population affect the relative prices and quantities traded of different services such as obstetric, paediatric and geriatric care? Use economic analysis and diagrams in your answer. What problems might arise if such changes were left entirely to the market system with no state intervention?

3. Use supply and demand analysis, with appropriate diagrams, to explain the situation described in the following case study.

Case study 5.3 ■ The market for nurses

According to the Royal College of Nursing, in early 1997 many hospitals had 20% of their nursing posts vacant and were having great difficulty in recruiting British nurses. As a result they were having to recruit from overseas. The problem stems from problems on both the demand and supply sides of the market.

There has been a large increase in the demand for nurses from private sector nursing homes, clinics and hospitals. According to official figures, numbers of nurses in that sector have increased by 56% between 1990 and 1995. The number of nurses on GP-led primary health teams has increased by 29% over the same period.

The supply of nurses has been affected by a new system of planning training places which was introduced in 1991. Under this system, the former health regions asked trusts to forecast their needs and it seems that most of them underestimated their requirements, perhaps because of overoptimistic forecasts of the number of nurses that could be replaced by support workers taking over the less skilled nursing tasks.

Because of the problem of shortages, another new system was introduced in April 1996. It involves more consultations with trusts, health authorities, colleges and the independent sector. There will be increases in the number of nurses in training over the next few years but it will take time for these increases to feed through to the workforce.

---

4. 'Prices, by conveying relevant signals on both demand and supply, act as a simple mechanism for the resolution of an immensely complex allocation problem. Prices are useful in "invisibly", but not costlessly, allocating resources' (McGuire, Henderson and Mooney, 1988). Using diagrams and examples, explain this statement.

CHAPTER SIX

The economic analysis of production

Objectives

▨ To demonstrate the relationship between the resource inputs and the service outputs produced.

▨ To show how variations in the quantities of inputs influence total outputs.

▨ To examine the measurement of outputs in health care services.

Introduction

A production function is a specification of the relationship that exists at any time, given the existing technology, between the inputs to production and the quantity of output. It is assumed that the production is taking place in the most technically efficient way. As noted in previous chapters, one of the most obvious problems that arises when we try to apply this concept in a health care context is the way output should be measured.

Production functions are important in economic analysis because of the close relationship between the process of production and the cost of that process. They deal with questions such as the degree of substitutability of inputs and the optimum combination of inputs required to produce a given output. We begin by examining the basic concepts and theory of the production function and then discuss its applications and limitations in health service organizations.

6.1 ▨ The production function

The output of an enterprise, denoted by Q, is a function of its inputs. The precise form of this production function will depend on the available technology, the characteristics of the organization, equipment, labour and materials employed by the enterprise. In specifying the production function we will assume that the enterprise is producing the maximum amount of output possible with the inputs at its disposal. In the discussion that follows we will assume that there are just two inputs, denoted by X and Y. In many production function studies and examples, the inputs X and Y are assumed to be quantities of labour and capital.

A simple production function can be represented by an equation such as:

$$Q = f(X,Y)$$

This equation represents the statement 'the amount of total output, Q, is a function of the amount of the first input, X, and the amount of the second input, Y'. The letter f stands for 'is a function of'. The precise form of the equation will depend on the nature of the production process.

Examples of the use of production function analysis in health care

The following examples were cited by Brown (1991). In a study based on an American urban health centre, Zechhauser and Eliastam (1974) measured output by the quantity of services supplied; inputs were the number of doctors and the number of physician assistants. Having estimated the parameters of the production function, they then used data on relative wage rates for doctors and physician assistants to calculate the optimum (cost-minimizing) ratio of doctors to physician assistants.

In another study based on Newfoundland cottage hospitals, Brown estimated a production function in which output was measured by the number of patient-days and the inputs were the number of beds and the number of hospital personnel. His results suggested that hospital productivity had declined over time.

Example of the use of production functions in social care

The approach by Davies and Knapp (1981) considers that the output of old people's residential homes is measured by the benefits to the well-being of the residents and also their 'significant others'. In their study they review the then existing methods of measuring such benefits. On the input side they divide inputs into three categories:

1. **Resource inputs**: the conventional factors of production – buildings, equipment, staff, consumables, etc.
2. **Non-resource inputs**: intangible inputs such as staff attitudes, characteristics of the social environment.
3. **Quasi-inputs**: personalities of the persons in care, resident experiences prior to admission, etc.

Non-resource inputs and quasi-inputs are both intangible; however, non-resource inputs are at least to a certain extent under the control of the organization whereas quasi-inputs are not. In other words, non-resource inputs are endogenous variables, whereas quasi-inputs are exogenous.

Output from the process of production of welfare can be measured on a number of dimensions including psychological well-being, physical health, social interaction and benefits to 'significant others'. The production function approach in this context is to hypothesize that output (welfare) is a function of both the resource and non-resource inputs, but with the particular values of the quasi-inputs being taken as given. If outputs and inputs are identified and measured for a large number of clients, with appropriate statistical analysis it is possible to estimate a production function relationship between outputs and inputs. The results can be used to help to evaluate the contribution of the different inputs to the production of welfare.

Average and marginal product

The production function can be used to explore the relationship between total output and variations in the quantities of the separate inputs. Of particular interest are the measures known as average product and marginal product.

The average product of X, AP_x is the total product divided by the number of units of X employed.

$$AP_x = Q/X$$

This measure is better known as the **productivity of the input,** i.e. output per person employed or output per bed. Changes in the measure are often used to assess efficiency. The marginal product of X, MP_x is the extra output that results from using an extra unit of X while holding the amount of Y constant.

$$MP_x = \Delta Q/\Delta X$$

(The symbol Δ simply means 'a small change in'.) For example, it might be of interest to measure the extra number of patients that could be treated in a hospital by increasing the number of beds but holding the number of medical personnel constant.

Where inputs have to be combined in fixed proportions, the marginal product of a single input will be zero. For example, an operation requires both a surgeon and operating theatre time. An extra surgeon will be unable to perform extra operations if no extra theatre time (and theatre staff) is available. Thus the marginal product of the surgeon, given no extra resources, is zero.

The short run in economic analysis

The short run is the period of time over which the amounts of some inputs cannot be varied. In other words, in the short run some factors of production are fixed in supply. Usually it is taken to be the case that the capital stock (buildings, equipment) is fixed while the labour force is the variable factor. The length of time corresponding to the short run will depend on the type of production process being considered. It may be a few months (the time it would take to build an extension on an existing facility) or it could be several years (the time it would take to plan and build a new hospital or to reorganize services – the planned closure of some London hospitals under the Tomlinson proposals will take many years to implement).

The law of diminishing marginal returns

The law of diminishing marginal returns is a short-run phenomenon, the short run being the time period which is too short to allow all factors of production to be varied. As noted above, we usually assume that the capital stock is fixed and that labour is the variable factor. For example, we would assume that the hospital size and equipment availability are fixed but the number of doctors, nurses, cleaners, etc. could be varied. The law of diminishing marginal returns states that as the quantity of a variable input increases, with the quantities of all other factors held constant, the resulting increases in output eventually decrease in size.

Consider a factory with a fixed amount of capital stock (factory buildings, machinery). If there is only one employee, this person will have to do all the different tasks necessary to produce the output. As more labour is employed, specialization and division of labour will be possible, enabling the capital stock to be used more intensively and causing output to increase rapidly (the marginal product of labour is high). Eventually, though, the addition of extra units of labour will result in smaller increases in output as the capital stock is now being used to its full capacity (the marginal product of labour, although still positive, is smaller than before). A point will be reached where further increases in the amount of labour employed lead to no further increase in output (the marginal product of labour is zero). It may even be the case that output will start to fall because there are so many employees they are hindering rather than helping the production process (the marginal product of labour is negative). In this case the relationship between total output and the amount of the variable input, labour, will be similar to that shown in Figure 6.1.

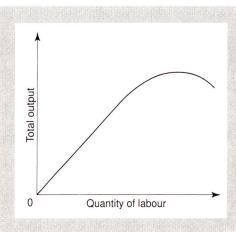

Figure 6.1 The total product curve.
In the short run, with some factors of production fixed in supply, adding more units of the variable factor, in this case labour, eventually results in little or no increase in output.

The total output curve initially rises quite steeply when the amount of labour increases, but after a point the curve rises less steeply and then flattens off. This illustrates the law of diminishing marginal returns.

In a health care context we might imagine a clinic with consulting rooms, a reception area and a general office. If staffed by one doctor without support staff, this doctor will have to keep records, answer the telephone and deal with correspondence as well as seeing patients. If extra staff are used such as a receptionist, a practice nurse, a second doctor, the number of patients treated will increase quite sharply. However, the total number will be limited by the fact that there is only a limited amount of physical space for consultations in the centre. Once a certain number of staff have been employed, adding more will not increase the number of patients who can have consultations at the clinic. From the total output curve we can derive the curves for average product (output per unit of labour) and marginal product (the extra output added by an extra unit of labour).

Average product is always positive. It rises when total output is rising fast and then falls when total output rises less fast. When average product is rising, marginal product must be larger than average product. This is because each extra unit of labour must be adding enough to total output to pull the average up. When average product is falling, marginal product must be below average product. This is because at this point the extra amount of output each extra unit of labour is adding is low enough to be pulling the average down. Eventually, when the point is reached where total output is falling, marginal product must be negative. The graphs for average and marginal product are shown in Figure 6.2.

The implication of the law of diminishing marginal returns is that in the short run the marginal cost of production will eventually rise as output increases. This is because each extra unit of labour time costs the same, but after a certain level of output, each extra unit of labour time will be adding less to total production than previous units did. Thus producing an extra unit of output is becoming more expensive.

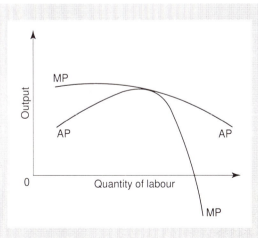

Figure 6.2 Average and marginal product.
Because the total output eventually stops increasing as more units of the variable input factor are added, average product starts to decline and marginal product becomes zero. It may even become negative if increasing the amount of the variable factor beyond a certain point actually causes total output to decline.

The long run in economic analysis

The long run is the minimum period of time over which the quantities of all inputs can be varied. In particular, the capital stock can be varied so that the scale of operations can be altered. In the long run the question of the degree to which inputs can be substituted for one another becomes more important. Some inputs can be substituted for one another in the short run, so the analysis which follows can be applied to short-run situations. However, when it comes to questions of substituting capital for labour, that is usually a long-run problem.

Substitutability of inputs

In many production processes, it is possible to substitute one input for another, at least to a certain extent. For example, in the delivery of health care, nurses may be able to provide some services usually seen as the province of doctors, such as prescribing or performing minor operations. Care assistants may be able to perform some services instead of nurses. To enable us to explore this concept further, it is useful to introduce the concept of the isoquant.

Even with only two inputs, drawing graphs to illustrate production functions requires three dimensions. To overcome this problem, curves can be drawn showing the different input combinations required to produce a given level of output, as shown in Figure 6.3. All points on the curve labelled 'Output level Q_1' represent the same level of output but produced by different input combinations. At point A, an input combination of x_a and y_a has been chosen. At point B, the same output level has been achieved with an input combination of x_b and y_b. If X represented labour and Y represented capital, then A would be a labour-intensive method of production whereas B would represent a choice of a more capital-intensive method. The choice of method would depend, at least in part, on

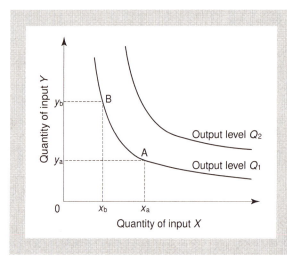

Figure 6.3 Isoquants: different levels of output.
A and B represent different combinations of inputs X and Y which can be used to produce the same amount of output Q_1. If X represents labour and Y represents capital, then A represents a more labour-intensive method of production than B. Q_2 is a higher output level than Q_1.

the relative cost of the different inputs. The curve labelled 'Output level Q_2' is another isoquant representing the input combinations required to achieve the higher level of output Q_2.

The isoquants drawn in Figure 6.3 are smooth, implying that inputs are divisible and can be smoothly substituted for one another. If inputs were perfect substitutes for one another the isoquants would look like those in Figure 6.4. Here the degree of substitutability is always the same, whatever combination of inputs is being used. This situation is unlikely to be encountered in practice. Figure 6.5 illustrates a situation where the inputs cannot be substituted for one another at all. They have to be combined in fixed proportions in order to produce the output, as in the example about surgeons and operating theatre time introduced in the discussion about marginal product.

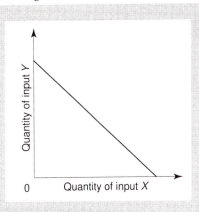

Figure 6.4 Isoquants: perfect substitutability of inputs.
Inputs X and Y are perfect substitutes for one another. They are interchangeable.

A non-medical example is bicycle production. Each bicycle requires (among other things) two wheels and a frame. An increase in the number of wheels available will not result in the production of more bicycles if no frames are available. In the same way, each surgical operation requires a surgeon and an anaesthetist. An extra intensive care bed cannot be used without the specialist staff to care for the extra patient.

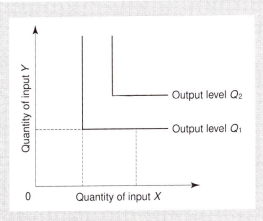

Figure 6.5 Isoquants: zero substitutability of inputs.
X and Y cannot be substituted for one another, providing extra units of input X without any extra units of input Y will not result in any extra output.

Example

The L-shaped isoquant shown in Figure 6.5 can be the result of rules and regulations in the medical profession. Until recently, in the UK, nurses were not allowed to prescribe medicines or carry out operations. Therefore they could not be used as substitute inputs for doctors at all. More recently, in the UK, there have been been isolated examples where specially trained nurses are allowed to carry out simple operations. Thus in some cases, the shape of isoquants in medicine can be altered by altering the rules.

Figure 6.6 shows an isoquant in which the inputs can be substituted for each other but they are not perfect substitutes. This can be seen from consideration of how much of one input is required to substitute for the other at different input levels.

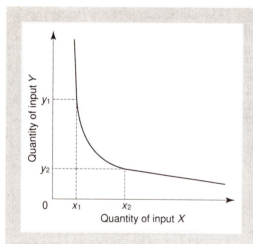

Figure 6.6 Isoquants: limited substitutability of inputs.
Inputs *X* and *Y* can be substituted for one another but only to a limited extent as they are not perfect substitutes.

Suppose the amount of *X* is reduced from A to B as shown on Figure 6.7. It can be seen that the amount of input *Y* must be increased from C to D in order to maintain the same output level. However, if the amount of *X* was reduced from E to F, the same amount as A to B, this time the amount of extra *Y* required to maintain the output level is much greater, G to H. This is because in the first case, when the amount of *X* was at A, there was a large amount of *X* available and the extra contribution made by the amount AB was probably rather small. However, at E, there is relatively little of input *X* in the production process. Each unit is probably making a large contribution and it is more difficult to compensate for the loss of the amount EF, since the inputs are not perfect substitutes. For example, several care assistants may be less effective in caring for a patient than a single skilled and experienced nurse who recognizes signs and symptoms and reacts appropriately.

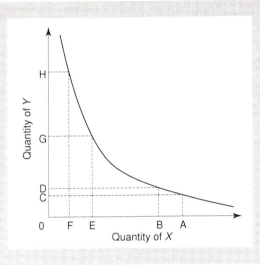

Figure 6.7 Isoquants: substitutability at different input levels.
The amount of Y needed to substitute for a small reduction in the amount of X will be low if relatively large amounts of X are being used. If not much X is being used, then much more Y will be needed to compensate for its loss.

Varying the skill-mix

Case study 6.1 ▓ Doctor–nurse substitution

A review of studies of doctor–nurse substitution was carried out by Richardson and Maynard (1995). Different studies suggested that between 30% and 70% of tasks performed by doctors could be performed by nurses instead. It was also estimated that 30% of doctors could be replaced by nurses, saving the health service millions of pounds.

The situation can be illustrated using an isoquant, as shown in Figure 6.8. On the horizontal axis, we measure units of nurse input and on the vertical axis we measure units of doctor input. The units of input could be hours, for example. The isoquant represents all combinations of doctor and nurse input that can be used to produce that particular level of output.

The suggestion is that the input combination is altered to use fewer doctors (d_2 is lower than d_1) and more nurses (n_2 is higher than n_1) to produce the same level of output. Since nurses are paid less than doctors, in the main, this change should save money. However, Richardson and Maynard advise caution in the interpretation of the results of the studies. They all used measures of intermediate output, such as the number of patients treated, and did not consider outcomes. Many of the studies had design flaws such as small samples or special circumstances which meant the results could not be generalised.

There are other problems which have to be addressed before a decision can be made about the cost-effectiveness of doctor–nurse substitution. First, measuring costs may not be straightforward. Salaried doctors are not necessarily paid overtime, whereas nurses usually are. What if nurses take longer than doctors to perform the same tasks? Is the quality of output the same? What if nurses have to be supervised? What happens if relative costs change?

All these questions need to be addressed before any fundamental decisions about skill-mix are taken.

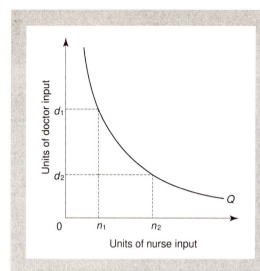

Figure 6.8 Varying the skill mix. The same level of service is maintained by substituting nurses for doctors.

Discussion

This case study illustrates some general problems associated with finding the lowest-cost input combination. It must be possible to measure the inputs in such a way that their true cost can be identified. Considerable attention must be paid to the appropriate definition and measurement of output, an issue which will be discussed in Section 6.3 and in Chapter 11.

6.2 ■ Returns to scale

In a long-term planning context, where the scale of operations can be varied, it is important for managers to consider the advantages and disadvantages of increasing the scale of organizations. For example, what are the advantages and disadvantages of building a few large hospitals as opposed to a large number of smaller local facilities? What are the advantages and disadvantages of having a smaller number of large high quality Accident and Emergency Departments with longer travelling times for patients, given the importance of the 'golden hour' after an accident?

A crucial question, which depends on the nature of the production function is: 'what happens to output if all the inputs are increased by the same proportion? Does output increase in the same proportion as the increase in inputs?' If so, we have **constant returns to scale**. However, it might be the case that over a certain range at least, output increases by a greater proportion than the proportionate increase in inputs. If so, we have **increasing returns to scale**. This situation suggests that it is a more efficient use of resources to produce on a larger scale.

It is not always the case that increasing the scale of operations produces such benefits. It is possible that output may increase by a lower proportion than the increase in inputs. In this case we have **decreasing returns to scale**. In this situation, smaller units provide a more efficient use of resources than larger units.

Clearly the nature of the returns to scale has significant cost implications and we shall return to this question in the discussion of costs. First, though, we must consider the important question of the measurement of output.

6.3 ▨ Measurement of output in health care

In the examples of production functions cited above, output was measured as the number of services provided in the first case and as the number of patient days in the second case. Other measures have been used in these types of studies, such as the number of completed consultant episodes or the weighted sum of services provided. All of these measures present difficulties when it comes to the interpretation of the results and comparisons between institutions.

Consider the patient-day. Patient service requirements are different for each type of case and at different points in their treatment profile. Some services are associated with admission and discharge and are therefore used at the beginning and end of the stay. The 'hotel' services – meals, laundry, etc. – may well be fairly constant throughout the patient's stay. Treatment inputs may well be high at the beginning of the patient's stay, particularly if operations are required, but then may fall to lower and lower levels until the patient is discharged. As the case-mix and severity of patient conditions varies both over time and between institutions, the results of any analyses based on this variable should be interpreted with caution.

As pointed out in earlier chapters, a much more serious criticism can be levelled at the use of measures which are based simply on counting either services provided or patients treated. These measures take no account of patient outcomes. Whether the patient is cured or not, lives or dies, makes no difference. And yet it is surely reasonable to consider that the output of a health care organization should somehow be related to the increase in levels of health of the patients treated. It should not be forgotten that an increase in the health of a patient will bring indirect benefits to those associated with the patient.

In many ways, measures such as services provided or patient-days are in fact inputs into the production of health and not outputs at all. They can be thought of as intermediate outputs. The resources of land, labour and capital produce the services and provide the patient-days. These in turn are inputs into the production of health. Looking at the production of the intermediate output provides a useful method of examining the **processes** by which health care is delivered. However, our analysis cannot be complete until we examine the final outputs of the system, and these final outputs are the improvements in health that the system was designed to produce. We will be examining the problems of the measurement and valuation of these final outcomes in Chapter 11.

Example

The following numerical exercise involving a hypothetical (and simple) production function will help to illustrate the points made in this chapter. The body of the table shows output measured as units of patient care per week. The inputs are units of nurse input and units of doctor input.

Units of nurse input	Units of doctor input				
	1	2	3	4	5
1	50	77	100	118	132
2	66	100	128	150	174
3	77	118	150	178	204
4	87	132	168	200	228
5	95	145	184	218	250

It may seem somewhat clumsy to refer to units of nurse input and units of doctor input rather than just 'nurses' and 'doctors' but it is an explicit recognition of the fact that nurses and doctors are not homogeneous. They vary considerably in skills, qualifications and experience, and any production function approach should take this into account.

From the table it can be seen that a combination of 2 units of doctor input and 3 units of nurse input produces an output of 118 patient care units per week, while a combination of 4 units of doctor input and 2 units of nurse input produces an output of 150 patient care units per week.

Average and marginal product

The average product of units of nurse input depends on how many units of doctor input are employed. For example, if we hold units of doctor input constant at 2, then from the table we have the following figures for units of nurse input and output of patient care (average product is calculated by dividing output by the number of units of nurse input. Marginal product is calculated by assessing how much **extra** output each extra unit of nurse input provides):

Units of nurse input	Output	Average product	Marginal product
1	77	77	*
2	100	50	23
3	118	39.3	18
4	132	33	14
5	145	29	13

With the number of units of doctor input held constant at 2, we can see that both the average product and the marginal product of units of nurse input decline as the number of units of nurse input increases. This illustrates the law of diminishing marginal returns. Note that the law of diminishing returns only applies when some inputs are fixed in supply.

Returns to scale

Now if we consider what happens when both the number of units of nurse input and the number of units of doctor input are allowed to vary (and assume that the capital stock and other inputs also vary in the same proportion) we can see that when 1 unit of doctor input and 1 unit of nurse input is employed, output is 50 units of patient care. If we double the quantities of both inputs to 2 units of nurse input and 2 units of doctor input, output is 100, also double. So doubling the amount of inputs has doubled the amount of output. Similarly, trebling the inputs trebles the output and so on. We have constant returns to scale.

Finally, we consider the optimum input combination. Suppose the management have a target output of 118 units per week. We can see from the table that this output can be achieved with either 2 units of doctor input and 3 units of nurse input, or 4 units of doctor input and 1 unit of nurse input (and some fractional combinations in between, but to keep the example simple we shall ignore them). Suppose units of doctor input cost £150 and units of nurse input cost £50. Then 2 units of doctor input and 3 units of nurse input will cost in total £450. The other combination will obviously be more expensive since the doctor input is so much larger. In fact it costs £650.

Now consider the cost of producing 77 units per week. This can be done with either 2 units of doctor input and 1 unit of nurse input, or 1 unit of doctor input and 3 units of nurse input. At the present prices of doctor and nurse units, the first combination costs £350 and the second combination costs £300, cheaper by £50. However, if a glut of doctors means that the cost of a unit of doctor input falls to £120 while the cost of a unit of nurse input rises to £90, the first combination now costs £330 while the second costs £390, more expensive by £60. Thus the choice of optimal input combination depends on relative prices. This will be explained further in Chapter 8.

Substitution of inputs

This last part is a little more complicated and you might want to omit it on a first reading. The explanation will require the use of fractions of units of nurse and doctor input. Consider the output level when we have 2 units of doctor input and 5 units of nurse input. From the table we can see that the output is 145. If we take one unit of nurse input away the output drops by 13 to 132. How many units of *doctor* input would be required to bring us back to an output level of 145? We can see that adding a whole unit of doctor input would take us up to 168, so we only need a fraction of that, about one-third. So when we have 5 units of nurse input, we do not need very much in the way of units of doctor input to compensate.

Now consider the output level when we again have 2 units of doctor input, but this time only 2 units of nurse input. The output level is 100. If we take 1 unit of nurse input away, the output level drops to 77. This time, to get back to the same output level, we require 1 whole unit of doctor input. So when we do not have many units of nurse input to start with, if one is taken away, we need more units of doctor input to compensate.

References

Brown, M. C. (1980) 'Production and Cost Relations of Newfoundland Cottage Hospitals', *Inquiry*, 17.

Brown, M. C. (1991) *Health Economics and Policy: Problems and Prescriptions*, McLelland and Stewart, Toronto.

Davies, B. and Knapp, M. (1981) *Old People's Homes and the Production of Welfare*, Routledge and Kegan Paul, London.

Richardson, G. and Maynard, A. (1995) 'Fewer Doctors? More Nurses? A Review of the Knowledge Base of Doctor–Nurse Substitution', Discussion Paper 135, Centre for Health Economics, University of York.

Zechhauser, R. and Eliastam, M. (1974) 'The Productivity Potential of the Physician Assistant', *Journal of Human Resources*, 9, pp. 95–117.

Questions for consideration

1. In real-life problems in health care, there are generally more than two inputs to the production process. Think about using a production function approach to analyse the behaviour of the following organizations. What would the inputs be? What would the output be? What measurement problems would you expect to encounter?
   (a) A hospital.
   (b) A GP fundholding practice.
   (c) A health authority.
2. Repeat the calculations in the exercise at the end of the chapter for the following production function, considering management output targets of 152 and 230.

Units of nurse input	1	2	3	4	5
	\multicolumn{5}{c}{Units of doctor input}
1	100	123	139	152	162
2	152	190	211	230	246
3	193	238	267	293	313
4	230	283	319	348	372
5	263	323	365	398	426

Comment on the nature of the returns to scale. Suppose the department had a total budget of £400 to spend on doctor and nurse inputs. If 1 unit of doctor input costs £100 and 1 unit of nurse input costs £50, what (approximately) is the highest level of output that can be attained?

CHAPTER SEVEN

The economic analysis of costs

Objectives

- To examine the different types of costs incurred in producing health care services.

- To show how different types of costs behave with varying levels of activity in the short and longer terms.

- To examine the most efficient size for health care organizations bearing in mind economies of scale and scope.

Introduction

In this chapter we look at the nature of costs and their relationship to the production process and to changes in the scale of that production. The process of the identification, classification and analysis of costs is vital to any organization. It provides a basis for pricing and for future investment decisions, for the identification of inefficiencies and opportunities for savings. It is important therefore that costs should be classified with as few ambiguities as possible. As this chapter will show, this is far from easy in the health care services.

7.1 ■ The classification of costs

Fixed costs

Fixed costs are those costs which do not vary at all with the level of activity of the enterprise over the time period under consideration (often one year). Examples are rent, rates, capital charges, insurance premiums and so on. Also included would be the salary costs of any staff on long-term contracts, such as consultants.

Variable costs

Variable costs are those costs which do vary continuously with the level of activity of the enterprise. Examples are patient food costs, costs of disposable bed linen, operating theatre consumables such as rubber gloves, and salaries of staff on short-term or piece-rate contracts. The cost of nurses recruited from agencies to cover short-term peaks in demand or staff sickness would be classed as variable costs.

Semi-variable costs

These costs have a fixed and a variable element. They do vary with the level of activity, but not in a continuous fashion. For example, a trained nurse may be able to care for up to ten patients. Because the nurse is an indivisible input, he or she is still required if there are only five patients on the ward. However, if the number of patients rises to twelve, two nurses will be required. Thus nursing costs do vary with the number of patients, but in a stepped fashion, as shown in Figure 7.1.

It is important to note that of course consultants, nurses, porters and cleaners are all *physically* indivisible inputs. As Dawson (1994) points out, what determines whether their wages or salaries are regarded as fixed or variable costs is the nature of the *contract* under which they are employed. If a consultant was paid on a per case basis, his or her remuneration would become a variable cost. What is more, if the consultant was employed on that basis, the risk of a loss of income in periods of low demand is shifted from the hospital to the consultant.

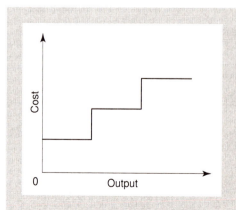

Figure 7.1 Semi-variable costs.
Semi-variable costs do increase with output, but are fixed over some ranges, jumping incrementally as output increases.

7.2 ▓ Direct and indirect costs

Costs can also be classified according to whether they can be directly identified with a particular activity or not.

> **Direct costs**, also known as separable costs, are those costs which can be directly identified with a particular product or service. In hospitals, drug costs and operating theatre costs would be classified as direct costs because they can be identified with a particular patient and thus with a service and specialty.
>
> **Indirect costs** are those costs which cannot be identified with a particular product or service. Note that this may be because the systems for tracing costs back to patients and specialties does not exist. It many cases it would be very costly to introduce such a system. Common examples of indirect costs of patient care in hospitals are catering and laundry expenditure.

It is important to note that the direct/indirect classification is almost entirely independent of the fixed/variable classification. Sometimes indirect costs are referred to as 'overheads' but this is confusing. Some indirect costs could be variable costs whereas true overheads are fixed costs.

The salary of an orthopaedic surgeon on a long-term contract is a fixed cost. It is also a direct cost as it can be directly associated with a particular specialty. The salary of a senior manager on a long-term contract is also a fixed cost, but it is an indirect cost as it cannot be associated with any particular activity. The provision of disposable bedding and linen within a hospital is a variable cost; whether or not it is a direct or an indirect cost will depend on the information systems within the hospital. Does a mechanism exist for recording the cost of this item for each patient? If so, it is a direct cost because it can be separated out by activity. However, the cost of doing this for each patient for items such as bedlinen, food and other services would be prohibitive. Thus, as noted above, the cost is likely to be recorded as an indirect cost.

This example illustrates an important point made by Dawson. She points out that the division of costs into direct and indirect is often an arbitrary one determined by the nature of contracts and the quality and detail of information systems. 'The Direct/Indirect/Overhead distinction simply relates to our lack of information (or the costs of acquiring information) on precisely what inputs are used for treating a particular patient for a particular problem' (Dawson, 1994, pp. 14–15).

7.3 ▓ Allocation of indirect costs

Even when all direct costs of each specialty and procedure, and the indirect costs of the organization have been identified, there is still the problem of deciding what proportion of the indirect costs should be allocated to each procedure/specialty in order to estimate the full cost. MacKerrell (1993), produced a simple example to show how different but entirely logical methods of apportioning indirect costs lead to very different results.

He took the example of a specialty which has been allocated indirect costs of

£200,000. Within the specialty, 400 procedures were carried out in the previous year at a total direct cost of £400,000. The average time taken to carry out each procedure was 30 minutes. How should the indirect costs be spread over the individual procedures?

MacKerrell then gives two examples of procedures (there are other procedures carried out within the specialty). Procedure A requires sophisticated equipment and expensive personnel. The direct cost is £1,000 and the procedure takes 1 hour. Procedure B is straightforward. The direct cost is £600 and it takes 2 hours. He then shows the effect of allocating indirect costs in three different ways.

1. Per procedure. We are told that last year 400 procedures were carried out. Indirect costs total £200,000 so the indirect cost per procedure is £500. There the full cost of Procedure A is £1,500 and of Procedure B is £1,100.
2. Per hour. We are told that last year 400 procedures were carried out at an average time of 30 minutes. This gives 200 hours altogether. Since indirect costs are £200,000, this represents an indirect cost of £1,000 per hour. Procedure A takes 1 hour. The direct cost is £1,000 and the indirect cost if also £1,000, giving a full cost of £2,000. Procedure B takes 2 hours. The direct cost is £600 and the indirect cost is now £2,000, giving a full cost of £2,600.
3. Per direct cost. The total direct costs of the specialty were £400,000. The indirect costs were £200,000. This method requires that we allocate the indirect costs in proportion to the direct costs. So every £1 of direct cost will incur 50p of indirect cost. Since Procedure A has a direct cost of £1,000, the indirect cost will be £500, giving a full cost of £1,500. Procedure B has a direct cost of £600, so the indirect cost will be £300, giving a full cost of £900.

In each case, the indirect costs are fully allocated to the procedures but the resulting cost estimates are very different.

7.4 ▨ Total, average and marginal cost

In this section we will look at the relationships between total, average and marginal cost of production. All of these economic variables are functions of the level of output which we will denote by Q. At this point we will not consider the question of how output is being measured, but the points made in the previous chapter still apply. In the internal market of the UK National Health Service, provider units are instructed by the Department of Health to charge prices for their services which are equal to short-run average total costs. We examine what this cost concept represents and its relationship with the level of activity of the organization.

In the short run some factors of production are fixed in supply and therefore total cost is the sum of total fixed costs and total variable costs. For brevity we write

$TC = TFC + TVC$
where TC = total cost, TFC = total fixed cost and TVC = total variable cost.

Average total cost is equal to total cost per unit. It is obtained by dividing total cost by the number of units of output, i.e.

$$ATC = TC/Q$$

where ATC = average total cost and Q = number of units of output.

ATC is also known as 'unit cost'. The UK Department of Health rules state that NHS Trusts should set their prices at the unit cost (ATC) of the service concerned with no cross-subsidy permitted.

Because total cost TC can be divided into fixed and variable elements, so can average total cost.

We have
$$\begin{aligned} ATC &= (TFC + TVC)/Q \\ &= TFC/Q + TVC/Q \\ &= AFC + AVC \\ &= \text{Average fixed costs + average variable costs.} \end{aligned}$$

Thus the unit costs of a service can be divided into fixed and variable elements. This may be a useful distinction; unit fixed costs will always fall as the number of units increases whereas unit variable costs may rise or fall depending on production conditions.

A very important concept is that of **marginal cost**. At any level of output, marginal cost is the increase in total cost that would result from the production of one extra unit. If total cost is increasing slowly as output increases that means that marginal cost is low. If total cost is increasing sharply as output increases, that means that marginal cost is high.

7.5 ■ Short-run cost curves

The total cost curve

We now consider how these different costs vary with the level of output. Figure 7.2 illustrates a total cost curve. Cost is measured on the vertical axis and output (Q) is measured on the horizontal axis. When Q is zero, total cost is positive because even when the firm is not producing anything it is incurring fixed costs. On the diagram fixed costs are represented by the vertical distance OA. At output Q_b the total cost of producing that output is given by the vertical distance from that point on the horizontal axis to the point B on the total cost curve. The average total cost of producing output Q_b is found by dividing the total cost by Q_b.

Marginal cost tells us the rate at which total cost is increasing. Graphically, the marginal cost at any point on the total cost curve is given by the steepness of the curve at that point. Where the curve has a steep slope, marginal cost is high; where the curve is flatter, the marginal cost is lower.

Total fixed costs and marginal cost

Suppose total fixed costs fell but total variable costs remained the same. The total cost curve would retain the same shape but would cross the vertical axis lower down, at C, say,

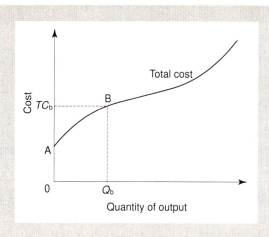

Figure 7.2 The total cost curve.
The total cost of production increases as the level of output increases. It does not always increase at the same rate. It may increase more slowly at some output levels than at others.

as shown in Figure 7.3. The new total cost curve is parallel to the old total cost curve. Its steepness at any point, which represents marginal cost, is unaltered. Thus changes in the level of fixed costs do not affect marginal costs. This result is obvious really. Since marginal cost is the cost of producing one extra unit and the fixed costs are the same by definition whatever the level of activity, the level of fixed costs can have no impact on the cost of production of one extra unit.

This result has important implications for the pricing of units of spare capacity. If a hospital or unit has spare capacity which would otherwise remain unused in the short run, it will be profitable to charge a price which does not necessarily cover the full cost, as long as it covers the marginal cost of production and perhaps makes a small contribution to overheads. For example, if the contract for cataract surgery only requires 90% of available capacity the remaining 10% could be used for patients of GP fundholders at a lower price to make a contribution as long as variable costs are covered.

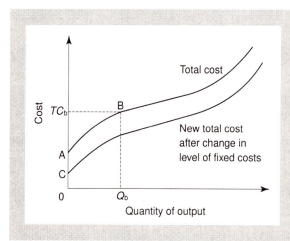

Figure 7.3 The total cost curve after change in fixed costs.
A change in the anticipated level of fixed costs will alter the height of the total cost curve but will not alter its shape. It will shift to a position parallel to the original curve. The slope will be unaltered.

The average cost curves

By definition, total fixed costs do not vary with the output level. Thus average fixed cost must fall as output increases, as the total fixed costs are spread over a larger and larger number of units of output. The graph of average fixed costs will have a shape similar to that shown in Figure 7.4.

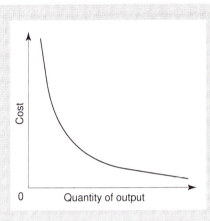

Figure 7.4 Average fixed costs. Because fixed costs are being spread over a larger number of units of output, average fixed costs decrease as output increases.

In the short run, when some factors of production are fixed, average variable costs are likely to fall and then to rise as output increases. This is because of the law of diminishing returns, introduced in the previous chapter. Given fixed capital stock, as the labour force increases, specialization and the efficient use of capacity means that output may well increase quite fast and this will drive the average variable cost down.

However, as capacity constraints are reached, extra units of output may become expensive to produce. For example, more night shift and weekend working might be required. Thus average variable costs may well begin to rise, giving an average variable cost curve as shown in Figure 7.5. The average total cost curve is calculated by adding the corresponding costs on the average fixed cost curve and the average variable cost curve, giving a short-run average total cost curve as shown in Figure 7.6.

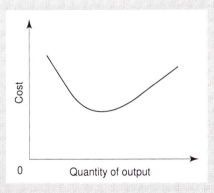

Figure 7.5 Average variable cost. Average variable cost may initially decline as output increases but it will eventually rise as using the fixed capacity more intensively becomes more expensive.

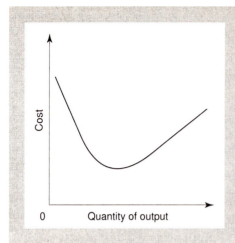

Figure 7.6 Average total cost.
At any level of output, average total cost is the sum of average fixed costs and average individual cost. In the short run it will eventually rise as output increases.

Average cost and marginal cost

If the production of an extra unit of the output causes average cost to fall, then it follows that the cost of producing this extra unit, the marginal cost, must have been lower than the previous average. Similarly, if the production of an extra unit of output causes average cost to rise, then the marginal cost of producing this extra unit must have been greater than the previous average.

To put it another way, if the marginal cost is greater than average cost then the average cost must be increasing; when the marginal cost is less than average cost, the average cost must be decreasing. It follows from this that if the average cost curve has a minimum point when we plot it on a graph, then the marginal cost curve must intersect the average cost curve at the minimum point of the average cost curve.

A very useful result follows from the consideration of the relationship between average variable cost and marginal cost. It may well be the case that over a certain range of output, average variable cost is constant. Thus the variable costs associated with the production of an extra unit will be the same over that range of output. But another way of describing the variable costs associated with producing one extra unit of output is marginal cost. Thus if average variable cost is constant, marginal cost equals average variable cost. The short-run average and marginal cost curves are shown in Figure 7.7.

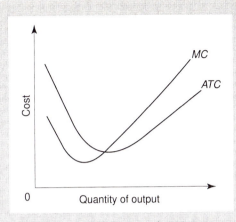

Figure 7.7 Average and marginal costs. The marginal cost curve cuts the average cost curve at its minimum.

| Case study 7.1 |

Teeling Smith (1990) described a Swedish study in which the costs of four different methods of reducing post-operative infections in total joint replacement were compared. The four methods were:

1. Prophylactic antibiotics (SA).
2. Cement impregnated with gentamyacin (PC).
3. The 'Charnley enclosure' to achieve a sterile environment for the surgery (SE).
4. Exhaust ventilated suits for the theatre staff (XS).

The first two methods cost a constant amount per case, whereas the second two involved purchase and installation of expensive equipment, whose cost per case fell as more operations were performed.

The graphs of average cost per case are shown in Figure 7.8. It can be seen that if fewer than 100 operations per year were performed, both antibiotic treatment and impregnated cement were the cheapest methods. However, if more than 150 operations were performed, providing a sterile environment became the cheapest method. Note that for the antibiotic treatment and the impregnated cement, marginal cost equals average variable cost.

The study went on to relate the cost of different methods compared to the cost of re-operations following post-operative infection. Again, the choice of which method was cheapest depended on the volume of activity.

Discussion

Both the antibiotic treatment and the impregnated cement treatment involve a constant cost per case. Thus the average cost is the (constant) cost per case and the marginal cost, the cost of treating an extra patient, is also the cost per case.

The Charnley enclosure and the exhaust ventilated suits involve an initial outlay and

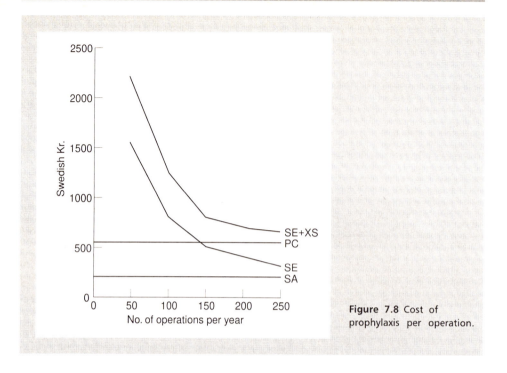

Figure 7.8 Cost of prophylaxis per operation.

no extra costs. Therefore as the costs are spread over a larger number of cases, the cost per case falls and the graph of cost per case looks like the average fixed cost graph in Figure 7.4. A relevant question here is whether this equipment could be used in the treatment of other conditions as well. This would reduce the cost per case further.

7.6 ■ Marginal cost and decision-making

The importance of marginal cost in the decision-making process can be illustrated with a simple example. Figure 7.9 shows a situation in which two hospitals, A and B, quote the same average cost for a service. However, they are operating at different points on their average cost curves (assumed to be the same for the purposes of this example). Clearly it would be a more efficient use of resources if patients were referred to hospital A (because an increase in activity will lead to a fall in unit costs) rather than hospital B (where an increase in activity will result in a rise in unit costs). However, if the average costs are the only data available, the decision-makers will not be aware of this.

In this situation, information about marginal costs would have been helpful. Since the average costs at hospital A are falling, marginal cost is below average cost. Since the average costs at hospital B are rising, marginal cost is above average cost. Thus if data on marginal cost were available, it would be clear that hospital A was the better choice. In practice it is unlikely that such information would be readily forthcoming. However, it

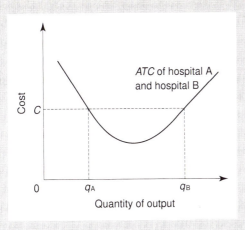

Figure 7.9 Marginal cost in decision-making.
Both hospitals quote the same average cost C for the service, but if A expands its volume of output its average cost will fall, whereas if B expands its volume of output its average cost will rise. Knowledge of marginal cost would be useful.

might be possible to estimate what would happen to average costs if the case-load should rise to a new level 5% or 10% above the present level.

A numerical example may be useful at this point to illustrate the cost relationships.

Example

Given the following data on total cost for different quantities of output, calculate average total cost, average variable cost, average fixed cost and marginal cost for each level of output. Graph your results.

Quantity	0	1	2	3	4	5	6	7	8	9	10
Total cost	100	141	168	187	204	225	256	303	372	469	600

Solution

We can see that when nothing is being produced (quantity is zero), the total cost is 100. This is the fixed cost element of production, the cost that does not vary with the level of output. If we subtract this amount from total cost, this leaves us with total variable cost.

Average total cost is calculated by dividing total cost by quantity for each output level except zero. Average variable cost is calculated by dividing total variable cost by quantity for each output level except zero. Average fixed cost is calculated by dividing total fixed cost by quantity for each output level except zero. Finally, marginal cost is calculated by taking the *difference* between the total cost figures for each extra unit of output. So, for example, when quantity increases from 3 to 4, total cost increases from 187 to 204. The marginal cost of producing the fourth unit is 204 minus 187, which equals 17.

The results of all the calculations are shown in the table below. Graphing these results gives us the curves shown in Figures 7.10–7.15.

Quantity	Total Cost	Total Fixed Cost	Total Variable Cost	Average Total Cost	Average Variable Cost	Average Fixed Cost	Marginal Cost
0	100	100	0				
1	141	100	41	141.0	41.0	100.0	41.0
2	168	100	68	84.0	34.0	50.0	27.0
3	187	100	87	62.3	29.0	33.3	19.0
4	204	100	104	51.0	26.0	25.0	17.0
5	225	100	125	45.0	25.0	20.0	21.0
6	256	100	156	42.7	26.0	16.7	31.0
7	303	100	203	43.3	29.0	14.3	47.0
8	372	100	272	46.5	34.0	12.5	69.0
9	469	100	369	52.1	41.0	11.1	97.0
10	600	100	500	60.0	50.0	10.0	131.0

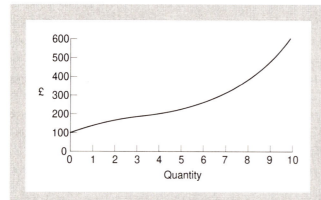

Figure 7.10 Total cost curve.

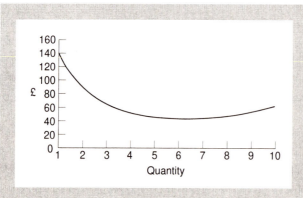

Figure 7.11 Average total cost (ATC).

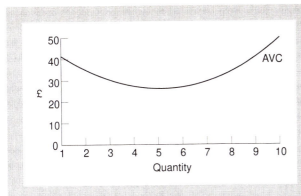

Figure 7.12 Average variable cost (AVC).

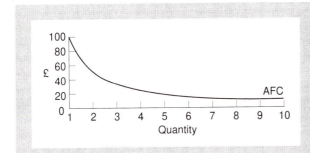

Figure 7.13 Average fixed cost (AFC).

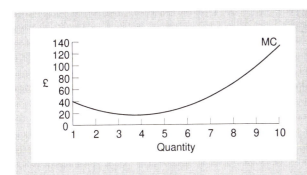

Figure 7.14 Marginal cost (MC).

Costs and pricing

In all organizations that produce goods or services for sale, the cost of production is an important determinant of the pricing decision and it will also determine whether the organization remains in that line of business. If buyers are not prepared to buy at the price necessary to cover all the organization's costs in the long run, then the organization will leave the market for that product.

A common approach to pricing in the private sector is to estimate the variable cost per

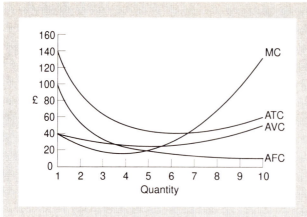

Figure 7.15 Short-run cost curves.

unit (AVC) and to add on a markup to cover overheads and give a 'satisfactory' profit. So, for example, if the variable cost is £10 per unit and it has been estimated that a markup of 50% will cover fixed costs and provide a satisfactory profit, then the selling price will be

$$AVC \times (1 + m/100)$$

where m is the percentage markup

$$= £10 \times (1 + 50/100)$$
$$= £10 \times 1.5$$
$$= £15$$

Economic theory can provide some guidance as to what the markup should be if the firm wishes to maximize its profits. It can be shown that where the price elasticity of demand is greater than 1 in numerical terms, the optimum percentage markup on *marginal* cost is given by

$$\{1/(E_p' - 1)\} \times 100\%$$

where E_p' is the numerical value of the price elasticity of demand (i.e. ignoring the negative sign).

Example

It is estimated that at the present level of activity, the marginal cost of providing an extra unit of service is £100. It is also estimated that the price elasticity of demand for the service is –3. What price should be charged for the service if the firm wishes to maximize its profits?

The numerical value of the price elasticity of demand is 3. Therefore the optimal markup on marginal cost is given by

$$\{1/(3-1)\} \times 100\% \qquad = 0.5 \times 100\%$$
$$= 50\%$$

The firm should charge £100 × (1 + 50/100) = £150.

Note that this applies only when the firm is making a single product, or a set of products for which the demands and production costs are unrelated. Where the firm produces products which are substitutes or complements, or where production costs are linked, the effect of price changes on the demands for a range of products must be taken into account. As noted above, if the variable cost per unit (AVC) is constant over a range of output, then over this range average variable cost equals marginal cost. Therefore the optimal pricing formula can be applied using variable cost per unit instead of marginal cost.

Note also that for optimal pricing the important distinction is between fixed and variable costs, not direct and indirect costs. In the NHS, providers have been instructed to charge prices for services equal to the full cost of production. According to the guidelines, direct and indirect costs have to be identified and the indirect costs have to be allocated to the different services in order to arrive at the full cost, which then becomes the price of the service. As we saw in the example from MacKerrell (1993), different methods of apportioning indirect costs can have very different implications for prices. Ellwood (1992), commenting on the results of the West Midlands survey of contract prices and cost methods 1991/2, remarked that 'The database revealed *vast* variations in the specialty prices' (our italics). She cited the example of a consultant episode in dermatology costing from £469 to £3,417 depending on which hospital was selected.

What do the prices charged by providers in the NHS represent? They are not marginal costs, nor market clearing prices, nor opportunity costs of resource use. They represent the application of accounting rules. It is clear that immense comparison problems arise if these rules are not applied consistently by each provider.

7.7 ▓ Long-run costs

In the long run the quantities of all factors of production can be varied and thus there are no fixed costs. All costs are variable in the long run. As noted in the previous chapter, the length of time which constitutes the long run will depend on the type of production process being considered. Long-run cost relations are a vital aid to an organization's long-term planning strategy.

Economies of scale

When planning for the longer term, clinicians and managers will be interested in the effect on unit costs of an increase in the scale of activity. There are a number of possible effects.

Constant returns to scale

If output increases by the same proportion as the proportionate increase in all the inputs, there are constant returns to scale. The implication of this is that unit costs will be unaltered by a change in the size of the organization. There are no cost advantages to be gained from becoming bigger or smaller.

Diseconomies of scale

If output increases by a smaller proportion than the increase in inputs, there are decreasing returns to scale. This means that unit costs rise as the scale of operations increases. (Doubling all the inputs produces less than double the output, therefore the cost per unit produced must be higher.) Becoming larger produces cost disadvantages. This may be because of problems such as increased bureaucracy, poorer communications and worse labour relations which are often encountered in larger organizations.

Economies of scale

If output increases by a larger proportion than the increase in inputs, there are increasing returns to scale. This means that unit costs are likely to fall as the scale of operations increases. Becoming larger produces other cost advantages. Economies of scale may arise because staff are able to specialize in their areas of expertise, administrative costs can be spread over a larger number of units of output, quantity discounts can be obtained from suppliers, more efficient use can be made of expensive diagnostic equipment and so on.

The long-run average cost curve

Long-run average cost curves are constructed assuming that all inputs, including the capital stock, can be varied (see Figure 7.16). The long-run average cost represents the unit cost of production for different scales of operation. We are trying to compare unit costs of different sizes of organization. The long-run average cost curve may have a shape similar to that shown in Figure 7.9. Here the long-run average cost falls initially as the size of organization increases and it benefits from factors producing economies of scale. Then for a time there are no further cost benefits from increasing size; long-run average cost is constant. Finally, as the organization becomes very large, problems with the increasing size create diseconomies of scale and long-run average costs begin to increase. The concept of long-run unit costs varying with the scale of operations is of vital importance to managers and to clinicians; what is the optimum size of a hospital, or a GP practice?

Minimum efficient scale

The optimum size of an organization is found at the minimum of the long-run average cost curve (although there may be a range of values which correspond to minimum average cost as shown in Figure 7.16). The minimum efficient scale (MES) of production is defined to be the output level at which long-run average costs are **first** minimized.

The relevance of this concept is to the determination of the likely number of competitors in a market. Where the MES is small compared to total market demand, it

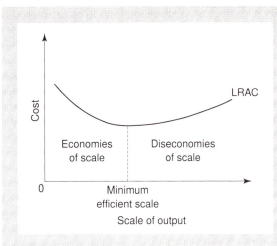

Figure 7.16 Long-run average cost curves.

follows that there will probably be a large number of small competitors in the market, because organizations do not have to be large to achieve lowest average cost. Competition is likely to be vigorous. Examples might be physiotherapists or chiropodists working from home.

However, if the MES is large, say over 50% of total market demand, it is likely that the market will be dominated by only one or two large providers. This is because, relative to the total market demand, size does bring cost advantages. To be profitable, a newcomer would have to enter on a large scale. An example might be a comprehensive cancer diagnosis and treatment centre.

Case study 7.2

In December 1996, a report, *Concentration and Choice in the Provision of Hospital Services* was published by the Centre for Reviews and Dissemination at the University of York. Its main findings were summarized by Sheldon *et al.* (1996) in the *Health Service Journal*. Commenting on the pressure to concentrate hospital services in order to gain better outcomes and economies of scale, they point out that the evidence does not support the assertion that increasing size will bring the expected benefits. Specifically, they report that:

1. Although a large number of studies do seem to show a positive relationship between volume and outcomes, the effect is probably overestimated in many studies, and that where there are benefits they seem to 'operate at relatively low levels of activity'.
2. For acute hospital services, most better quality studies suggest that economies of scale 'appear to be fully exploited at a relatively low level (in the range 100–200 beds)'.
3. There is evidence of diseconomies of scale. 'A range of 300–600 beds is consistent with the evidence.'
4. There is evidence that for services such as health education and screening, there is 'a reduction in utilization with increasing distance'.

> They point out if economies of scale do not exist to the extent expected by planners, then the concentration of services in a few large centres will have a negative effect on patient access without any compensating benefits.

Discussion

This case study illustrates an important point about the measurement of outcomes. In many of the studies looked at by the authors, outcomes were measured by looking at hospital mortality statistics, but variations in the figures could well be the result of variations in case-mix and severity. For long-term planning of hospital provision, a study like this provides vital information about the extent to which services should be concentrated at larger hospitals, but it is important to make sure that like is being compared with like.

Economies of scope

Economies of scope occur when the cost of joint production is less than the cost of producing several related items separately. They play an important role in decision-making for organizations with multiple outputs such as hospitals. For example, joint provision of A and E services, intensive care beds and acute services may well be cheaper because of common use of inputs such as surgeons, specially trained nurses and diagnostic equipment. Consideration of these potential economies may provide useful insights when evaluating current and prospective service provision. Another example would be a health centre with GPs, community nurses, dentists and other practitioners sharing reception and computer services.

When considered separately, some services may appear to be loss-making. Nevertheless they may provide 'customers' for other more profitable services. For example, low-cost health screening by private hospitals might generate a demand for some of their other services.

Case study 7.3 ■ Hospital costs

Total hospital costs = number of cases × cost per case
                      = number of cases × average cost per day × length of stay

Reducing one particular component of cost may not lead to a reduction in total cost. All factors which affect costs should be considered. A reduction in length of stay will not reduce total cost if it is offset by a larger proportionate increase in average cost per day. In addition, an attempt to reduce hospital costs by reducing length of stay may increase costs in other parts of the health service, for GPs for example.

According to the Audit Commission, hospital costs are split approximately in the following proportions between fixed and variable costs:

Overhead costs (generally fixed)	40%
'Hotel' costs (mostly variable)	25–35%
Treatment costs (mostly variable)	25–35%

The existence of fixed costs which are a high proportion of total costs means that falling demand will reduce income more than it reduces total costs and that closing down spare capacity (shutting wards, for example) will not necessarily result in significant cost savings.

Discussion

This illustrates the problem facing many hospitals in which fixed costs are a high proportion of total costs. When demand falls, revenue falls but total fixed costs remain the same. The financial viability of the hospital may be threatened. This explains why many hospitals might prefer to hire staff on short-term or hourly contracts, thus converting some fixed costs to variable costs and shifting the risk of loss from the hospital to the staff.

7.8 ■ Other cost concepts

Sunk costs

Sunk costs are costs which are not affected by a particular decision and are therefore irrelevant to that decision. They are costs which cannot be recovered. For example, some costs may have been incurred in evaluating different project proposals. If these costs are irrecoverable no matter which project is chosen then they are therefore irrelevant to the decision about which project to choose.

Incremental costs

Incremental cost is a broader concept than marginal cost. Marginal cost refers to the cost of varying output by one unit whereas incremental costs refer to the cost of changing a production method or introducing a new service. Incremental costs include any cost variation arising from a decision. In practice, these costs are the ones that are more likely to be examined when evaluating a change of policy or a change of service.

Historical costs

Historical costs are a record of costs incurred as a result of past decisions (which may have been in error). They may not be the most appropriate costs to use when making decisions about the future. Historical costs may also be inaccurate because of changes in input prices and inflation rates.

7.9 ■ Estimating cost functions

A cost function is a specification of the relationship between cost, usually average cost (*AC*), and output (*Q*). We write:

$AC = f(Q$, other relevant variables)

(average cost is a function of the output level Q and other relevant variables such as case-mix).

Cost functions might be estimated in order to look for evidence of economies of scale, to estimate marginal costs and to make comparisons of the efficiency of one hospital or department with other hospitals or departments of the same type. However, there are considerable problems associated with such exercises. One obvious problem is the measurement of output, Q. As noted in Chapter 6, Cullis and West (1979) point out that measures such as inpatient-days or number of inpatient cases are deficient.

In any statistical comparison, like must be compared with like if valid and reliable conclusions are to be drawn. This means that the 'other relevant variables' included in the analysis should be accurately measured and comprehensive. Whichever method of measuring output and whichever 'other relevant variables' are used, it has to be assumed in cost function analysis that each hospital in the study is operating efficiently, i.e. minimizing the cost of producing its output. This may not be the case, especially if there is lack of competition in the market in which the hospital is operating.

Cost functions in mental health services have been estimated by Beecham, Knapp and Fenyo (1991) and Knapp and Beecham (1990) to name but two of many. Using a production of welfare approach they derive the associated cost functions and use them to examine, for example, whether more expensive services are associated with better outcomes. They are positive about the use of cost functions in this context:

> The cost function has impeccable theoretical credentials – it follows directly from the economic theory of production, and is based on assumptions which have been exhaustively debated in a wide variety of market and not-market contexts....

but sound a note of caution:

> It is, however, a data-hungry tool, which limits its application, and in the hands of the inexperienced, uninitiated or unscrupulous it is as dangerous and misleading as any other empirical tool. (Knapp and Beecham, 1990)

The comprehensive analysis of the use of cost functions in health care is beyond the scope of this book. However, the increasing emphasis on the importance of costs and efficiency in health care is likely to increase the use of this tool of analysis.

References

Beecham, J., Knapp, M. and Fenyo, A. (1991) 'Costs, Needs and Outcomes', *Schizophrenia Bulletin*, 17 (3), pp. 427–39.

Cullis, J. G. and West, P. A. (1979) *The Economics of Health: An Introduction*, Martin Robertson, Oxford.

Dawson, D. (1994) 'Costs and Prices in the Internal Market: Markets vs the NHS Management Executive Guidelines', Discussion Paper 115, Centre for Health Economics, University of York.

Ellwood, S. (1992) *Cost Methods for NHS Healthcare Contracts*, Chartered Institute of Management Accountants.

Knapp, M. and Beecham, J. (1990) 'Costing Mental Health Services', *Psychological Medicine*, **20**, pp. 893–908.

MacKerrell, D. K. D. (1993) 'Contract Pricing: A Management Opportunity', in Tilley, Ian (ed.), *Managing the Internal Market*, Paul Chapman Publishing Ltd, London.

Sheldon, T., Ferguson, B. and Posnett, J. (1996) 'Provision Revision', *Health Service Journal*, 12 December.

Sheldon, T., Ferguson, B. and Posnett, J. (1996) 'Concentration and Choice in the Provision of Hospital Services: A Summary and Implications', CRD Report No. 8, Centre for Reviews and Dissemination, University of York.

Teeling Smith, G. (1990) 'The Economic Impact of Medicines', *Office of Health Economics Briefing*, no. 27, London.

Questions for consideration

1. 'Obviously, if we were examining the cost structure of any industry we would expect to find it stated in terms of the total cost, average cost or marginal cost of each quantity of output. Thus for the electricity supply industry, frequently analysed by econometricians, costs can be related to the kilowatt-hours of electric power produced' (Cullis, J. G. and West, P. A. (1979) *The Economics of Health: An Introduction*, Martin Robertson, London).

   (a) Why is it more difficult to analyse hospital costs than the costs of the electricity supply industry?

   (b) What are the advantages and disadvantages of using the inpatient day rather than the inpatient case as a measure of output?

2. For the following total cost function, calculate average total cost, average variable cost, average fixed cost and marginal cost for each output level. Draw graphs to illustrate your results. For what value of output is average total cost minimized?

Q	0	1	2	3	4	5	6	7	8	9	10
TC	152	235	300	353	400	447	500	565	648	755	892

3. It is estimated that the average variable cost of producing one unit of a particular service is £80, and that this is constant over a wide range of output levels. It is also estimated that the price elasticity of demand for the service is –4. What price should be charged for the service in order to maximize profit?

4. Consider the following example, similar to the one produced by MacKerrell.

   A specialty has been allocated indirect costs of £500,000. Within the specialty, 500 procedures were carried out in the previous year at a total direct cost of £600,000. The average time taken to carry out each procedure was 1 hour. Procedure A requires sophisticated equipment and expensive personnel. The direct cost is £1,200 and the procedure takes 45 minutes. Procedure B is straightforward. The direct cost is £300 and it takes 2 hours 15 minutes. Allocate the indirect costs to each treatment using a per direct cost basis, a per hour basis and a per procedure basis. Comment on your results.

CHAPTER EIGHT

Marginal analysis

Objectives

- To show how marginal analysis can be used to make the best decision with available resources.

- To show how decisions to increase or reduce inputs impact on subsequent revenues.

- To examine the implications of substituting one input for another.

Introduction

Management decisions, whether in the private or public sectors, often involve maximizing or minimizing some economic variable. For example, possible objectives might be:

1. Given demand and cost conditions, find the level of output that
   (a) maximizes revenue, or
   (b) maximizes profit.
2. Given demand and cost conditions, find the maximum possible output level that can be produced subject to the constraint of not making a loss, or making a specified rate of return.

Marginal analysis is a technique used by economists to aid this sort of decision-making. It involves the consideration of the costs and benefits associated with a small increase or decrease in activity. From the results of the analysis, rules can be determined for the optimum level of the activity.

As we have seen in an earlier chapter, at any point on the total cost curve, the value of marginal cost is given by the steepness, or *slope*, of the curve. This tells us the rate at which costs are increasing at that level of output. The cost of producing an extra unit will be high when costs are increasing sharply. This is a general property of marginal variables. If the total cost, or revenue, or profit curves are smooth, then the value of marginal cost, or revenue or profit respectively is given by the slope of the curve. If the curve is sloping upwards from left to right, the marginal value will be positive; the total is increasing as output increases. If the curve is sloping downwards from left to right, the marginal value will be negative; the total is decreasing as output increases. If the curve is horizontal, the marginal value will be zero because the total remains unchanged as output increases.

Marginal analysis can be carried out using a mathematical technique known as calculus. In this chapter we introduce the techniques without calculus; mathematically minded readers are referred to the managerial economics texts in the references at the end of this chapter.

8.1 ▨ Marginal analysis and efficiency

Rules for the optimum size of a public sector programme can be determined from the consideration of **marginal social benefit** and **marginal social cost.** Marginal social benefit (MSB) is defined to be the extra benefit to society resulting from the provision of one extra unit of the service (or treatment). Marginal social cost (MSC) is the cost to society as a whole of the resources used to provide one extra unit of the service (or treatment).

It is assumed that, at least above a certain level of provision, MSB will decline with each extra unit provided. When most needs have already been met, the extra benefit of extra units of service will be lower than when the first few units were provided. At the same time, the MSC of providing extra units will rise. To begin with, the resources used to supply the treatments may not have been very productive in their alternative uses. However, as the programme expands and more resources have to be brought in, they may have to come from programmes where they were providing significant benefits. Thus the opportunity cost of the resources rises as more are used. The MSB and MSC curves are shown in Figure 8.1.

The optimum size of the programme is found where the downward sloping MSB curve intersects the upward sloping MSC curve. Thus the rule for finding the size of programme which maximizes the benefits to society is:

> As long as MSB exceeds MSC, expand the programme. Stop at the level of activity where MSB = MSC.

Another way of stating the same rule is to consider **net marginal social benefit** which is equal to marginal social benefit **minus** marginal social cost. The rule for maximizing the benefits to society would then be:

> Expand the programme as long as net marginal social benefit is positive. Stop at the point where net marginal social benefit is zero.

Note that when there are external benefits, the marginal social benefit curve will be to

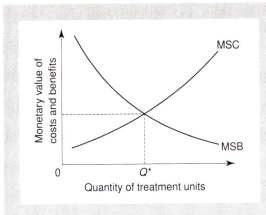

Figure 8.1 Marginal analysis: the optimal size of a treatment programme. For the efficient use of resources, expand the programme until MSC = MSB.

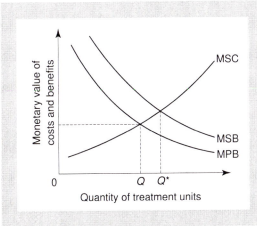

Figure 8.2 Marginal analysis: the effect of external benefits. Where there are external benefits, a market system will result in Q units being supplied, rather than the efficient level Q*.

the right of the demand curve (the marginal *private* benefit (MPB) curve) as shown in Figure 8.2. Thus a market system without intervention will result in a lower supply of such goods and services than would be efficient from the point of view of society as a whole. Since many health care services provide external benefits, this explains why a market system might lead to underprovision of some services.

Example

Suppose we can make monetary estimates of the costs and benefits of a health programme with a single output and that there is no budget constraint. The estimates are as follows:

'Size' of programme (Units of output)	Total benefits (£m)	Total cost (£m)
1	50	10
2	80	20
3	105	30
4	125	40
5	140	50
6	150	60
7	155	70
8	155	80

We can find the optimal 'size' of the programme by considering the *marginal* benefits and costs. We do this by calculating the *extra* benefits and costs that an extra unit of the programme would provide. (When the size of the programme is zero, there are no benefits and costs.)

'Size' of programme (Units of output)	Marginal benefits (£m)	Marginal cost (£m)
1	50	10
2	30	10
3	25	10
4	20	10
5	15	10
6	10	10
7	5	10
8	0	10

This table makes it clear that, for example, when the programme is expanded from 3 to 4 units in size, the extra benefit is £20 m, while the cost of the extra unit is £10 m. The extra benefit exceeds the extra cost. However, if the programme is expanded from 6 to 7 units in size, the extra benefit is £5 m, while the extra cost is £10 m. Here, the extra cost exceeds the extra benefits provided. The resources could be more usefully employed elsewhere.

The optimal size of the programme is 6 units because we can see that up to that point, the extra benefits exceed the extra costs. The sixth unit provides £10 m extra benefits and costs £10 m. The total cost of the programme is £60 m and the total benefit provided is £150 m.

This illustrates the general rule stated above that in order to maximize *net* benefits, a programme should be expanded while marginal benefit exceeds marginal cost. Expansion should stop at the point where marginal benefit equals marginal cost.

8.2 ▦ Marginal analysis and revenue maximization

Total, average and marginal revenue

Total revenue (*TR*) is equal to the quantity sold (*Q*) multiplied by the price at which the product is sold (*P*).
Thus

$$TR = PQ$$

Average revenue (*AR*) is equal to total revenue divided by the number of units sold.
Thus

$$AR = TR/Q = P$$

Because the average revenue at any particular quantity level is equal to the price, it follows that when average revenue is plotted against *Q* on a graph it shows the relationship between price and quantity. In other words, the average revenue curve is identical to the demand curve.

Marginal revenue (*MR*) is equal to the extra revenue obtained from selling one extra unit. When the firm faces a downward sloping demand curve, the total revenue function may well reach a maximum value and then start to decline, as shown in Figure 8.3. This is because of the inverse relationship between price and quantity sold; in order to sell more of its product the firm must lower its price.

> **Example**
>
> Suppose a firm can sell 1,000 units per week of a product at £6.50 per unit. Total weekly revenue (price × quantity) will be £6,500. Now the firm wishes to increase its sales by 20% to 1,200 units per week. However, it finds that in order to achieve this level of sales it has to drop the price to £5 per unit. Total revenue will now be £6,000, lower than before.

Marginal revenue at any point on the total revenue curve is given by the slope of the curve at that point; at the maximum of the total revenue curve marginal revenue is clearly equal to zero. This is an illustration of a very important property of marginal variables (cost, revenue or profit):

For a function to be at a maximum (or a minimum) its marginal value (slope) must be zero.

We saw this in the earlier example about the maximization of the benefits of a public sector programme to society. Here the rule was to keep expanding the programme while net marginal social benefits were positive. The maximum benefit was obtained when net marginal social benefit was zero.

Thus to maximize revenue, the rule is:

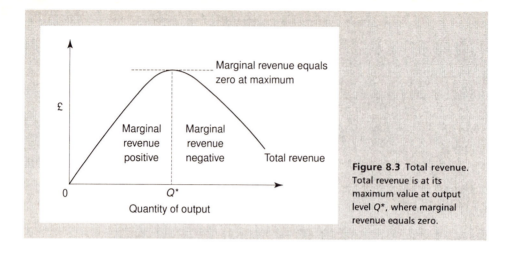

Figure 8.3 Total revenue. Total revenue is at its maximum value at output level Q^*, where marginal revenue equals zero.

Expand sales while marginal revenue is positive; stop at the point where marginal revenue is zero.

8.3 ■ Marginal analysis and employment

In the short run, some input factors are fixed, and as we saw in Chapter 6, total output will increase as amounts of the variable input are increased, but with eventually diminishing marginal returns. We can use marginal analysis to find the optimal amount of the variable input to employ. To do this we must introduce the concept of *marginal revenue product* (MRP).

The marginal revenue product of an input is calculated by taking the marginal product that the input is expected to produce, and multiplying this by the price at which this extra output can be sold. For example, if the marginal product associated with one extra unit of the input is 5 units of output, and each of these units of output can be sold for £200, then the marginal revenue product is given by:

$MRP = 5 \times £200 = £1,000.$

In general, marginal revenue product is equal to marginal product (the extra product associated with one extra unit of input) multiplied by marginal revenue (the extra revenue obtained from selling the extra units of output):

$MRP = MP \times MR$

If the price of the output does not change as output increases, then marginal revenue per unit equals price per unit, so marginal revenue product equals marginal product multiplied by the price of the output.

From this we can decide whether it is worth employing this extra (marginal) unit of input. Clearly, if the extra unit of input costs more than £1,000 to employ, the enterprise will make a loss on this extra unit. If the extra unit of input costs less than £1,000, the enterprise will receive more revenue from this unit than it costs to employ it. Thus it will be profitable to employ the extra unit.

The general rule is that employment of an input should be expanded as long as the marginal revenue product exceeds the cost per unit of the input.

Example

Suppose each unit of output can be sold for £100, and the cost of the variable input is £400 per unit. Given the total product figures shown below, we can find the optimal level of employment of the variable input using marginal analysis.

Units of input	Total product
1	50
2	60
3	68
4	74
5	78
6	80

We calculate marginal product and marginal revenue product by first calculating the *extra* output each extra unit of input provides (marginal product), and then multiplying this by the price at which these units of output can be sold (marginal revenue product).

Units of output	Marginal product	Marginal revenue product
1	50	5000
2	10	1000
3	8	800
4	6	600
5	4	400
6	2	200

For example, if the number of units of input is increased from 2 units to 3 units, total product rises from 60 to 68 units so marginal product is 8. These 8 units can be sold for £100 each, giving marginal revenue product of £800.

Since the units of input cost £400 each, it is worth employing the third and fourth units. The fifth unit adds the same to revenue as to cost, so the enterprise will just break even on this unit. It is not worth employing the sixth unit as it adds more to cost than to revenue. Thus the optimal level of employment is 5 units. If the cost of inputs increased, say to £500 per unit, then the optimal level of employment would fall. The fifth unit would now add more to cost than to revenue and the optimal level of employment would fall to 4 units.

8.4 ■ Marginal analysis and profit maximization

Consider an enterprise with a fixed stock of capital (buildings, equipment) but which is able to vary some inputs such as labour. Managers of the enterprise wish to find the level of output at which profit will be maximized given the existing demand and cost conditions they face.

The analysis here proceeds in exactly the same way as in the case of finding the size of a health programme which maximized total net benefits. A firm is an organization which uses factors of production in order to produce output for sale. In elementary economic analysis it is assumed that private sector firms seek to maximize profits. In Chapter 10 we will examine other possible objectives that enterprises may have.

Profit is defined to be equal to total revenue minus the total costs of production. As the firm produces more and sells more, its total cost will rise and so will its total revenue. A positive profit will be made if total revenue exceeds total cost. We wish to find the output level at which profit is at its maximum level – in the case of positive profits, the output level at which total revenue exceeds total cost by the greatest amount. We can use marginal analysis to find a general rule giving the output level at which profit will be maximized.

At any level of output, we consider the extra cost of producing one extra unit (marginal cost MC) and we consider the extra revenue to be gained when it is sold (marginal revenue MR). As long as marginal revenue exceeds marginal cost, the extra unit is adding to profit. Producing units for which marginal cost exceeds marginal revenue will reduce profit. Thus the rule for profit maximization is to expand production as long as marginal revenue exceeds marginal cost.

In the short run we expect the marginal cost of production to start rising as output increases because some factors are fixed in supply. After a certain point, trying to expand

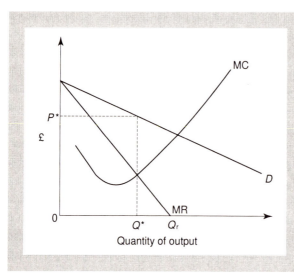

Figure 8.4 Profit maximization: marginal cost = marginal revenue. Profit is maximized at output level Q^* where marginal cost equals marginal revenue. The price of the output is p^*. (Note that revenue would be maximized at output Q_r, where marginal revenue is zero.)

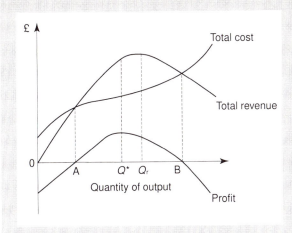

Figure 8.5 Profit maximization. Another way of illustrating profit maximization is to look at the total revenue and total cost curves. Profit is maximized at Q^*, where the difference between the two curves is greatest. (Note that this is a lower output level than Q_r, the revenue maximizing level of output.)

production with limited facilities will be expensive (overtime must be paid, temporary extra space rented and so on). Thus eventually marginal cost will rise. Expansion of output should stop at the point where marginal cost equals marginal revenue. This can be seen in Figure 8.4, where the profit-maximizing level of output, Q^*, corresponds to the level where the marginal cost curve intersects the marginal revenue curve.

Another way of illustrating the same problem is to look at the total cost and total revenue curves as in Figure 8.5. Profit is given by the vertical distance between the total cost and total revenue curves. Note that when total cost exceeds total revenue, profit is negative. The firm is making a loss. At output levels A and B, the firm is breaking even. Output Q^* is the profit maximising level of output. At that output level the profit curve is at its highest, and the slopes of the total cost and total revenue curves are equal (marginal cost equals marginal revenue).

8.5 ▪ Marginal analysis and maximization of output subject to a minimum profit constraint

Some enterprises may have the objective of producing as much output as possible but are required either not to make a loss or to achieve some minimum rate of return. We can adapt the profit maximization analysis and diagram in the previous section. Figure 8.6 shows the output levels A and B where the firm breaks even. If the firm seeks to maximize output subject to not making a loss, it should produce at output level B. If a certain minimum profit level z_{min} is required, the maximum output possible consistent with that is Q_m.

The following section is more technical and can be omitted without affecting your understanding of the rest of the text.

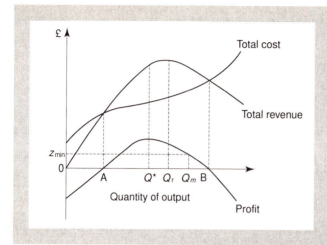

Figure 8.6 Profit maximization: subject to a minimum profit constraint. For output maximization subject to a no-loss constraint, the enterprise should produce output at B, the high breakeven point. If there is a minimum profit requirement z_{min}, the enterprise should produce output Q_m, the highest output consistent with this minimum profit requirement.

8.6 ■ Marginal analysis and isoquants

The marginal rate of technical substitution (MRTS)

Given two inputs X and Y

$MRTS = \Delta Y/\Delta X$ = slope of isoquant (when Y is measured on the vertical axis)

It is the amount of change in Y required to keep output constant given a unit change in X. For example, if the $MRTS$ equals -2, then it means that if the amount of X is increased by 1 unit, therefore to stay at the same output level, Y must decrease by 2 units. Another way of looking at it is to say that if X increases (decreases) by a small amount, Y must decrease (increase) by twice that amount for output to remain unchanged.

With limited substitutability the MRTS will not be constant; the slope of the isoquant decreases as X increases as shown in Figure 8.7. The MRTS is related to the marginal products of the inputs; it can be shown that

$MRTS = -MP_X/MP_Y$

This is because if we reduce X by a small amount X, output will fall by an amount Q, given by

$Q = X.MP_X$

To restore output to its previous level we require an increase in Y sufficient to bring this about. When Y increases by the small amount Y, the increase in output is given by $Y.MP_Y$. If this is also equal to Q, as required, then we have

$-(X.MP_X) = (Y.MP_Y)$

(The left-hand side is negative because it is a fall in output.)

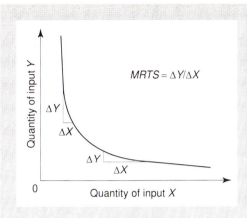

$MRTS = \Delta Y/\Delta X$

Figure 8.7 Marginal rate of technical substitution.
In general, the MRTS will vary according to the relative usage of the inputs.

Rearranging gives

$\Delta Y/\Delta X = -MP_X/MP_Y$

which is the required relationship, the important result that

At any point on the isoquant, its slope, which measures the rate at which inputs can be substituted for one another, is equal to the ratio of the marginal products of the inputs.

8.7 ■ Marginal analysis and the optimal combination of inputs

Consider the case of two inputs X and Y costing P_X and P_Y respectively. The total cost of the inputs is given by

$P_X.X + P_Y.Y$

If the total amount available for the firm to spend on inputs is B, then the budget constraint can be written

$B = P_X.X + P_Y.Y$

This is the equation of a straight line. For example, suppose that input X costs £250 per unit and input Y costs £500 per unit. If the total budget is 1,000, then the budget constraint is

$1,000 = 250X + 500Y$

If no units of Y were bought then 4 units of X could be afforded; if no units of X were bought then 2 units of Y could be afforded. These give the end points of a straight line as shown in Figure 8.8.

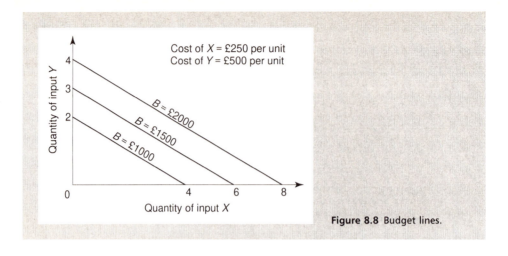

Cost of X = £250 per unit
Cost of Y = £500 per unit

Figure 8.8 Budget lines.

Any combination of X and Y on the straight line will satisfy the budget constraint. If the total budget is 1,500, the constraint becomes

$$1,500 = 250X + 500Y$$

and if it is 2,000, the constraint becomes

$$2,000 = 250X + 500Y$$

The budget lines corresponding to these constraints are also shown in Figure 8.8. Note that the budget lines are parallel; the higher the total budget, the further from the origin is the budget line.

The budget line equation can be rearranged to give

$$Y = B/P_Y - (P_X/P_Y).X$$

This is the equation of a straight line with intercept B/P_Y and slope equal to

$$-(P_X/P_Y).$$

Note that the slope of the budget line measures relative prices.

We illustrate the production of a given output at the least cost by drawing the isoquant and a budget line on the same graph. We know the slope of the budget line because it is the ratio of the input prices. All possible budget lines are parallel. If we slide the budget line as far as possible in the direction of the origin while still touching the isoquant, we find that the lowest possible cost is given by the input combination at the point of tangency between the isoquant and the budget line as shown in Figure 8.9.

At this point the budget line and the isoquant have the same slope.

Therefore $-(P_X/P_Y) = MRTS = -(MP_X/MP_Y)$

Rearranging, we find that the optimal combination of inputs for a given level of output is found by setting

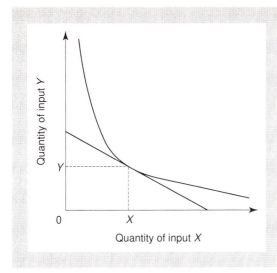

Figure 8.9 Optimal (least-cost) combination of inputs.

$$MP_X/P_X = MP_Y/P_Y$$

Thus a profit maximizing firm will do the following

(a) produce output up to the point where $MC = MR$, and
(b) use the least-cost combination of inputs to produce that level of output.

Summary of chapter results

1. For the efficient use of resources expand programme until $MSB = MSC$.
2. Expand use of an input to the point where MRP = cost of input.
3. For revenue maximization, expand output until $MR = 0$.
4. For profit maximization, expand output until $MC = MR$.
5. For the optimal combination of inputs, the ratio of input prices should equal the ratio of the marginal products of the inputs.

References

Hirshey, M. and Pappas, J. L. (1995) *Fundamentals of Managerial Economics* (5th edn), Dryden Press, Fort Worth, London.
Mansfield, E. (1993) *Managerial Economics: Theory, Applications and Cases* (2nd edn), Norton, New York.

CHAPTER NINE

Market structures

Objectives

- To introduce the more complex forms of market in which health care providers usually operate.

- To show how the structure of a market influences the patterns of management and competition adopted by hospitals and other institutions.

- To examine the causes and consequences of market failure.

- To introduce transaction cost economics and its implications for organizational structure and contracts.

Introduction

The purpose of this chapter is to introduce the different types of market structure that are generally encountered in the market sector of the economy. Such structures are emerging and evolving in the quasi-markets introduced in many public services to replace the bureaucratic models for delivery of services.

Because of the degree of regulation in the internal market of the NHS and other public services, organizations within those markets do not have the degree of freedom to set prices and output that would be available to a private sector organization. Nevertheless institutions must compete for business and the degree of competition will be influenced by the structure of the market. In addition, the NHS buys many of its inputs such as labour, drugs and equipment in less regulated markets. Any private work done in NHS hospitals will be taking place in a more competitive environment. As the system develops, Trusts may demand more freedom in setting prices; it is useful to be aware of the market forces that are shaping many aspects of the internal market and of the consequences if they were allowed to operate more freely.

Markets are a means of decentralized decision-making. Resources are allocated in response to price signals, with less input from bureaucratic structures than is the case in a centrally planned system. The benefit of a market system is to be found in its incentives for efficient production and responsiveness to changes in consumer demand.

However, the extent to which these incentives will exist is very dependent on the type of market structure which is in existence. It has also to be borne in mind that market structures evolve; they should not be viewed as static entities. In addition, markets may fail. Problems such as lack of information may lead to perverse incentives for decision-makers and an inability of the markets to allocate resources efficiently.

9.1 ▧ Market structures

'Market structure' refers to the competitive environment in which buyers and sellers are operating. It can be described on the following four dimensions.

Buyers and sellers

The number and size distribution of both actual and potential purchasers and providers is an important determinant of the degree of competition in a market. In health care, the geographical distribution of providers is an important determinant of the degree of competition for services; a hospital in Manchester cannot realistically offer outpatient services to patients in Exeter.

Product

The more substitutes there are for a product or service, the greater will be the degree of competition in the market. It is common practice for firms in the private sector to try to differentiate their product from other similar products by imbuing their product with some real (or imagined) quality. The purpose of this is to try to reduce the number of substitutes and thus reduce the amount of competition they face.

GPs or hospitals may try to limit the amount of competition they face for certain types of patient or service by attempting to differentiate their service from those of other providers by offering enhanced levels of service – more convenient surgery times, extra services such as physiotherapy and counselling, quicker access to consultants, more comfortable waiting areas.

The physical characteristics of the product or service will also affect the degree of competition. Where a product can be easily transported long distances, or where the patients are able and prepared to travel long distances to receive the service, the organization is able to compete over a wide geographical area.

Information

The behaviour of buyers and sellers within a market will be influenced by the amount of information they have available about present and future prices and costs. For providers, information about the likely demand for a service and the expected costs of providing that service will be important determinants of the supply decision, as will the prices charged and the costs faced by competing institutions. For purchasers, accurate information about the prices, quality and the costs of services offered by competing providers will be vital in determining the optimal allocation of their budget.

In the private sector, information, particularly about costs, is generally regarded as being commercially sensitive and is generally kept strictly confidential. In quasi-markets such as the NHS, the value of such information is recognized and providers are encouraged to be open about their costs and prices.

However, as Dawson (1994) points out, in many markets the actual price paid may well differ from that quoted. For example, in the housing market or the second-hand car market, there is an asking price but the price paid is arrived at by negotiation between buyer and seller. It is usually in the interest of both to keep the actual price paid a secret. This does not mean that the markets are uncompetitive as buyers will generally indulge in search behaviour to find the best deal. Nevertheless, it makes it more difficult for organizations to plan and for the market to be monitored effectively.

Barriers to entry and exit

Barriers to entry exist when there are factors which give existing firms in a market an advantage over potential entrants. These barriers can be legal in the form of patents, such as those enjoyed by pharmaceutical companies over new drugs, or other restrictions such as those preventing unqualified persons from practising as doctors. They may be financial, in the form of huge capital requirements. Customer loyalty and reluctance to try new suppliers may make it difficult for new firms to enter a market. Existing firms can erect barriers to new entrants by price behaviour – setting low prices to deter new entrants or threatening to set low prices if new firms enter the market so that the new firms are unprofitable.

There can also be considerable barriers to exit from an industry. It may be the case that the provider has invested in physical assets which are very specific to one purpose and cannot easily be employed in another line of business. Examples might be specially designed computer systems or sophisticated diagnostic equipment. In that case, even if market conditions are unfavourable, it will be more expensive for the supplier to leave the industry than to stay. Legal requirements such as redundancy payments to staff may also make exit from an industry an expensive process.

9.2 ▮ Types of market structure

Perfect competition

The word 'perfect' in this context does not mean 'desirable' or 'ideal'. Strictly speaking, it means 'extreme'. A perfectly competitive market is the most competitive of all the theoretical market structures and it is often used by economists and others as a benchmark against which to compare other market structures. Because it leads to a situation in which prices will be set equal to minimum average costs and no supplier will be able to make excess profits in the long run, it is also held to be desirable and the theoretical results are used to justify policies to promote greater competition throughout the economy.

The characteristics of a perfectly competitive market structure are as follows:

1. There must be a large number of buyers and sellers so that no individual buyer or seller can influence the market price. **All buyers and sellers are price-takers**.
2. The product sold by the firms in the industry must be **homogeneous** so that there is nothing to distinguish the product of one producer from that of another.
3. There are **no barriers to entry to or exit from** the industry. Resources can move in and out of the industry without hindrance.
4. There must be **full information** available to buyers and sellers about price and cost conditions.

Truly perfectly competitive industries are unlikely to arise in practice; perfect information about market conditions is not available in practice and there are often barriers to new entrants to an industry in the form of patents and other legal restrictions, problems with availability of capital and difficulty in breaking into the market because existing firms have established relationships with customers and suppliers. The product itself in most cases is not homogeneous; each supplier wishes to differentiate their product from others on the basis of characteristics such as quality.

In a perfectly competitive market, the industry demand curve is downward sloping and the market price for the product is determined by the interaction of demand and supply. However, each individual firm is a price-taker; it cannot affect the market price. Thus the demand curve facing the firm in perfect competition is horizontal (perfectly elastic). Since the price does not vary with each individual firm's output, the demand curve is also the marginal revenue curve. The extra revenue that the firm receives when an extra item is sold is equal to the price.

Figure 9.1 shows how the profit-maximizing output of the firm in perfect competition is determined in the short run. The output level where marginal cost equals marginal revenue is at Q^*. At this level of output, the average cost of production is equal to the distance $0C$. The firm is making a profit represented by the shaded area.

It can be shown that if a market is perfectly competitive, in the long run, producers will be efficient and will not make excess profits. Prices will be low, equal to the minimum average cost of production. (It should be noted that the relevant costs in this discussion

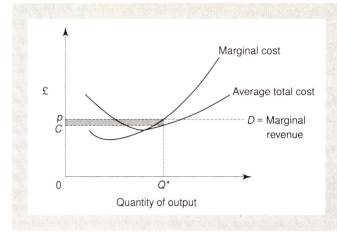

Figure 9.1 Q* is the profit maximizing level of output. At this level of output, price *P* is greater than average total cost *C*, so the firm is making economic profits (the shaded area).

are the opportunity costs of production. These include a rate of return to the entrepreneur.)

The long-run situation is shown in Figure 9.2. Because there are no barriers to entry, new producers have entered the market attracted by the profits being made by the existing firms. The extra supply has driven the price down until is is equal to minimum average cost.

Monopoly

At the other end of the spectrum from perfect competition is monopoly. A monopolist is a single supplier that constitutes the whole industry. For a monopoly to exist there must be considerable barriers to entry to the industry. It may be the case that the product in question can only be provided profitably on a large scale and therefore it is not profitable for more than one producer to exist. The demand curve facing the monopolist is the industry demand curve and thus it is downward sloping.

The profit-maximizing output level of the profit-maximizing monopolist is shown in Figure 9.3. Again, it is found by putting marginal cost equal to marginal revenue. The price corresponding to this output level Q* is found from the demand curve *D*. At this level of output, average cost is 0C and profit is represented by the shaded area. However, because of the considerable barriers to entry associated with the monopoly, the profits are not competed away.

Monopolies are unpopular because it is felt that they are in a position to use their market power to the disadvantage of the purchaser; they can restrict their output in order to keep prices higher and make excess profits. Because of the barriers to entry, monopolies can continue to make high profits at the expense of the consumer. Monopoly markets may well emerge in health care; if patients are reluctant to travel for treatment then the local hospital may become the monopoly supplier for some services in that geographical area.

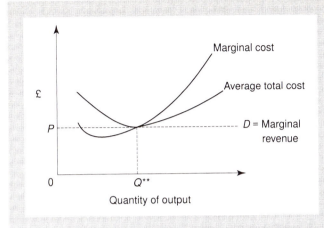

Figure 9.2 Perfect competition: long-run profit maximization.
In the long run, competition between firms drives down the price. Economic profit is zero (but remember costs include financial rewards to the owner of the firm). Price is equal to minimum average total cost in the long run.

There may well be a case for allowing monopoly supply of certain services. Some products can only be supplied at low cost if they are produced on a large scale. It is also the case that studies have shown that the treatment of some cancers has a better success rate at large specialist centres.

Monopolistic competition

In monopolistic competition there are a relatively large number of producers selling similar but differentiated products. There are few barriers to entry and exit; full information on price and costs is available to all participants. Each firm has a relatively small

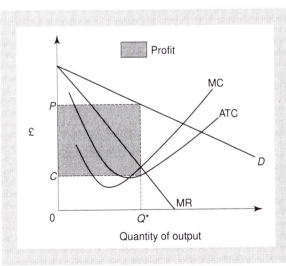

Figure 9.3 Monopoly: profit maximization.
Q^* is the profit-maximizing level of output (MC = MR). The corresponding price is found from the demand curve. At Q^* the average cost is C.

market share and therefore only a small amount of control over the market price. The producers act independently of one another. Each firm faces a downward sloping demand curve; the price elasticity of demand will depend on the extent to which the firm has differentiated its product from those of its competitors.

It is thought that the market for services provided by hospitals may be monopolistically competitive. The services provided by the hospitals, although similar, are not identical. They are differentiated by geographical factors, among other things. The hospitals themselves may wish, for competitive reasons, to differentiate their services from those of other hospitals (Culyer and Posnett, 1990).

Monopsony

Monopsony is rather like monopoly except that instead of having a single seller, there is a single buyer. If, for example, there is only one employer in a geographical area then this employer will be the single buyer of labour and will therefore be a monopsonist. Clearly a monopsonist is in a position to bargain for a low price. The NHS is a monopsonistic employer for many categories of medical personnel.

It may be the case that if hospital trusts are free to set their own rates of pay, competition between them for skilled staff may cause pay rates to rise.

A purchaser with a large budget has considerable market power. If its purchasing accounts for a large proportion of the income of some providers, then it has the power to negotiate effectively for lower prices. There is a danger that this power could be used to create severe financial difficulties for some providers. At least in theory, some providers could be put out of business by a large purchaser or some services could be made unviable. Thus large purchasers may have the power to shape the market in which they operate. They may have to weigh up the benefits and disadvantages associated with having either a large number of smaller providers or a small number of large providers of certain services.

Bilateral monopoly

If in a market there is a single buyer facing a single seller, such as a single employer facing a single union, or a single purchaser facing a single provider, this is known as bilateral monopoly. Because of the restrictions imposed by the medical profession on entry and because of the position of the NHS as a very large employer, the medical labour market is almost a bilateral monopoly. Decisions tend to be made by negotiation, since there is no competition on either side.

In the case of doctors, their powerful professional organization provides a **countervailing power** that offsets the monopsony buying power of the NHS. However, the NHS is also an employer of workers who are in greater supply, either less highly unionized or who are reluctant to use industrial action. Their countervailing power is lower, and this is reflected in their pay and conditions of service.

Oligopoly

In an oligopoly, the industry is dominated by a few large firms. There are very high barriers to entry. The decisions of any individual firm will be affected by the actions and expected reactions of its competitors. Because of this, access to information about firms' costs, prices and quality is very restricted. Oligopolistic markets tend to be highly competitive, but the competition often tends to take place in non-price ways – better service, more advertising, special offers – because each firm realizes that it is not in its interest to begin a price war.

In some oligopolies, firms form a cartel; they make a formal agreement to fix prices and output. In that case they are acting as a monopoly supplier. Cartels are illegal.

9.3 ▨ Quasi-markets

In welfare and public services, the system of organization in which the activities of purchasers and providers are separated and the purchasers contract to buy services from various providers is called a quasi-market. Most quasi-markets are heavily regulated by the state, both in terms of prices and in terms of the range and quality of services provided. Nevertheless, the purpose of introducing quasi-markets is to inject competitive forces which will improve efficiency and responsiveness. The degree of competition will depend on the market structures which evolve and in most cases it will be possible to describe these market structures in terms of one of the categories introduced earlier.

Le Grand and Bartlett (1993) suggest the following criteria for judging the success of quasi-markets.

Efficiency

As noted in Chapter 3, efficiency should be measured with respect to not just the number of cases treated, but also the outcomes. Le Grand and Bartlett make the point that evaluation and monitoring of outcomes is essential to the success of quasi-markets but is also very difficult and adds to the cost of the contracting process.

Responsiveness

As we saw in Chapter 5, in conventional markets excess demand or supply and the resulting price movements act as signals to suppliers to respond to changing consumer demands. Most quasi-markets have pricing rules which do not allow prices to act directly as signalling devices. However, as users' needs change, purchasers are meant to detect this through the process of needs assessment and to alter their sets of demands. Providers who are flexible enough to anticipate and to respond quickly to these altered demands will survive; unresponsive and inflexible providers will not. Thus, it is hoped, quasi-markets will provide a framework for greater responsiveness than did the old hierarchical system.

Choice

Quasi-markets are intended to provide users with more choice, both between types of service and between providers. The ability of users to choose between providers means that providers are more likely to aim to be efficient and responsive. Thus one of the criteria for judging the success of quasi-markets will be whether in fact users do have more choice. Is it the case that some have more choice and some have less? Where a GP fundholder has a contract with a particular provider, it may be difficult for the patient to have him or herself referred elsewhere, for example.

Equity

As noted earlier, equity can be defined in many ways. In health care, equity is often interpreted as meaning equal levels of access to services. Recent controversies about 'queue-jumping' by patients of GP fundholders suggest that perhaps the quasi-market in the UK NHS has decreased equity. Nevertheless, it could be argued that if no one is having to wait longer than before, and some patients are being seen sooner than before, then this is a welfare gain.

9.4 ▦ Market failure

Both in conventional markets and in quasi-markets, market imperfections will mean that incorrect signals are given to participants and therefore resources are not allocated efficiently. There are many possible sources of market failure.

Market structure

The degree of competition is strongly dependent on the number of competing providers. We might be thinking in terms of several hospitals competing to provide a single service or a range of services.

Where there are few suppliers, the degree of competition is likely to be low. In a conventional market, the monopoly supplier may restrict output, charge high prices and make excess profit. In a quasi-market, there may be little incentive to reduce costs, to respond to changing demands or to innovate. The monopoly power could be the result of geographic location and the preference of patients to be treated near their homes.

Measurement of the degree of competition

The degree of competition in a market is often assessed using measures of concentration such as the total market share held by the largest four, or five, or eight firms in the industry. The larger the market share held by the biggest firms, the more concentrated the industry and the lower the degree of competition.

Some studies of concentration make use of the Hirschman-Herfindahl Index (HHI) which is calculated by summing the squares of the market shares of all the firms in the industry. The index is affected by both the number of firms in the industry and their size distribution. The maximum size of the HHI is 10,000, obtained if there is only one firm in the industry – a true monopoly with a market share of 100%. The larger the value of the HHI, the greater the degree of concentration. American anti-trust law defines any industry with an HHI of more than 1,800 as having a significant degree of monopoly power.

Example

Suppose there are four firms in the industry each with a market share of 25%. The HHI will be equal to:

$$(25)^2 + (25)^2 + (25)^2 + (25)^2 = 625 \times 4 = 2,500$$

Now suppose that the firms are unequal in terms of market share and that the shares are 60%, 25%, 10% and 5%. Here one firm is dominating the industry. This is reflected in the value of the HHI which becomes:

$$(60)^2 + (25)^2 + (10)^2 + (5)^2 = 3,600 + 625 + 100 + 25 = 4,350$$

This is much higher than the previous value, even though the industry contains the same number of firms.

Case study 9.1

Appleby *et al.* (1993) measured the degree of competition in general surgery facing each of 39 hospitals in the West Midlands region in 1988/9. The study had three main stages.

1. The definition of each hospital's market and market share. This was done by examining patient flows by District. The hospital's market area included a District if the District contributed at least 3% of the hospital's total finished consultant episodes (FCEs), both as inpatient and day cases.
2. The identification of competitor hospitals. A hospital was defined to be a competitor if, from at least one of the Districts in the first hospital's market area, it drew at least 3% of the District's total episodes.
3. Calculation of an index of competition faced by each hospital. This was a two-stage process. First, an HHI for each District was calculated by summing the squares of the market shares of all competing hospitals in the District. Then, since each hospital's

market area contained a number of Districts for which HHIs had been calculated, for each hospital these HHIs were weighted by the patient numbers coming from each District. This gave an index showing the degree of competition faced by each hospital.

The results showed a wide variation in the degree of competiton faced by each hospital. For full details of the methodology and the results for each hospital, see Appleby (1993). The hospital with the highest-valued index (least degree of competition) was St Cross, Rugby, with an index of 6,790. The hospital with the lowest index value, 90, was the Lichfield Victoria, S.E. Staffordshire. Of the 39 hospitals in the study, 10 had an index value greater than 1,800, the value used in the USA to define a monopoly.

Discussion

The conclusion is that there may be significant degrees of monopoly power in the market for hospital services across the country. Competition between hospitals may be difficult to achieve because of significant barriers to entry. It is worth noting that for competition to exist in a market, it is not necessary to have new entrants in existence. The *threat* of entry can be perceived as potential competition. However, because of the significant capital requirements of entry to the hospital sector, the threat of replacement of the management team may act as a competitive force.

Large providers may well have a significant degree of monopoly power. However, it should be pointed out that in many cases, because of economies of scale and scope, large providers may be able to produce at lower average cost that small providers. In addition, large providers may provide a better quality service. For example, in health care, it has been shown that cancer patients have longer survival times on average if they are treated at large specialist centres.

There may also be advantages associated with large purchasers. There can be coordinated planning of services. Buying in large batches may lead to discounts. The monopsony power of the large buyer may also force providers to charge lower prices. However, large purchasers may be bureaucratic and out of touch with the needs of all their users. In addition, a large purchaser may act too aggressively in forcing down prices if it faces a large number of small providers, thus creating severe financial problems for them.

To summarize, for efficiency it would seem that each quasi-market requires a large number of purchasers and providers. However, the existence of economies of scale may favour the large provider. If the provider has a large degree of monopoly power, it might be more advantageous for users if the purchaser was also large to provide countervailing power in the market. Unfortunately, this may mean too close a relationship between the small number of negotiators on each side – thus reducing incentives for efficiency.

On the employment side, the monopsony power of the large employer can help to keep wage levels down. If a large number of small providers compete for scarce staff, wage levels may rise.

Information problems

Competitive forces will be weak and resource allocation may be inefficient if there is little or no accurate information available to participants about costs and quality of services. However, producing detailed and accurate information about costs and quality can itself be costly. Specialized staff and equipment are required. In addition, hospital trusts may be reluctant to release what they consider to be 'market-sensitive' information. In particular, information asymmetries between purchasers and providers can lead to market failure.

Adverse selection

This type of market failure is sometimes known as the problem of hidden information and is usually presented as a problem faced by insurance companies. Individual premiums are calculated according to the risks assessed for groups of similar individuals in the community. Those individuals with greater risk of claiming than the average in their group will be paying lower premiums than they should. They have little or no incentive to try to reduce their own risk. Those individuals with risks lower than the average will be subsidizing the high-risk group. If, by chance, the insurance company has unwittingly insured a number of high-risk individuals, it will lose money.

The problem is that the insured individuals have more information than the company about the likelihood of their making a claim. It is in their interest to make their risk *appear* low in order to keep their premiums down. It is for this reason that insurance companies are very insistent about disclosure by potential clients of all relevant information, and will refuse to meet claims if it is suspected that relevant information has been withheld.

Scheffler (1989) suggested that adverse selection could be a problem for GP fundholders in the UK if the practices had relatively small numbers of patients. Insurance companies have very large numbers of clients and so face only a small risk of a number of claims large enough to threaten their financial viability. They also take great care to screen out bad risks. GP fundholders typically have smaller numbers of patients and face a greater risk of adverse selection: that a significant number of patients cost more than had been budgeted for. Initially GP fundholding schemes in the UK were limited to those with more than 11,000 patients. More recently, this lower limit has been reduced to 7,000. Although there is an upper limit to the cost that practices have to face for any individual patient, the existence of a group whose costs fall just below this limit could cause financial problems. There will be a tendency to try to screen out potential problem patients. As a result, some individuals in poor health may find it difficult to be accepted by a GP. The practice of screening potential clients and accepting only those with a low risk of being expensive is known as 'cream-skimming'. If financial incentives to purchasers and providers in a quasi-market encourage cream-skimming, then the allocation of services is likely to be more inequitable.

Scheffler points out that in the USA, Health Maintenance Organizations (HMOs), which undertake the care of patients for a fixed fee per annum, are much larger and that those with less than 50,000 patients have financial problems. He gives examples of the way in which HMOs have tried to screen out potentially high-cost patients. One HMO, seeking to recruit more elderly clients because of the higher capitation fees they received for their care, invited applications at a sponsored dance for the elderly held on the second floor of a building with no lift.

Moral hazard

This is another type of market failure, sometimes known as the problem of hidden action, which is usually presented as being a problem for insurance companies. Briefly, the problem is that once an individual is insured, he or she may take less care and become more likely to make a claim. In order to reduce the problem of moral hazard, insurance companies usually insist that the insured individual pays some portion of the claim – the 'policy excess'.

The existence of moral hazard is sometimes used as an argument against providing free health care. If an individual does not have to pay the cost of health care, he or she may be more likely to indulge in risky activities. Perhaps smokers would be more likely to give up if they thought they might have to pay for their own medical treatment.

If a provider made a contract with a purchaser to provide items of service at an agreed quality standard, and then, to save costs, supplied a service of a lower quality, knowing that the purchaser was not in a position to monitor the quality provided, this would be an example of moral hazard – hidden action by the provider.

Imperfect information may also prevent individuals from making the best decisions about the type of health care they need. The role of the doctor is to act as the agent of the uninformed patient, demanding the appropriate type of health care on the patient's behalf. However, in a private health care system, the doctor's income depends on how much and the type of health care the patient uses. Thus there may be a tendency by some doctors to overtreat their patients. The existence of supplier-induced demand may lead to a misallocation of resources.

Transaction costs and uncertainty

In addition to the costs of producing cost and quality information, in a quasi-market there are also considerable costs associated with drawing up and monitoring contracts, sending out and organizing the settlement of bills, collection of debts and settlement of disputes. In the health services needs and outcomes may be difficult to predict and quality is not easy to measure. The question of whether the extra costs created by the information and administrative requirements of the quasi-markets outweigh the saving generated by the incentives for greater efficiency has to be considered when deciding whether quasi-markets are an improvement on the old system. The problems associated with contracting in the health service are covered in more detail in the section on markets and hierarchies (Section 9.5).

Objectives

In conventional economic theory, it is assumed that consumers attempt to maximize their total utility from the goods and services they consume and that firms aim to maximize profits (although it is widely accepted that firms may have other goals as we shall see in Chapter 10). In a quasi-market providers must be motivated at least in part by financial considerations; without the fear of bankruptcy or some financial penalty they may not price services in a way which reflects costs and they may not respond to market signals. Purchasers must be motivated to pursue the interests of users.

Externalities

As we saw in Chapter 3, the production or consumption of certain goods may impose costs on or provide benefits to other members of society which are not taken into account by the individual producer or consumer. These extra costs which are not included in production and consumption decisions are called externalities. If there are externalities, then market forces will not by themselves bring about an efficient allocation of resources.

Mobility of factors of production

The market system will work efficiently only if resources can be readily shifted to alternative uses in response to changes in market conditions. Factors of production, particularly labour, may not be easily shifted into alternative occupations or regions because of lack of training, difficulty in finding accommodation, lack of information about available jobs and so on. At the moment, the proposals to close some London hospitals and move the resources into primary care are running into considerable opposition.

9.5 ■ Markets and hierarchies

Hospitals are complex organizations. Services are provided by a wide range of staff to patients with conditions that differ in type, severity and prognosis. Within hospitals activities are generally coordinated hierarchically, with those at the top of the hierarchy having the power to direct those at lower levels. However, some functions, such as computer services or cleaning, are being bought in from outside firms through market transactions. Different staff in the hospital will be on long-term contracts, short-term contracts or paid by the hour. Some will be supplied through agencies while others are recruited directly by the hospital.

In the UK the services provided by the hospital are those which have been purchased through internal market transactions by purchaser organizations such as health authorities or GP fundholders. However, this arrangement is relatively recent. Before

1989 and the introduction of the internal market, health services used to be coordinated hierarchically, with one body taking overall responsibility for both the planning and provision of services.

Divisions between hierarchies and markets are observed in the wider economy. Pharmaceutical companies are large organizations with production, marketing, research and administrative functions generally carried out within the company, coordinated hierarchically. However, they are likely to buy in supplies such as stationery, equipment and raw materials through market transactions. Large pharmaceutical companies increasingly buy in statistical services for use in drug trials. A university-based statistical service may offer high credibility due to the combination of perceived academic expertise and also some sense of objectivity since those providing the service do not have a direct interest in a particular outcome from the trials.

Organizations, particularly hierarchies, are a common alternative to markets as a way of coordinating activities and allocating resources. An important question arises. Why are some activities coordinated within organizations and others bought in by the organization through the market system?

9.6 ▦ Transaction cost economics

This question has been extensively studied by Willamson (1985) using a transaction cost framework. All transactions, whether within organizations or between firms in markets, incur costs. The total cost of an activity is made up of production costs and transaction costs. The reason for the existence of organizations such as firms is that the cost of the required transactions is less if the firm's activities are carried out internally than if they are undertaken as market transactions.

The nature of transaction costs

Transaction costs can be very broad in scope. For example, if a particular activity is outsourced, there may be a risk of loss of control and failure to meet important deadlines. If technical activities are outsourced, learning opportunities for those in the firm may be forgone. The subcontractor benefits from the 'experience curve' effects. Subcontractors may have to be closely monitored, imposing additional costs of inspection on the firm. On the other hand, there may be benefits. Outsourcing may bring with it the need to collaborate with other firms, bringing with it the possibility of shared experience. For example, hospital doctors may collaborate with doctors working for pharmaceutical companies.

The assumptions of transaction cost economics

There are two main assumptions about the parties to transactions. The first is **bounded rationality**, the assumption that when the problem is complex and/or the outcomes of decisions are uncertain, decision-makers cannot possibly undertake all the calculations necessary to compare all possible courses of action (March and Simon, 1958). The second is **opportunism**, the assumption that in some circumstances one of the parties to the transaction might try to turn the situation to his or her own advantage, for example, if information about cost or quality was unavailable to the other party to the transaction. Williamson does not assume that opportunistic behaviour will *always* take place, just that it is a possibility that cannot be ignored.

The problem of possible opportunistic behaviour is increased if there are few possible trading partners. With large numbers of potential trading partners, a company faced with opportunistic behaviour could do business with someone else, and the risk of this would be a deterrent to a potential opportunist. Opportunistic behaviour becomes more risky and less attractive in this situation. However, with small numbers of potential trading partners this is not an option, so the risk of facing opportunistic behaviour increases.

Dimensions of transactions

Williamson defines three important **dimensions of transactions**:

1. Asset specificity – the degree to which each or either party to the transaction has to obtain and maintain assets which are very specific to the transaction and which have a much lower value in alternative uses. As well as physical capital equipment, the assets might include human capital and specific operating routines and computer software.
2. Uncertainty/complexity – the extent to which the transaction has a complex specification and/or uncertain outcomes. Where there is unpredictability and a wide range of needs, as for example, in the long-term care of the elderly, forecasting costs is fraught with difficulty.
3. Frequency – the number of times the transaction is likely to take place over a given period. For example, the transfer of a seriously injured patient requiring specialist neurological treatment from a local hospital to a London hospital is an event that takes place much less frequently (thankfully) than the referral of a patient by a GP to the local hospital for a blood test.

Market or organization?

The main results of Williamson's work suggest that where there is a high degree of asset specificity and much complexity and/or uncertainty, then transaction costs will be reduced if the transactions are carried out within organizations rather than across markets. This is particularly true if the frequency is high as well. In such situations, contracts will be complicated to draw up, difficult to enforce and monitor, and expensive. Thus it will be a great deal cheaper and less risky to carry out the activity in-house rather than buy it in from outside.

9.7 ▧ Contracts

It is argued that placing contracts for services with providers may increase efficiency and reduce costs because of the increased competition on the supply side. The was one of the motivations behind the introduction of the internal market in the NHS. However, the contracting process may have its own inefficiencies. For example, the provider may have more information than the purchaser about costs and quality, and have an incentive to behave opportunistically if quality, costs or activity are difficult to monitor. The efficiency of the contracting process in health and social care where quality is not readily observable is discussed by Propper (1993).

Factors affecting the efficiency of contracting are as follows:

1. Industry specific factors – the degree of market power of purchasers or providers. For example, when there are few providers purchasers will not be in a strong position when negotiating contracts.
2. Ease of specifying, measuring and monitoring the quality of output. In some cases there may be standard protocols or procedures, in others not.
3. The choice of which goods or services to include in the contract – the franchise design. For example, who does the investigations? Who carries out the treatment?
4. The specific features of the contract – the contract design.

The process of contracting in the health service is covered in some detail in Hodgson and Hoile (1996). However, the following brief outline will illustrate some of the points made above.

Types of contract

Fixed price: the purchaser pays a fixed sum which is determined at the bidding stage. The provider has to cover any cost overrun. Thus all the risk of unforeseen increases in cost is being borne by the provider. It is likely that providers will have an incentive to build in a risk premium. Also there may be few bidders, meaning less competition for the contract. The purchaser may well have to pay a higher price. Experience of fixed-price contracts for health care in the USA, where prospective payment systems are ever more common, suggests that such payment systems have led providers to reduce quality and discharge patients earlier (Ellis and McGuire, 1986; Walsh, 1995).

Cost-plus: the purchaser pays all the costs including any overruns. Here the risk of unforeseen increases in cost is being borne by the purchaser. Naturally, this sort of contract is very attractive to potential suppliers. No doubt there will be much competition to be awarded the contract, which will bring the price down. But since the purchaser bears all the cost overruns, there is no guarantee that the provider who would have been the cheapest actually gets the contract. In addition, there is an incentive for the provider to inflate the costs artificially, or at least to make no effort to keep costs down.

Walsh (1995) discusses public sector contracting in some detail. He points out that different degrees of trust between client and contractor will result in different contract terms. At one extreme are punishment-based contracts, where the assumption is that the interests of the client and contractor are completely opposed. If the contractors fail to meet some or all of the conditions in the contract, they are punished by the withholding of some of the payment, for example. The NHS internal market does include provision to 'fine' providers who fail to meet contracts. (Recent examples of behaviour by the recently privatized railway companies in the UK suggest that fining a failing provider does little to sort out the problems involved.)

At the other extreme are cooperative contracts. Here there is a much greater degree of trust between client and contractor. If the contractor fails to meet all the obligations of the contract, the client's response is to work with the contractor in an attempt to overcome the problems. Where it is expected that the client/contractor relationship will continue, the cooperative contract has many advantages over the punishment-based form. The following case study illustrates this point.

In the health care market, because of complexity and uncertainty surrounding many medical treatments and outcomes, contracts are often incomplete. There are some issues and problems which cannot be completely specified in the contract conditions. Thus there has to be considerable emphasis on trust between the parties to the contract.

Case study 9.2

A report from the NHS Trust Federation in 1995, called *Good Practice Guidelines for NHS Contracting*, criticized what it called 'macho' contract negotiations, saying they had resulted in 'lost opportunities for building patient care'. The Federation guidelines are intended to reduce the confrontational element in the contracting process. The report blamed both trusts and health authorities for poor practice, saying that both sides seemed reluctant to share information about clinical outcomes and costs. Providers often ignored strategic plans of purchasers, while purchasers went through the tendering process too quickly rather than negotiating with providers.

Discussion

In the NHS, given the preference of many patients to be treated at hospitals near their homes, it is clearly the case that the relationship between a health authority and its local trust hospitals is going to be long-lasting. The implication of the report is that the 'macho' approach to negotiations is reducing the potential benefits to patients. The new Labour government may well introduce a new system of organization which changes the framework for such negotiations in the future.

Forms of contract in the health service

In the NHS internal market there are three basic forms of contract, the block contract (sometimes with indicative volume), the cost and volume contract and the cost per case contract. Contracts may well include specifications of quality and timing of activity, together with information and monitoring requirements. Ellwood (1992), in her discussion of the results of the 1991/92 West Midlands Survey of contract prices and cost methods, produced a table showing the pattern of contract income of the average provider hospital.

Type of contract	% of contract income
Block	28
Block with indicative volume	61
Cost and volume	8
Cost per case	3

As well as discussing the type of contract, she also examines the cost methods used to calculate contract prices.

Features of types of contract

Block contract

This is an agreement to provide a given range of services for a stated total cost. It is a particularly important type of contract where consumption is patient-led, for example, Accident and Emergency services. The more sophisticated type of block contract includes indicative activity levels. These types of contract are relatively low risk to the provider, especially if there is no indicative volume. The hospital can let waiting lists rise if there is a possibility of overspending.

Cost and volume contract

The contract states the cost of units of different services and the quantity of each that will be required. Such contracts may include volume thresholds below which a fixed price is paid, and above which a set price per case is paid up to a specified volume ceiling. Such contracts carry greater risks for the providers, since they will have to meet cost overruns.

Cost per case contract

The contract states the price of a unit of service but does not include any commitment to a particular quantity. For the provider this means that there is much uncertainty about the amount of income that will be received.

When the internal market was introduced, the majority of contracts were block contracts, keeping transaction costs low. In 1993 the National Health Service Management Executive instructed purchasers and providers that simple block contracts were no longer acceptable. Since then there has been a reduction in the proportion of block contracts and a corresponding increase in the proportion of cost and volume contracts. GP fundholders, although making use of some long-term contracts, make a greater use of spot contracts and cost per case contracts. For providers, taking extra patients on spot contracts from GP fundholders can be more profitable than doing more work under a block contract, since the former brings in extra revenue.

Case study 9.3

The chief executive of Mid-Barsetshire General Hospital Trust has reacted angrily to the demand by Barsetshire Health Authority that the trust should lower its prices by an average of 5% in the next round of contracts. Barsetshire HA is a major purchaser of the Mid-Barsetshire General Hospital Trust's services and withdrawal of its contracts would make the Trust's financial position precarious. 'They have us over a barrel and they know it,' the chief executive is reported to have said. 'We cannot deliver the quality of services required if our prices are squeezed down any further.'

Barsetshire Health Authority says it has no choice but to seek price cuts. It is responding to demands from the government to make efficiency savings. At the same time it has a £3 m budget deficit caused by high-spending GP fundholders and an unexpected spate of young accident victims who need 24-hour nursing care at home.

Discussion

The chief executive obviously feels that the health authority is behaving opportunistically, using its monopsony power as a large purchaser to force price cuts on to the provider. The assets held by the provider are transaction-specific; it would be difficult and expensive to convert them to other uses. They are also place-specific. Given the preference of patients to be treated near their homes, the trust is dependent on contracts from the local health authority. The health authority is complaining that it is short of funds because of unforeseen circumstances, emphasizing the problem that uncertainty creates for planning in health services.

References

Appleby, J., Smith, P., Ranade, W., Little, V. and Robinson, R. (1993) 'Competition and the NHS: Monitoring the Market', in Tilley, I. (ed.), *Managing the Internal Market*, Paul Chapman Publishing Ltd, London.

Culyer, A. and Posnett, J. W. (1990) 'Hospital Behaviour and Competition', in Culyer, A., Maynard, A. and Posnett, J. W. (eds), *Competition in Health Care: Reforming the NHS*, Macmillan, London.

Dawson, D. (1994) 'Costs and Prices in the Internal Market: Market vs the NHS Management Executive Guidelines', Discussion Paper 115, Centre for Health Economics, University of York.

Ellis, R. and McGuire, T. (1986) 'Provider Behaviour under Prospective Reimbursement', *Journal of Health Economics*, 5, pp. 129–51.

Ellwood, S. (1992) *Cost Methods for NHS Health Care Contracts*, Chartered Institute of Management Accountants.

Hodgson, K. and Hoile, R. W. (eds) (1996) *Managing Health Service Contracts*, Saunders, London.

Le Grand, J. and Bartlett, W. (eds) (1993) *Quasi-Markets and Social Policy*, Macmillan, Basingstoke.

March, J. G. and Simon, H. A. (1958) *Organizations*, Wiley, New York.

Propper, C. (1993) 'Quasi-Markets, Contracts and Quality in Health and Social Care: The US Experience', in Le Grand, J. and Bartlett, W. (eds), *Quasi-Markets and Social Policy*, Macmillan, Basingstoke.

Scheffler, R. M. (1989) 'Adverse Selection: The Achilles Heel of the NHS Reforms', *The Lancet*, April, 29, pp. 950–2.

Walsh, K. (1995) *Public Services and Market Mechanisms; Competition, Contracting and the New Public Management*, Macmillan, Basingstoke.

Williamson, O. E. (1985) *The Economic Institutions of Capitalism*, Free Press, New York.

Questions for consideration

1. In a private sector multi-product firm, what competitive advantages might the firm gain if it keeps its methods of costing and pricing each of its products confidential?

2. 'To take a familiar starting point, a profit-maximizing monopolist hospital selling an undifferentiated single service will select an output rate lower and a selling price higher than a profit-maximizing competitive hospital industry . . .' 'Hospital Behaviour and Competition', Culyer and Posnett, 1990.

   (a) Using diagrams, explain this statement.

   (b) Another model for hospital behaviour is output-maximization subject to a no-loss constraint. Using diagrams, suggest how such a hospital selling a single undifferentiated service would choose its optimal price–output combination: (i) in a perfectly competitive industry and (ii) as a monopoly.

   (c) It has been suggested that under some market structures, hospitals might engage in non-price competition. Explain, using relevant examples, what is meant by 'non-price competition'.

3. Consider the following case study and analyse the outsourcing problem using a transaction cost economics framework.

Case study 9.4

Battle is raging in the boardroom at Marketshire Hospital Trust over whether or not to transfer computer services at the trust to an outside contractor. Those in favour of outsourcing point to the benefits of using an outside company which already has expertise in this area and which provides similar services to other trusts; costs are likely to be lower than providing the services in-house. Those against point to the high transaction costs, the advantages of having all the information and computing services under a single management structure and the problems associated with allowing outside companies access to confidential and sensitive data.

4. '[GP] Fundholding needs to be treated for what it is; a subcontract for a cluster of services centred around primary care from a commissioning authority. As with any subcontract, there are problems of cost-shifting and exploiting loopholes.' Donald Light, Professor of Comparative Health care Systems, University of Medicine and Dentistry of New Jersey, in an article in the *Health Service Journal*, 20 July 1995.

   Analyse this statement, using a transaction cost economics approach.

5. Describe the type of market, in terms of numbers of purchasers and providers, and competitive behaviour that are likely to develop for inpatient treatments for medical conditions which are:

   (a) common, require routine inexpensive treatment, predictable outcomes, high success rate;

   (b) common, expensive to treat, high success rate;

   (c) rare, expensive to treat, high success rate;

   (d) rare, expensive to treat, low success rate;

   (e) common, chronic, requiring regular cheap treatment;

   (f) rare, chronic, requiring regular expensive treatment.

   In each case, what sort of contract is likely to be drawn up between purchaser and provider?

CHAPTER TEN

The firm and its objectives

Objectives

- To examine the different possible objectives of the firm and show how these influence its behaviour.

- To examine different models of hospital objectives showing how they influence behaviour.

- To look at different organizational forms in health services such as sole practitioners and group partnerships.

Introduction

In the chapter on marginal analysis, we examined a simple model of the firm and deduced the rule for determining the output level at which profits are maximized. We found that the profit-maximizing firm should expand its output up to the point where marginal cost is equal to marginal revenue. Apart from the obvious difficulties associated with finding this level of output in practice, there is also the question of whether firms do aim to maximize profits or whether they pursue other objectives.

This question is important because the objectives of the organization, together with the market structure in which it operates, will determine its competitive strategy. A firm which aims to maximize its profits will have a different pricing policy from one which aims to increase its market share as much as possible. A hospital which aims to make profits may use different pricing rules from a not-for-profit hospital.

In early (classical) economic theory the typical firm was assumed to be small, the owner managed the firm and it operated in a competitive environment. Thus the objective of profit maximization meant in effect that the owner was trying to maximize his income, a not unreasonable assumption in the circumstances. Because the market structure was so competitive, any firm that did not try to maximize profits would be in danger of going bankrupt.

However, the typical modern enterprise is very different from the simple structure described above. Managers run the enterprise but the shareholders are the owners. There is no guarantee that the interests of these different groups will coincide exactly. This is known as the principal–agent problem – the managers are agents for the principals (shareholders), and the managers may have their own objectives. For example, the shareholders' desires for high dividends may conflict with managers' desires to retain earnings in order to fund investment for growth.

Modern enterprises are complex, producing a variety of outputs and operating in market structures which often are not very competitive. Where the industry is oligopolistic, competitive strategy may be aimed at maintaining or increasing market share rather than at maximizing profit.

10.1 ▓ Alternatives to profit maximization as an objective of the firm

Alternatives to the objective of profit maximization have been proposed. Baumol (1967) suggested a model in which the firm aims to maximize sales revenue, possibly subject to a minimum profit constraint. We saw a simple version of this in Chapter 8. The revenue-maximizing firm expands output up to the point where marginal revenue equals zero. Typically, this occurs at a higher output and a lower price than the profit-maximizing level of output. Essentially the firm is sacrificing profit in order to achieve a higher market share.

This approach can lead to problems. For example, in the late 1980s, the Ford Motor Company achieved a high market share by heavy price discounting on company cars, but began to make losses. The policy was changed in favour of a strategy to increase profits. If a minimum profit constraint is introduced, the firm still lowers prices and expands output past the profit-maximizing point, but stops short of the revenue-maximizing point.

Marris (1963, 1964) proposed a model in which the firm's objective is growth. Managers see growth as a desirable objective because it brings security, higher salaries and greater status. Thus, as pointed out above, managers may wish to retain profits to fund growth, while shareholders would prefer higher dividends. There is a danger that if low dividends are paid, the share price will fall and the firm may be in danger of being taken over. Managers must try to find the best balance between dividends and retained profits.

Williamson (1967) proposed a model in which managers aim to maximize their own utility. Their utility functions include measures of status and personal comfort such as high salaries, number of subordinates, executive cars and lavish offices among other things. Managers use their managerial discretion over expenditure to acquire these items. Shareholders may object (shades of British Gas!) and managers recognize that a certain minimum level of profit must be made. Nevertheless, in this model managers are not aiming to maximize profits, but rather to satisfice.

The models of Baumol, Marris and Williamson are all based on the maximization of some objective function, be it revenue, growth or managerial utility. In each case, the conflict between the objective of profit maximization and other objectives can be resolved to a certain extent if firms establish contracts with the managers in which their salaries are linked to the performance of the firm. The final model to be discussed in this section is very different because there is no objective function to be maximized.

The model of Cyert and March (1963) presents the firm as a coalition of groups, managers, shopfloor workers, shareholders, different departments and so on, each with different interests and objectives. The firm cannot be described as having a single goal. The different interest groups each have different goals, and the behaviour of the firm at any time is determined by the outcome of the bargaining process that takes place between the groups.

Not all groups can achieve their goals simultaneously as the goals are bound to be inconsistent. For example, workers want higher wages while shareholders want higher profits. Some groups have to be compensated by 'side-payments' such as fringe benefits if their particular goals cannot be met.

This is essentially a behavioural model. It focuses on the processes by which the firm's goals emerge. It emphasizes the fact that bargaining involves compromises, that the firm's goals will change as different interest groups become stronger or weaker. The model implies that profit-maximization as a single goal is unlikely to be paramount over any extended time period.

10.2 ■ Hospital objectives

Hospitals are extremely complex organizations producing a wide range of services. There are major difficulties in defining the output of hospitals. In addition, some hospitals are run on a 'for-profit' basis, while others fall into the 'not-for-profit' category. However, just because a hospital is run on a 'for-profit' basis, it does not follow that the objective is to maximize those profits. Many hospitals compete in a market, as in the USA, or in a quasi-market, as in the British NHS. In either case, the hospital's objectives will determine its competitive strategy.

Many models of hospital behaviour have been developed over the last 30 years or so. This is not intended to be a complete review but rather an introduction to some of the more influential ones.

Newhouse (1970) put forward a model to describe the behaviour of non-profit hospitals. In it he assumed that the hospital's objective was to maximize both quantity and quality of the services provided, subject to a limit on the size of the hospital's deficit. The arguments for including quality in the maximand follow from the premise that as the administrators of the hospital cannot be judged on profits in a non-profit enterprise, they must be judged on other criteria such as the prestige of the institution and the quality of its facilities and services. The medical staff also have a role to play in the decision-making process and they also care about quality of facilities and services.

According to the Newhouse model, managers in not-for-profit hospitals have little incentive to look for efficiency savings as they do not receive a reward for achieving a budget surplus. Worse still, managers assume that quality is a function of input prices – the higher the price, the better the quality. Thus hospital administrators will seek highly priced inputs.

The model does not include explicitly any factors relating to competition between hospitals although Newhouse does point out that non-profit status acts as a barrier to entry, since there are no profits to attract a new entrepreneur. Thus the non-profit hospital sector will tend to be inefficient. The presence of quality in the objective function, together with the lack of a profit motive, leads to a bias towards producing higher quality services than a profit-maximizing hospital and a tendency for hospitals to duplicate expensive and sophisticated equipment.

The model has been criticized because of its lack of consideration of the interdependency among hospitals even though many of them operate in markets which have oligopolistic structures. By contrast, Lee (1971) does take into account competition between hospitals in her 'conspicuous consumption' model. The model is reminiscent of the managerial utility maximization theory of Williamson. Lee assumes that hospital administrators attempt to maximize their utility. Their utility functions include such variables as salary, power, prestige, security and professional satisfaction. All of these variables are dependent on the prestige and status of the hospital in which they are employed.

The visible symbols of the hospital's status are the range of services provided, the amount of expensive and sophisticated equipment and the number of high-status clinical staff. The high-status clinical staff demand the best and most sophisticated equipment and facilities. In order to attract and maintain the numbers of such staff, hospitals must compete to provide the best facilities. Although the hospitals acquire the inputs ostensibly for patient care, they are essentially the price paid to attract the best physicians. The price one hospital has to pay will of course depend on the prices other hospitals are prepared to pay.

This desire to attract physicians with facilities and equipment leads to the acquisition of these expensive inputs without regard to the extent to which these inputs can be used to generate extra production and revenue. The pricing system used by some hospitals encourages this oversupply; there is no necessity for the increased expenditure to be covered by increased revenue if the cost can simply be spread over all the hospital output.

The administrators run the hospital with the objective of minimizing the gap between its actual status and the desired status. The competition between hospitals will be similar to that found in oligopolistic markets. Activities and purchases of expensive equipment will be justified on the grounds that the other hospitals are doing the same and that the status gap must be kept to a minimum.

The model suggests that hospitals will use more resources than those required to produce a given level of output, equipment will be underutilized and there will be a tendency to use higher quality inputs than necessary.

Pauly and Redisch (1973) introduce a model with features that make it more similar to conventional models of the profit-maximizing firm. They point out that not-for-profit hospitals are faced with weaker market forces because of lack of competition and the profit motive. They see hospital physicians as seeking to maximize their incomes. They are in control of the hospital and the hospital objective is to maximize the net income per member of staff. The hospital faces a conventional downward-sloping demand curve for its services. If the number of physicians is assumed to be constant in the short run then the analysis becomes identical to that of the profit-maximizing firm in the short run.

The model can be used to examine the effects of changes in demand and cost conditions, and of different staffing policies. Predictions from the model include duplication of facilities, quality consciousness and a hospital size smaller than that required for minimum average cost.

The model introduced by Harris (1977) differs from the others in that it places more emphasis on the internal organization of the hospital, viewing it as consisting of two separate firms. On the demand side are the clinicians who demand services from the supply side which consists of service departments such as X-ray, radiology, operating rooms and staffing, pathology and so on. Patient-care decisions are taken by the medical staff. Thus the hospital, although one organization, is 'split into two disjoint pieces, each with its own objectives, managers, pricing strategies and constraints' (Harris, 1977).

There are similarities here with the behavioural model of the firm by Cyert and March, in the sense that some sort of bargaining process must take place between two major interest groups, the demand side (physicians) who want well-equipped hospitals with plenty of spare capacity and the supply side (administration) who have budget constraints and who have personal objectives relating to status, working conditions and numbers of subordinate staff. The objectives of the hospital – increases in quality, quantity or revenue, for example – may alter according to which group happens to have the upper hand.

The number of groups whose interests are likely to conflict with the budget-constrained administrators could be increased to include nurses, who might wish for higher wages and also fewer patients per nurse, and patients, who desire speedy access to high-quality medical care and who have option demands for emergency facilities.

Morrissey *et al.* (1984) introduce a model in which the hospital is viewed as a 'bundle' of characteristics, these being the various services the hospital provides. (A similar approach is used in studies of house prices: houses are heterogeneous commodities with different characteristics such as number of bedrooms, garden size, location, etc. The *hedonic* approach to house price analysis involves attempting to estimate the implied values of the different characteristics.)

In this model the physician is a net income maximizer; he employs hospital services and his own time and skill to produce medical care. The not-for-profit hospitals are assumed to be aiming to maximize medical staff net income (which implies that the hospitals will supply services to physicians at minimum cost). The for-profit hospitals aim to maximize net present value. The consumer (patient) is aiming to maximize utility which is a function of health and other goods. In turn, health is a function of the consumer's initial endowment of health and the medical services purchased.

This model was used to explore the effect of price controls on hospital behaviour. It predicted, among other things, a lowering of quality and the likely 'unbundling' of some services.

Ellis and McGuire (1986) developed a model in which hospitals were assumed to be profit maximizers with the physician being the agent for both the patient and the hospital. The physician is assumed to maximize a utility function which includes both patient benefits and hospital profits. The model was used to explore the effects of the prospective payment scheme (PPS) where the hospital receives a fixed fee for treating the patient. Thus the hospital bears the marginal cost of treating the patient and the patient receives the marginal benefit.

The physician has to trade off the hospital's profit against the benefits to the patient. If the physician is the perfect agent, defined in this case as one who values $1 of cost to the hospital as being of equal weight to $1 of benefits to the patient, the amount of treatment the patient receives will be set at the point where marginal benefit equals marginal cost. Net total benefits to the patient will be maximized. However, if the physician weights $1 of costs to the hospital more highly than $1 of benefits to the patient, the amount of treatment prescribed will be lower.

Thorpe and Phelps (1990) model a not-for-profit hospital with some market power, i.e. facing a downward sloping demand curve. The hospital maximizes its utility function which is a function of the number of days of care provided (N) and the service intensity per day (S) subject to demand conditions and a breakeven constraint.

The equilibrium level of output is higher than the profit-maximizing level, so marginal cost is greater than marginal revenue at that point. The effect of binding price control is to reduce average cost; this is achieved by reducing service intensity. The authors' empirical analysis of New York hospitals showed that price controls resulted in a reduction of average length of stay and a substantial reduction (about 10%) in the staffing levels of non-medical personnel.

As noted above, this section was intended to give the flavour of different economic models of hospitals, their objective functions and the consequent implications for behaviour. Readers who wish to know more are recommended to consult the references at the end of the chapter.

10.3 ▧ Other health care providers

The hospital is far from the only form of health care provider despite the vast resources which hospitals consume. Two other key organizational forms are typical in health care provision, namely the sole practitioner typified by the so-called 'single-handed general practitioner' or the office-based medical specialist, not forgetting a wide range of independent therapists who sell their services direct to the consumer.

The self-employed physician or family doctor often seeks a measure of independence in patterns and style of work. Such a practitioner can decide how much work to do depending on whether he or she is keen to maximize income or simply seeks to satisfice. He or she is usually working in a branch of medicine where the capital requirements are modest or where there are a range of services which can be purchased when required. For instance, many independent clinicians will want to be able to purchase pathology tests either on a cost per item basis or through a longer-term contract. Few such practitioners will dispense with a secretary/receptionist although this may be a family member. Some independent practitioners will effectively work in networks through which patterns of referrals take place enabling a degree of flexibility and realizing some economies in the transactions which take place when a patient requires complementary services to those provided directly by the sole practitioner. This also enables civilized arrangements to be made for out-of-hours cover.

In principle an independent practitioner can decide the price and terms of the service he or she provides as long as that price is also paid by the consumer and not subject to the reimbursement of a third party or agent or even to governmental regulation. In some cases the independent practitioner will be able to work on a part-time basis and so integrate their clinical work with other activities.

Independent practice has a number of drawbacks including the limited opportunity for exploiting the advantages which are connected with the division of labour. It is likely that availability of capital resources will be low and that economies of scale and of scope will be hard to achieve. Where capital equipment is purchased it may be underutilized since the flow of patients requiring any particular procedure may be limited. Additionally, any support services such as secretarial/reception services and associated capital assets ranging from computers to office space may also be underutilized.

The partnership form of organization attempts to achieve the benefits of the division of labour while minimizing the underutilization of capital and human resources. A partnership will have certain objectives which will be described in a formal agreement which spells out the responsibilities of partners, the ownership of assets, responsibilities for liabilities and arrangements for the distribution of revenues. Such an arrangement is not limited to the time and talents of a single individual. The requirements of six partners are certainly not six times the requirements of a single practitioner and it might be possible to achieve synergistic improvements in efficiency and perhaps also in effectiveness. Such an organization will seek to outsource some activities which cannot be efficiently provided within the partnership and will need to look carefully at the make-or-buy decision. Should it employ its own counsellors or should it buy in counsellors on a sessional basis? Should it purchase a small X-ray machine or should such services be provided by specialist providers from other organizations?

The optimal size of a partnership will be subject to objective considerations about demand and patterns of service requirements among consumers but will also be determined by subjective views about the working environment desired by partners. Where demand exceeds supply partnerships may face very little pressure from competitors but where supply exceeds demand it may be necessary to compete on the basis of price or services offered. This may mean amenity-based competition by differentiating the service or it might mean reducing prices to attract customers. In very competitive situations competition will include both differentiating services and offering attractive prices. Differentiated services may take the form of bundling related services so that a patient only needs to make one rather than several visits to the surgery, making arrangements so that pharmaceutical services are available, providing telephone consultations so that patients do not need to leave their homes or offices, etc.

References

Baumol, W. J. (1967) *Business Behavior, Value and Growth*, Harcourt, Brace and World, New York.
Cyert, R. M. and March, J. G. (1963), *Behavioral Theory of the Firm*, Prentice Hall International, Englewood Cliffs, NJ.
Ellis, R. P. and McGuire, T. G. (1986) 'Provider Behaviour under Prospective Reimbursement: Cost Sharing and Supply', *Journal of Health Economics*, 5, pp. 129–51.
Harris, J. E. (1977) 'The Internal Organization of Hospitals: Some Economic Implications', *Bell Journal of Economics*, 8, pp. 467–82.
Lee, M. L. (1971) 'A Conspicuous Production Theory of Hospital Behaviour', *Southern Economic Journal*, 38, pp. 48–58.
Marris, R. L. (1963) 'A Model of the Managerial Enterprise', *Quarterly Journal of Economics*, 77, pp. 185–209.
Marris, R. L. (1964) *The Economic Theory of Managerial Capitalism*, Macmillan, London.
Morrissey, M., Conrad, D., Shortell, S. and Cook, K. (1984) 'Hospital Rate Review: A Theory and an Empirical Review', *Journal of Health Economics*, 3, pp. 25–47.
Newhouse, J. P. (1970) 'Toward a Theory of Nonprofit Institutions: An Economic Model of a Hospital', *American Economic Review*, 60, pp. 64–74.
Pauly, M. and Redisch, M. (1973) 'The Not-For-Profit Hospital as a Physician's Cooperative', *American Economic Review*, 63, pp. 87–100.
Thorpe, K. E. and Phelps, C. E. (1990) 'Regulatory Intensity and Hospital Cost Growth', *Journal of Health Economics*, 9, pp. 143–66.
Williamson, O. E. (1967) *The Economics of Discretionary Behaviour*, Kershaw, London.

CHAPTER ELEVEN

Measurement and valuation in health care

Objectives

- To introduce the complex issues of measurement and valuation, pointing to key developments and remaining problems.

- To show why reliable and valid measures are needed if we are to achieve defensible answers to the key economic questions.

- To discuss the theory and practical use of multi-dimensional measures in health care management.

Introduction

The 1990s have seen a strong call for evidence-based medicine as a response to scarce economic resources with which to fund health care (see Frater, 1996). The argument seems simple: if we can discard ineffective practices we might be able to redirect funds, whether public or private, to more effective remedies. Who is to define effective and ineffective? Should it be the provider, the beneficiary or indeed a third party or agent? Is the determination of effectiveness a technical judgement or a social valuation and how can we measure these judgements of effectiveness and social or personal value?

Measures, if they are to be useful, need to be both **reliable** and **valid**. A reliable measure will come to the same reading when measuring identical phenomena or remeasuring a phenomenon which has not changed. A valid measure will measure the phenomenon in question and not some proxy which might not give a true indication of the object of interest. Unfortunately, we often have to rely on measures that are not 100% reliable or 100% valid since measurement itself is expensive and the phenomena which we are measuring are highly complex.

For instance, some managers in the past have taken the level of complaints as a reliable and valid proxy measure for the quality of care within their services. While this measure is undoubtedly cheap, it is subject to all sorts of external influences and an increasing number of complaints may bear little relation to the quality of care. Alternatively, an external audit may be a very expensive way of assessing the quality of care and usually only relates to the time at which the audit was conducted.

Similarly, the degree of efficacy of a clinical procedure achieved in a controlled clinical trial in which all patients have been carefully selected may not be achievable in the local District General Hospital (DGH) in which external influences cannot be so easily avoided and patients may be suffering from multiple pathologies. Thus the measure might not be valid outside the research setting in the context of the DGH.

In summary we want reliable and valid measures if we are to be able to answer the key questions:

1. Who to treat?
2. Which range of alternative treatments should be used?
3. What conditions to treat?
4. Which treatments/services to expand and which to reduce?

Given limited budgets all decision-makers will seek value for money – but how can this be assessed? (See Glynn, Perkins and Stewart, 1996.) Even if the cost of a treatment can be measured accurately, there is the problem of measuring the improvements in health status that the treatment produces and then, ideally, putting a value on this improvement.

Many approaches seek a single reliable and valid measure of health status and to identify such a measure would indeed be the Holy Grail of evidence-based medicine, but in practice things are not quite so simple.

11.1 ■ Health status measurement

Health status measurement presents difficulties because health is multi-dimensional and because value-judgements are required about the quality of the patients' lives. Different individuals may value apparently similar health states differently. An athlete may take a more serious view of a sprained ankle than a TV critic.

In medicine, we are often concerned with improvements in health status. Some patients are more seriously ill than others before treatment begins. Ideally, a value-added approach should be used when comparing treatment outcomes. This is one of the disadvantages of crude hospital 'league tables' which compare death rates from different causes. We need to know the health status of the patients before they were treated if we are to come to conclusions about the effectiveness of health care procedures and services.

11.2 ■ Scales of measurement

Before we can look at particular measurement procedures it is important that we understand the main types of scale in use, their advantages and drawbacks.

Ordinal scales

Such scales are devised by the ranking of health states. We judge whether one health state is better than another but we do not try to decide how much better one state is than another. Florence Nightingale, who in addition to her other accomplishments also took an interest in medical statistics, used an ordinal scale to classify her patients – she used three categories – relieved, unrelieved and dead.

Ordinal scales have their drawbacks. For example, suppose Treatment A costs £1,000 while a new Treatment B (for the same condition) costs £10,000. We find that Treatment B produces a more highly ranked state of health than Treatment A. Since we cannot judge **how much better** the outcome is with Treatment B, we cannot judge whether it is better value for money. This is a problem, because if the budget is limited, using Treatment B will mean that fewer patients can be treated. We need to have a more informative measurement scale to make this sort of decision. The majority of developments take the form of ordinal scales and do not help us to decide how to allocate funds between a variety of services for maximum benefit. Few would be willing to completely sacrifice middle-ranked services until all those in need of top-ranked services had been dealt with.

Cardinal scales

There are two types of cardinal scale, interval and ratio. Temperature is measured on an interval scale. If two numbers on the scale are a certain distance apart this will indicate the same difference in temperature wherever the two numbers are on the scale. For example, a jump from 20°C to 30°C is a 10 degree rise in temperature, as is a jump from 30°C to 40°C. However, we cannot say that 40°C is twice as hot as 20°C. To see why, convert from Centigrade to Fahrenheit. 20°C is equivalent to 68°F, and 40°C is equivalent to 104°F. The problem is that on temperature scales, the choice of the zero point is arbitrary. On the Centigrade scale, the freezing point of water is at 0°C, whereas on the Fahrenheit scale it is 32°F.

Distance is measured on a ratio scale. A movement from 20 metres to 30 metres from a fixed starting point is a change of 10 metres. Similarly, a movement from 30 metres to 40 metres from a fixed starting point is a change of 10 metres. In addition, we can say that 40 metres is twice 20 metres. When measuring distance, there is no ambiguity about what is meant by zero. Pulse rate is measured on a ratio scale. We can say that a pulse rate of 120 per minute is twice as fast as a pulse rate of 60 per minute.

From the point of view of valuing health states for use in cost-benefit analysis the cardinal ratio scale is most useful because we can say, for example, that one health state is three times better than another. However, this is the most difficult type of valuation to carry out.

Mooney (1992, 1994) uses the example that having pneumonia is worse than having a cold, which in turn is worse than not having a cold (or anything else, presumably). This is an ordinal measurement. Supposing a cold cure costs £50 and to cure pneumonia it costs £1,000. Should we treat one case of pneumonia or 20 colds? Only if we judge it to be twenty times worse to have pneumonia than it is to have a cold.

Measures of health status

Economists, clinicians and others have attempted to use a variety of techniques to measure health status and to identify the value added by health services.

Clinical measures are one of the simplest approaches in the sense that they are often single dimensional. For instance, the measurement of lung capacity before and after treatment might be thought to give evidence about the impact of treatment for lung disease, while the measurement of cholesterol levels might be thought to demonstrate the impact of drug treatment or patient compliance following advice from a GP. However, even these measures are not unambiguous and might indicate a variety of clinical processes. Indeed, clinicians frequently require a range of measures of symptoms over an appropriate time period before coming to any conclusions in the diagnostic and treatment process.

Clinical measures require an understanding of single or multiple disease processes and frequently diagnoses will have the status of hypotheses with considerable levels of uncertainty which are matched by similar uncertainty about prognoses.

Functional Measures can be described as multi-attribute measures and may include clinical indicators and other indicators related to activities of daily life or other capabilities which are regarded as important for the individuals or groups being measured. Some measures are specific to particular disease groups while others are generic and designed to be used across a wide range of conditions.

Wilkin *et al.* (1992) have pointed to the need for precision in the use of language when we talk about human function. They make an important and widely supported distinction between impairment, disability and handicap.

- *Impairment* is used to refer to any disturbance or interference with the normal structure and functioning of the body, including mental functions. This might normally be assessed by one or more clinical measures.
- *Disability* is the loss or reduction of functional ability and activity consequent on impairment. This would be measured by a functional measure.
- *Handicap* is the value attached to an individual's status when this departs from the norm – this must be related to some notion of social status or social functioning. Such an assessment and the implications for policy or action are likely to be a matter of competing values and may be very difficult to agree.

It follows that we cannot assume that a particular impairment in terms of the norms for an individual of a particular age and gender will result in either a significant disability or handicap. For instance, long sight is a clear impairment experienced by a large proportion of the middle-aged population which is corrected by spectacles and for many does not result in significant disability or handicap.

Functional measures focus on disability and typically look at what are called activities of daily living (ADL). Basic ADL measures look at bathing, dressing, toileting, transfer, continence and feeding (Mahoney and Barthel, 1965). Instrumental ADL (IADL) measures look at activities in terms such as shopping, cooking, housekeeping, laundry, use of transport, managing money, managing medication, use of telephone, etc. (Lawton and Brody, 1969). While it can be seen that these indices do not apply universally, they do provide some means of assessing the impact of an impairment and of action to remedy the resulting disability. For instance, the IADL measure will not make much sense in looking at the impact of an impairment among young children without considerable modification.

These indices can be used in terms of yes/no answers or they can be graded according to severity.

11.3 ■ Health profiles

The profile is an attempt to provide a consistent set of descriptors for a condition which can be used in the description of changes in health status.

One of the best-known profiles is the sickness impact profile (SIP) which has 12 dimensions and 136 items (Bergner *et al.*, 1981). While this is thought to be a methodologically sound instrument it is so long that it takes a lot of effort to deliver and has been less popular in research programmes than might otherwise have been the case. The Nottingham health profile is a relatively simple instrument compared with the more complex SIP and is much easier to use (McEwan, 1983).

Such profiles are expensive to construct in a valid manner and can be attacked relatively easily on the basis of the samples used and the degree to which the sample is regarded as truly representative of the population in question.

Nottingham health profile (McEwan, 1983)

The profile measures 13 dimensions using 45 items. The dimensions are:

1. Physical mobility.
2. Pain.
3. Sleep.
4. Energy.
5. Social isolation.
6. Emotional reactions.
7. Employment.
8. Social life.
9. Household work.
10. Sex life.
11. Home life.
12. Holidays.
13. Interests and hobbies.

Such a profile can be used to assess the health status of an individual and should be sufficiently reliable to detect changes in health status over time. It may still be difficult to determine whether these changes are attributable to a particular intervention or whether they would have occurred anyway due to the natural history of the disease or other intervening factors. There are a number of serious problems which can arise in the administration of these profiles which limit their reliability and need to be guarded against:

▓ A doctor may carry forward an impression of a patient's function from one rating to the next to make the ratings consistent.
▓ The rater may upgrade the score of a patient who is thought to be a complainer.
▓ Imprecision may occur if different raters use different frames of reference.

Other sources of bias may occur where the process of judgement is inconsistent. For instance:

▓ Two observers with the same information make different judgements (one only needs to look at the legal system to see how the courts come to different decisions about fact and severity of crimes).
▓ A judge may be unable to explain how he or she used the information or how different bits of it were weighted in coming to a view.
▓ Even if a judge is fully aware of all the information he or she may use it inconsistently.

Even if we can prevent these sources of bias which reduce the reliability of functional measures we are still faced with the difficulty of handling different dimensions such as pain and quality of life in a single measure. There is no obvious way of scaling such variables although one or two attempts have been made which we discuss below.

11.4 ▓ Valuation in health care

Health care purchasers whether individuals, insurance companies or public authorities inevitably make value judgements in their decisions about what services to buy and what services, and potential benefits, must be forgone. There are a number of questions which need to be asked of a health care intervention:

▓ *For whose benefit is the intervention being carried out?* Is it an individual procedure for the benefit of a single patient, a preventative measure with individual and collective benefits, or a health programme targeted at a community or similar group?
▓ *Is the procedure worth doing?* Is it possible to use the resources which could be consumed in another way that is more effective or more worthwhile?

In principle, questions to do with clinical effectiveness are open to scientific investigation using random controlled trials and other similar methods. Questions which ask whether there is a better use for the resources or whether a clinical procedure is worth doing at all imply that we can value the benefits which arise from the treatment or the programme and then make a decision based on the comparative value of two or more procedures and programmes. For instance, a number of purchasing authorities have decided that while it is clinically possible to remove tattoos which individuals have voluntarily purchased, it is not a priority for scarce public funds and since there is no contract for such a service it is not available in local trust hospitals.

It is rare for purchasers in the UK to exclude clinical procedures by explicitly deciding not to contract for them, but there are a number of examples and there is some evidence that this trend may be growing (Howell, 1993). For instance, a Trust acute hospital may not have a contract for family planning and so vasectomies will not be available.

In the pre-market NHS such decisions would not have been made explicitly since GPs would have made their own decision on whether to treat or refer and physicians or surgeons would have decided whether to treat or not on an individual basis. Professor Grimley Evans shows how this resulted in discrimination against the elderly in acute medicine and perhaps the most notable example of this is the exclusion of the elderly from some forms of treatment for end-stage renal failure (Grimley Evans, 1993).

It was still the case that authorities in the pre-market situation would make decisions on whether to fund programmes such as a community anti-smoking campaign which are usually more expensive than providing individual treatments.

Neither is it the case that such decisions were, or are, made on entirely rational grounds. There is seldom a situation in which a zero-sum review of activity is undertaken and decisions about the level and range of activities are made *ab initio* (Lindblom, 1959). More usually shortage of funds will cause a review of existing programmes and adjustments will be made to the planned level of activity in a number of the existing programmes. The shortage may result from the fact that new funds do not match bids for service developments (Hunter, 1980), or that a combination of medical inflation and increased needs does not translate into an effective demand for services.

Two important developments where rational procedures have been adopted are the development of QALYs and the Oregon Programme. The former approach is limited to the provision of comparative information as a decision aid while the latter is a public programme which has been developed for resource allocation and programme management.

11.5 ■ Attempts to identify shared values

Measuring the values which communities place upon various health and functional statuses is fraught with difficulties. For instance, the values which underpin perhaps the most popular compound measure are those underpinning the QALY approach.

Quality-adjusted life years (QALYs)

Many medical treatments are assessed in terms of their effectiveness by looking at survival rates – the percentage of patients still alive after five years, for example. This measure tells us nothing about the quality of the extra years of life a treatment might provide.

Rosser (Rosser and Kind, 1978) asked various groups of doctors to describe the criteria by which they judged the severity of illness in patients. She identified two key components of severity, namely *observed disability* and *subjective distress*. From these components, following structured interviews with 70 raters (medical patients, psychiatric patients, medical nurses, psychiatric nurses, healthy volunteers and doctors), a two-dimensional classification of illness states was developed ranging from Disability 1: No Disability to 8 Unconscious; and Distress A: No distress to D: Severe distress.

QALYs are calculated by first measuring the extra years of life that a treatment provides and then combining this figure with a value from the matrix of illness state ratings. The maximum value is 1 for patients with no disability and no distress.

Rosser's study has been criticized on various grounds, including the fact that the sample size was small and not necessarily representative of the population.

11.6 ▓ Matrix of illness state ratings

Disability rating	Distress rating			
	A	B	C	D
	No	Mild	Moderate	Severe
1. No disability	1.000	0.995	0.990	0.967
2. Slight social disability	0.990	0.986	0.973	0.932
3. Severe social disability and/or slight physical impairment	0.980	0.972	0.956	0.912
4. Physical ability severely limited	0.964	0.956	0.942	0.870
5. Unable to take employment, largely housebound	0.946	0.935	0.900	0.700
6. Confined to chair or wheelchair	0.875	0.845	0.680	0
7. Confined to bed	0.677	0.564	0	−1.486
8. Unconscious	−1.078	*	*	*

Note: 1.000 = Healthy, 0 = Dead, * = not applicable.
Source: Rosser and Kind (1978)

Based on the average sample scores, the extra years of life are adjusted for quality of life, giving the QALY. The benefit of the treatment can be measured in terms of the extra QALYs gained, as in Figure 11.1, where quality of life, maximum value 1, is measured on the vertical axis and time in years is measured on the horizontal axis. The lighter shaded area represents the extra QALYs provided by the treatment.

Treatments can then be compared on the basis of the QALYs they provide. Costs per QALY for each treatment can be calculated, the costs being considered on a marginal basis, i.e. what is the cost of treating an extra patient?

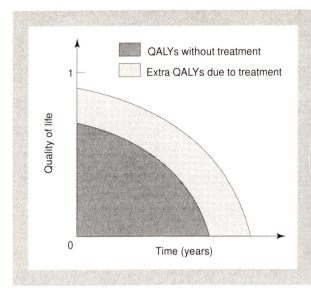

Figure 11.1 Clinical data can be used to estimate the extra QALYs a treatment will provide. The cost per QALY can then be calculated.

Treatment	Cost per QALY (£)
Home renal dialysis	17,300
Heart transplant	8,000
Kidney transplant	3,500
Heart bypass	2,000
Hip replacement	1,000
Stroke prevention	750
Anti-smoking campaign	250

Source: Alan Maynard (1991), 'Developing the Health Care Market', *Economic Journal*, September.

As stated above, the 'QALY league table' should be based on the marginal cost of purchasing extra QALYs. In other words, they are answering the question: 'Given the existing allocation of resources, what is the cost of purchasing one extra QALY using each of the procedures in the table?' In other words, how best can additional resources be spent? In a health care system where rationing is necessary this type of information is clearly useful, but the following points must be borne in mind:

1. It assumes one QALY is of equal value to everyone, which may not be the case.
2. As an activity expands and less and less promising cases are accepted for treatment the cost per QALY will rise (diminishing marginal returns). The implication of this is that the marginal cost per QALY is likely to vary from area to area or hospital to hospital as it will depend on the volume of this work already being undertaken. Also the cost per QALY may well vary over time as the level of activity alters.

3. Costs per QALY may change if the resources used change in price.
4. Costs per QALY may vary from area to area because of variations in the way treatments are carried out.
5. Expanding an activity may induce economies or diseconomies of scale. This is not the same point as that in 2. This refers to the situation where a substantial investment in new capacity is undertaken in order to significantly expand the number of cases treated.
6. Activities which are expensive now in terms of cost per QALY may be subject to technical improvements and other positive development; they should be supported so that the development work can proceed in order to obtain the benefits of future lower cost per QALY.
7. The benefits implied by the QALY are measured solely in terms of the health benefit of the patient. No other beneficiaries are taken into account.

As a decision aid this approach provides useful indications, and indeed the Department of Health holds information for interested parties on QALY studies of various conditions/treatments, but it is far from being recognized as a standard approach by practitioners and managers and part of this caution must stem from its research basis in the structured interviews.

A second approach has been adopted in the US State of Oregon and widely discussed elsewhere:

Case study 11.1

Oregon legislators created a health commission with the following remit: The commission shall actively solicit public involvement in a community meeting process to reach a consensus on the values to be used to guide health resource allocation decisions.

This instruction was carried out through the following procedures:

1. A telephone survey of 1,001 respondents to place a numerical value (0 = death, 100 = perfect health) on a series of symptoms and functional impairments, thus rating the severity of the condition and the associated quality of life and providing a local set of valuations.
2. Forty-seven meetings with interested parties were conducted by Oregon Health Decision, an organization designed to consult and assess community views. They ranked the issues raised by attendees according to the frequency with which they were discussed in the manner of a content analysis. They found that 'prevention' and 'quality of life' were mentioned at all meetings while 'length of life' and 'personal responsibility' were mentioned at less that 50% of meetings.
3. Twelve public meetings were held on the health plan when it was finally drafted.

In addition the health commissioners ranked diagnosis-treatment pairs according to the following three attributes: value to society; value to an individual at risk of needing the service; essential to a basic health care package.

The net benefit of a treatment-diagnosis pair was calculated by comparing the 'with treatment' outcomes (weighted by their estimated probabilities) with the corresponding 'without treatment' outcomes.

$$\text{net benefit} = \frac{\text{with treatment}}{\text{outcome * probability}} - \frac{\text{without treatment}}{\text{outcome * probability}}$$

The diagnosis-treatment pairs were ranked and a decision made on an annual basis of the balance between the numbers admitted to the programme and the range of treatments available to them.

Thus the procedure combines a mechanism for measuring clinical effectiveness and social valuation recognizing that there are considerable problems in measuring both elements. The measurement of costs did not take place to permit cost-effectiveness analysis since the calculation of a common cost basis was too complicated (see Kirk, 1993).

Discussion

What patterns of measurement were adopted in Oregon and to what extent did they provide a reliable and valid measure of clinical effectiveness and social valuation of the quality of life?

These two approaches raise important questions about who should be involved in the rating of disability.

In the approaches described in this chapter rating has been undertaken by citizens, experts and clinicians, politicians and patients. None of these groups can be regarded as disinterested but neither can they be regarded as ignorant of the conditions or impact of treatments. If their ratings differ, the researcher will want to account for the difference, to identify consistent bias in ratings and to assess the reliability of individual ratings – i.e. do they give consistent ratings to identical conditions?

Making decisions about treatment

The approaches of QALYs and Oregon are concerned with the allocation of resources to particular services. For many years public health services have left allocation decisions to clinicians who have to choose whether and how to treat particular patients. This clearly links questions of clinical judgement and social valuation and puts particular pressure on clinicians in times of resource scarcity.

According to Brooks (1995) there are four aspects which should be considered in making decisions in the case of a particular individual or patient:

1. *Medical indications* – principle of beneficence – clinicians should avoid doing harm to patients.
2. *Informed patient preferences* – right to accept or reject advice. There are some difficult considerations where the patient is not competent, e.g. brain dead or where the adult agent is competent but society does not agree with their values, e.g. Jehovah's Witness parents and refusal of blood transfusions for their children.
3. *Quality of life considerations* – these are primarily understood as judgements of the patient which are of course influenced by the judgement of the doctor.

4. *External factors* – these include benefits or burdens on others, externalities, safety of others, costs to society, use of scarce medical resources, family wishes, needs for medical research and teaching.

Siegler (1987) suggests that these decisions are becoming increasingly more difficult for the individuals concerned: 'In the past external factors were not accorded great weight in resolving clinical–ethical decisions, but this is obviously changing in the current era which emphasizes cost containment and parsimony.' Another approach is to try and assert common values across a health care system by reference to ethics, politics and other social values.

Common values

The current Chief Medical Officer Dr Kenneth Calman, in the context of a conference about rationing in health care, produced a summary of the guiding principles which underpin the provision of health care services and provide a framework for decision-making in the NHS (Calman, 1993).

The ethical framework rests upon the principles of:

1. *Justice* – the service should be fair and should be seen to be fair.
2. *Beneficence* – it is assumed that health care services are provided to benefit the individual concerned.
3. *Non-maleficence* – there is a particular requirement that health services should not harm individuals.
4. *Utility* – health services should provide the greatest good to the greatest number.
5. *Autonomy* – the needy individual should be entitled to all available resources.

He points out that these principles are frequently in conflict causing the problems experienced by managers and clinicians.

From this ethical framework he proposes a framework for decision-making in the NHS:

1. *A caring society* – the NHS starts with the presupposition that society cares for its members.
2. *Public health matters* – this implies that there must be an integrated network of primary public and environmental health services.
3. *A primary care service* – should be available to all.
4. *Hospital-based services of proven value* – should be available to all.
5. *Expensive/special services* – should be planned on a national basis.
6. *New procedures* – should be evaluated on a national basis.

It can be seen that such statements of values are at a very high level of abstraction which does not solve the need to make particular decisions or to develop reliable and valid measures with which alternative courses of treatment can be assessed.

The following case study shows an attempt to identify values from the general population on a national basis in the UK.

Case study 11.2 ■ Public opinion and health care priorities

An attempt to measure public opinion about health priorities is reported in the 16 March 1996 *British Medical Journal* (Bowling, 1996). A set of questions were inserted in the UK Office of Population, Censuses and Surveys May–June 1995 survey conducted by skilled interviewers. A random stratified sample of households was designed to identify adults who were the unit of study. A response rate of 75% was achieved which comprised 2,005 adults.

They were asked to rank 12 particular services which were described in such a way as to elicit particular biases such as treatment for life-threatening conditions for children and treatment for life threatening conditions for those aged over 75.

They were asked to agree or disagree with statements about contentious issues such as investment in new technology or the significance of personal responsibility in matters of health and treatment and were asked multiple-choice questions to determine who should make rationing decisions or determine health spending priorities. Finally, they were asked how they would allocate a notional sum of £100,000 between competing services.

The health service given highest priority was 'treatments for children with life-threatening illness' with 'special care and pain relief for people who are dying' being next. The service given the lowest priority was 'treatment for people aged 75 and over with life-threatening illness'. Also there was some support for the suggestion that people with self-inflicted conditions, such as smokers, should be given lower priority for care.

From this research conclusions were drawn about the pattern of public values in respect of health priorities and particularly a widespread view among respondents that it is appropriate to consult the public on health planning and resource allocation priorities.

Discussion

The study looked at the ranking of broad groups of treatments for specific groups of people. By contrast, in Oregon, people were asked to rank individual procedures. The author comments that 'priorities chosen by the public do not necessarily offer the most equitable solutions in relation to the original aspiration of the NHS of equal treatment for equal need'. Ethical issues are raised by the proposition that people with self-inflicted conditions should be seen as lower priority cases for treatment.

References

Bergner, M., Bobbit, R. A., Carter, W. B. and Gilson, B. S. (1981) 'The Sickness Impact Profile: Development and Final Revision of a Health Status Measure', *Medical Care*, vol. 19, pp. 787–805.

Bowling, A. (1996) 'Health Care Rationing: The Public's Debate', *British Medical Journal*, vol. 312, pp. 670–4.

Brooks, R. G. (1995) *Health Status Measurement: A Perspective on Change*, Macmillan, Basingstoke and London.

Calman, K. C. (1993) 'Decision-making and the National Health Service: Making Choices in the Real World – A Philosophical Approach', in Tunbridge, M. (ed.), *Rationing of Health Care in Medicine*, Royal College of Physicians of London, London.

Drummond, M. F. (1991) in McGuire, A., Fenn, P. and Mayhew, K. (eds), *Providing Health Care: The Economics of Alternative Systems of Finance and Delivery*, Oxford University Press, Oxford.

Frater, A. (1996) 'Measuring Clinical Effectiveness' in Glynn, Perkins and Stewart (eds), *Managing Health Care: Achieving Value for Money*, Saunders, London.

Glynn, J. J., Perkins, D. A. and Stewart, S. (eds) (1996) *Managing Health Care: Achieving Value for Money*, Saunders, London.

Grimley Evans, J. (1993) 'Health Care Rationing and Elderly People', in Tunbridge (ed.), *Rationing of Health Care in Medicine*, Royal College of Physicians of London, London.

Howell, J. B. L. (1993) 'The District Health Authority Decision Process' in Tunbridge, M. (ed.), *Rationing of Health Care in Medicine*, Royal College of Physicians of London, London.

Hunter, D. (1980) *Coping with Uncertainty*, Research Studies Press, Chichester.

Kirk, E. P. (1993) 'The Oregon Experience', in Tunbridge (ed.), *Rationing of Health Care in Medicine*, Royal College of Physicians of London, London.

Lawton, M. P. and Brody, E. M. (1969) 'Assessment of Older People: Self Maintaining and Instrumental Activities of Daily Living', *The Gerontologist*, 9, pp. 179–86.

Lindblom, C. E. (1959) 'The Science of Muddling Through', *Public Administration Review*, 9, pp. 70–88.

McEwan, J. (1983) 'The Nottingham Health Profile, A Measure of Perceived Health', in Teeling Smith, G. (ed.), *Measuring the Benefits of Medicines*, Office of Health Economics, London.

Mahoney, F. I. and Barthel, D. W. (1965) 'Functional Evaluation: The Barthel Index', *Maryland State Medical Journal*, 14, pp. 61–5.

Maynard, A. (1991) 'Developing the Health Care Market', *Economic Journal*, September.

Mooney, G. (1992) *Economics, Medicine and Health Care* (2nd edn), Harvester Wheatsheaf, Hemel Hempstead.

Mooney, G. (1994) *Key Issues in Health Economics*, Harvester Wheatsheaf, Hemel Hempstead.

Rosser, R. M. and Kind, P. (1978) 'A Scale of Valuations of States of Illness. Is There a Social Consensus?', *International Journal of Epidemiology*, 7, pp. 347–58.

Siegler, M. (1987) 'Decision Analysis and Clinical Medical Ethics: Beginning the Dialogue', *Medical Decision Making*, vol. 7, pp. 124–6.

Tunbridge, M. (ed.) (1993) *Rationing of Health Care in Medicine*, Royal College of Physicians of London, London.

Wilkin, D., Hallam, L. and Doggett, M. A. (1992) *Measures of Need and Outcome for Primary Care*, Oxford University Press, Oxford.

Questions for consideration

1. Answer the following questions with reference to the case study below:

   (a) How are we to assess a conflict of interests and a conflict of valuations of risk and benefit?

   (b) Do the valuations and judgements of one group outweigh those of another?

   (c) How are we to balance clinical uncertainties and differences in social valuations?

Case study 11.3 ■ Making babies, BBC TV, 16 May 1996

Professor Robert Winston is head of the In-Vitro Fertilization service at the Hammersmith Hospital in London. He presented a case to his clinical team of about 30 members for their opinions. A couple had been referred to the clinic for treatment since her fallopian tubes were ruptured and so she could not conceive naturally. She had been HIV positive for about 10 years without symptoms. If IVF treatment was successful there was a small chance that the baby would be born with the virus. After an intense discussion it became clear that the members of the team took a different view from Professor Winston and did not want to accept the risk that their treatment might lead directly to a baby being born with the HIV virus.

Professor Winston was not able to persuade them as a group that the benefit to the couple outweighed the risk to the potential baby or that the prospective parents had the right to make their own decision. The matter was complicated since the parents were paying for the service.

Listeners were told at the end of the programme that despite his doubts Professor Winston had proceeded with a supportive embryologist.

---

2. 'The commonly used measures of health service output are far from ideal. For example, the performance of health care systems at the national level is frequently measured in terms of changes in infant mortality. The same approach is used at the level of individual interventions, which may be assessed in terms of case fatality rates or five-year survival rates.' M. F. Drummond, in McGuire, A., Fenn, P. and Mayhew, K. (eds) (1991) *Providing Health Care: The Economics of Alternative Systems of Finance and Delivery*, Oxford University Press).
   (a) Why are the commonly used measures of health service output 'far from ideal'?
   (b) What difficulties are associated with measuring output in the health service?
   (c) What other approaches to measuring health service output would you recommend, and why?

3. The following case studies demonstrate how an NHS trust and a health authority purchaser use rational procedures to identify priorities for treatment and resource allocation. Read the case studies and critically assess the methods in terms of their implications for equity and for efficiency of resource use.

Case study 11.4 ■ Ranking patients for treatment

For many years the NHS has been subject to the criticism that an undersupply of medical care was the cause of waiting lists. Successive government waiting list initiatives focused on the objective of reducing the maximum waiting time and performance was heralded with phrases such as 'a sign of progress is that no one waits for more than 2 years for a non-urgent operation'. Some doctors complained that this meant that there were times when waiting list considerations caused them to treat relatively trivial complaints before they treated more urgent complaints in order to meet waiting list targets.

Salisbury hospital devised a points-scoring process to ensure a fair process of prioritizing those on the waiting list. Patients were scored on five criteria:

- Seriousness of disease.
- Pain or distress.
- Disability or dependence on others.
- Loss of occupation.
- Time waiting for admission.

The score which can be adjusted to take account of changes in circumstances is used to rank patients on the waiting lists. The system is attractive to consultants who believe that it helps them to identify and deal with clinical priorities and it takes account of other beneficiaries such as family carers. Thus, a patient who is self-employed and whose business is threatened by inability to work would score higher on that category than someone who suffers no serious financial loss. The scores are added together enabling a ranking of priorities on the waiting list. This approach cuts across conventional approaches to waiting lists and may cause problems with the government's performance indicators under the Patient's Charter.

Case study 11.5 ■ Wakefield Health Authority: How does an authority decide whether or not to purchase new services?

Facing a shortage of funds and an excess of proposals for new developments Wakefield Health Authority decided to devise a more rational mechanism for deciding what new services to fund and what existing services to develop.

It developed a simple cumulative scoring system based on seven weighted criteria. Put simply, the highest scoring proposals were to be the strategic priorities for development funds. Scoring was undertaken by a panel of managers and public health specialists with inputs from a panel of members of the general public and a survey of GP opinion.

The criteria with weightings are listed below:

1. Health gain – the degree of benefit plus the number of likely direct beneficiaries (24%).
2. Strength of evidence of clinical effectiveness (18%).
3. Prevention rated high versus treatment rated low (18%).
4. Appropriate setting of care and improved access to service (12%).
5. Promotion of equity – improved equity within the district was rated high (12%).
6. Public preference (8%).
7. GP preference (8%).

Scores on each criterion were cumulated to give the following priorities: counselling services in primary care, improvement in palliative care services, and improved access to terminations.

CHAPTER TWELVE

Financial analysis and economic appraisal

Objectives

- To introduce the criteria of financial analysis for evaluating projects.
- To discuss the need for the wider perspective of economic appraisal in health services.
- To describe the essential features of the process of economic appraisal.

Introduction

The purpose of this chapter is to introduce readers to the important decision-making aid of economic appraisal. Economic appraisal is a set of techniques used to judge whether a proposed project (or an existing project) involves the *efficient* use of resources.

It is important to draw the distinction between financial analysis and economic appraisal. A company carrying out a financial analysis of an investment project will be concerned with the monetary benefits and costs to the company – specifically those that show up in the company's balance sheet. An economic appraisal or economic evaluation is more usually carried out when public sector projects and the use of public funds are under consideration. Here a wider range of costs and benefits will be considered as the objective is the optimum use of funds for the whole community. However, before we begin to examine techniques of economic appraisal, it will be helpful to examine the decision criteria that may be used in financial analysis. In order to do this we must first introduce the concept of discounting and net present value (NPV).

12.1 ■ Decision rules in financial analysis

Net present value (NPV)

The effects of a project are likely to be spread over time. Individuals are likely to discount (place a lower value) on future costs and benefits. This is partly because of uncertainty about the future and partly because of the rational view that benefits available now may be invested to produce further benefits in the future and are therefore worth more than equivalent monetary benefits in the future.

Example

The promise of £100 in one year's time is not worth £100 today. It is worth the sum of money, which if invested today, would grow to £100 in one year's time. Suppose the appropriate rate of interest is 10%. What sum of money, invested now at 10%, would grow to £100 in one year's time? This is the present value of £100 in one year's time.

If a sum of money, £S, is put in a bank or building society account for one year at an annual rate of interest of 10%, it would by the end of the year have grown to:

£S (the original sum) plus £S × 10/100 (the interest)

We can write this as £S × (1 + 0.10). If we require this to equal £100, then we can see that £S must be equal to:

£100/(1 + 0.10) = £90.91

This is the present value (PV) of £100 in one year's time using a discount rate of 10%.

This process is called discounting £100 for one year at 10%. The factor by which £100 has been multiplied, 1/(1+0.10), is called the discount factor. There are tables of these, or the calculations can easily be done in a spreadsheet.

How much is £100 worth in two years' time, using the same interest rate? By the same method, a sum of money, £S, put in a bank for two years at an annual interest rate of 10% would grow to:

£S × (1 + 0.10) × (1 + 0.10)

If this is required to equal £100, then we can see that £S must be equal to:

£100/(1 + 0.10)^2 = £82.64

This is the **present value (PV)** of £100 in two years' time using a discount rate of 10%.

Notice that the higher the discount rate, the lower the present value will be. For example, if we had been using a discount rate of 20%, then the present value of £100 in one year's time would be:

£100/(1 + 0.20) = £83.33

Notice also that the further in the future the payment is made, the lower its present value will be. £100 in two year's time is worth less in present value than £100 in one year's time.

The **net present value (NPV)** of a project is the present value of its future net income stream. To calculate NPV, the monetary benefits and costs for each time period must be estimated and then discounted back to the present time period.

The NPV of net income in period t will be given by:

$$NPV = (B_t - C_t)/(1 + r)^t$$

where B_t is the estimated monetary benefit from the project in period t, C_t is the cost incurred by the project in period t and r is the discount rate. The choice of the appropriate discount rate will be discussed later in the chapter.

The NPVs for each year of the project's life are added together to give the NPV of the entire project. One possible decision rule in financial analysis is:

Go ahead with the project if the NPV is greater than zero.

If several mutually exclusive projects are being considered a logical rule would be:

Choose the project with the highest NPV.

If there is a budget constraint, rules for the optimal choice of project(s) can be devised although these are beyond the scope of this chapter.

The net benefit investment ratio (NBIR)

This is another criterion for decision-making in financial analysis. The NBIR is defined to be:

$$NBIR = \frac{PV \text{ of (benefits minus operating costs)}}{PV \text{ of investment costs}}$$

Essentially the project with the highest NBIR is the one which provides the greatest net receipts per unit of investment. Both NPV and NBIR are sensitive to the choice of discount rate.

The internal rate of return (IRR)

To find the IRR we calculate the benefits and costs for each year of the project's life and then ask which discount rate would make the NPV equal to zero. This can be done quite readily using a spreadsheet with goalseeking or 'what-if' facilities.

A very high IRR suggests that the project is worth undertaking since the NPV would be positive even for high interest rates. Another way of looking at this is to think of the IRR as representing the interest rate that the project could afford to pay to borrow the funds to finance the project. If only one project is being considered then the decision rule would be something along the lines of:

Go ahead with the project if the IRR exceeds a certain minimum rate (chosen by the company to represent the opportunity cost of investment funds).

If several projects are being considered then a possible decision rule would be:

Choose the project with the highest IRR (as long as the IRR is above a certain specified minimum).

The benefit–cost ratio (BCR)

The BCR is given by:

$$BCR = \frac{\text{PV of project benefits}}{\text{PV of project costs}}$$

The decision rule based on the BCR would be:

Go ahead with the project if the BCR is greater than 1 (i.e. if discounted benefits exceed discounted costs).

It can be shown mathematically that in fact these decision criteria are equivalent (Perkins, 1994).

12.2 ■ Economic appraisal

Any use of resources in health care involves costs and (hopefully) provides benefits. Resources are scarce so that not all projects which provide benefits can be undertaken. We need to be able to assess the costs and benefits of competing projects in order to make rational decisions about the best use of those scarce resources. The increasing requirements for accountability and value for money in the public sector have led to an increased recognition of the need for economic appraisals.

The types of problem for which the techniques of economic appraisal would be appropriate include decisions such as:

■ Should an existing hospital be extended or should a new hospital be built?
■ Should screening for breast cancer be extended to all women over 40?
■ Should treatment for cancer be concentrated at one centre or offered at several smaller centres throughout the region?
■ Should the number of intensive care beds be increased (and if so, by how much)?

Types of analysis

If a given output can be produced at minimum cost or, equivalently, the maximum output is produced with a fixed budget, then we have **technical** or cost efficiency. **Cost-minimization analysis** is concerned with just this problem – how to achieve a given objective at minimum cost. If projects are being compared it is implicitly assumed that they are equally effective. Teeling Smith (1990) gives an example in which the costs of treating periarthritis ('frozen shoulder') with physiotherapy were compared with the costs of treatment by an injection of triamcinolone. Trials showed that both treatments were equally effective, but the cost of physiotherapy was £48.50 per patient while the cost of the injection was £2.10.

In **cost-effectiveness analysis (CEA)** costs are measured in money terms and the health benefits are measured in whatever units are most appropriate to the problem in hand, for example, lives saved or years of life gained. Problems arise when assessing competing projects for which the outcomes are not readily comparable.

Szczepura (1995) cites studies in which the treatment of moderate myocardial infarction by intravenous streptokinase was compared with treatment of the same condition with intravenous tissue plasminogen activator. Costs per life saved were estimated and compared for the two treatments.

In **cost-utility analysis (CUA)** costs are measured in money terms and the benefits (usually) in quality-adjusted life years (QALYs), although there are other possible outcome measures such as Healthy Year Equivalents (HYEs). Szczepura cites another study of the streptokinase treatment for moderate myocardial infarction in which the outcomes were measured in QALYs and costs per QALY were then estimated.

Cost-benefit analysis (CBA) appears similar to financial analysis in that both the costs and benefits are measured in money terms; if the costs and benefits are spread over an extended period of time discounting techniques are used. The differences between financial analysis and cost-benefit analysis are considerable, though. In cost-benefit analysis the prices used are not necessarily market prices but rather the opportunity costs. Cost-benefit analysis is a very demanding technique because of the need to estimate the benefits in money terms.

Many of the costs and benefits relate to intangibles such a level of health or degree of anxiety and prices have to be imputed. All costs and benefits should be taken into account in cost-benefit analysis; in financial analysis the firm will ignore externalities.

12.3 ■ Why not leave it to the market?

Perfectly competitive markets will attain efficiency if there are no externalities. If there are externalities market prices will not reflect the opportunity costs of production and the allocation of resources will not be efficient. Economic appraisal techniques examine *all* costs and benefits, i.e. they consider externalities.

Note that in the financial analysis of a private sector project, market prices of resources would be used. The company is concerned only with the benefits and costs to itself; it is not so concerned about externalities except to the extent that it has to pay taxes or comply with legislation. In economic appraisal in the public sector, the aim is to seek the maximum benefit for the community as a whole. Where a quasi-market exists, as in the British NHS, conflicting objectives may cause problems. For example, managers of hospital trusts, which operate on private business principles, may consider financial analysis techniques to be the most appropriate and neglect externalities. The community which the hospital serves may object to the decisions made using such principles.

By looking at all the costs a truer assessment of efficiency can be made. For example, a financial analysis may suggest that a hospital can cut its costs by discharging patients sooner. But if those patients discharged early make more use of GPs' and health visitors' time, all that may have happened is that costs have been *shifted*, not reduced. As was explained in Chapter 3, the hospital may report efficiency gains but the health service as a whole has not seen an improvement in efficiency.

Closing a hospital may reduce a health authority's costs but if patients and staff have much further to travel, costing them both money and time, and if some patients die because they have further to travel in an emergency, then again costs have been *shifted*, but not necessarily reduced.

In the field of health care externalities are common. In addition we are frequently dealing with non-marketable goods and services, the benefits of health care are difficult to measure and value, there is a lack of competition and consumers are poorly informed. Economic appraisal is a way of determining the allocation of resources, given that we cannot rely on market prices. Even in a private health care system, these problems of market failure will still exist. Market prices will not be equal to the true opportunity cost of resources.

> Ignorance, prohibition of competition, externalities, prices that do not reflect opportunity costs and, therefore, the potential for inefficiency, are the norm, not the exception, in the health services. (McGuire, Henderson and Mooney, 1988)

Social efficiency

Most public projects create losers as well as winners. A new airport will benefit those whose journey times are shortened and made more convenient; those living near the new runways will have to live with extra noise and may suffer financial loss if the values of their homes are reduced. Building a new modern hospital and closing older ones will provide better services and surroundings for staff and patients but may lead to longer journeys and more inconvenience for some of them. Because of this, the criterion of potential Pareto improvement is often used. A project will provide a potential Pareto improvement if it makes at least one person better off *and the benefits are such that the losers could be compensated from the gains of the beneficiaries*, in other words, there will be increase in social efficiency.

If the aim is equity as well as efficiency then an additional value-judgement is required. What is the appropriate trade-off between equity and efficiency?

Measuring benefits in money terms

In CBA the benefits and costs are often measured with reference to consumers' surplus. Given a downward sloping demand curve, the consumers who choose to buy a good at a particular price include some consumers who would have been prepared to pay a higher price. They thus obtain a benefit from being able to buy the good at the market price rather than the higher price. The total benefit is measured by the area under the demand curve, as shown in Figure 12.1. If more of a good is available at a lower price, the consumers' surplus will increase. The increase in the consumers' surplus is given by the change in area under the demand curve as shown in Figure 12.2.

We can use the concept of consumers' surplus to try to calculate the value of a 'free' service, such as a consultation with a GP. Consider the following (rather contrived) example. Suppose visits to a GP's practice are running at the rate of 1,000 per week. A survey among patients reveals that if £25 was charged per visit only 500 per week would attend and if £50 was charged per visit, no-one would attend. This data gives us the demand curve as shown in Figure 12.3.

Since the service is presently free, the consumers' surplus is given by the triangle 0QP, with base 1,000 and height £50. The area of this triangle (half the base × the height) = 500 × £50 = £25,000.

Thus the benefit to the patients of free consultations at this practice is estimated to be £25,000 per week, which works out at £1,300,000 per annum.

In CBA studies, consumers' surplus is often measured by the compensating variation (CV).

CV: the maximum a consumer would be willing to pay for a benefit or the minimum the consumer would be willing to receive to accept some loss. CV is measured with respect to the consumer's existing utility level.

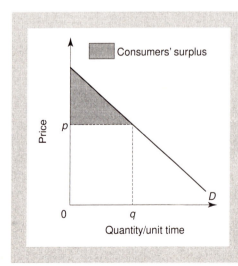

Figure 12.1 At price *p*, quantity *q* is demanded.
There are some consumers who were willing to pay more than *p*. The extent to which they benefit from paying the lower price is given by the shaded area.

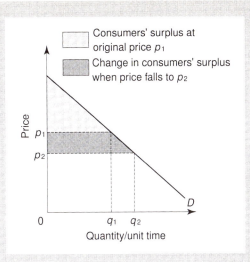

Figure 12.2 When the price of a good falls, consumers' surplus increases. We can use this to estimate the benefits to the community of providing subsidized or free goods and services.

Example

Suppose the waiting time to see a consultant is 12 weeks. The GP finds that the maximum her patients would be prepared to pay to cut the waiting time to 6 weeks is £60 per patient. The GP becomes a fundholder and arranges for the consultant to see patients at her surgery, cutting their waiting time from 12 weeks to 6 weeks. The implied monetary value of the benefit to the patients of this particular change is £60 per patient. Earlier diagnosis and earlier treatment may lead to better outcomes and lower costs in the future for both patients and the health service. We now have an estimate of the value patients place on these benefits. But are they the best judges.

Time preference and discounting

As stated above, where benefits of a project are spread over an extended period of time, they should be discounted to find their present value.

What is the appropriate rate of interest?

There are conflicting views about the choice of an appropriate interest rate for cost-benefit analysis. One school of thought suggests that the prevailing market rate of interest should be used, because if public funds obtained from taxes are used to fund projects on which the rate of return is less than the market rate, then those funds are not being used efficiently.

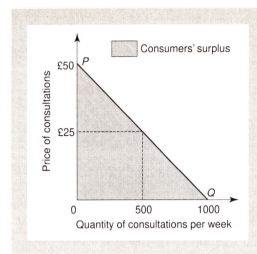

Figure 12.3 Given data on estimated demand at different prices, we can estimate the monetary benefit to patients of providing free GP consultations.

Another view is that if a high discount rate is used, only projects with benefits obtainable in the fairly near future will go ahead. However, many public projects have benefits which may be felt for generations to come. The present generation may give a very low weight to benefits not felt by themselves; the market rate of interest will reflect this and be too high. A variation on this view is the idea that individuals may well be prepared to sacrifice a greater amount of present consumption in order to invest in projects which will benefit future generations, *but only if other people will do the same*. Since no single individual can dictate what others will do, no one will undertake the greater sacrifice, even though everyone would agree with doing it. Therefore the government, acting on behalf of society as a whole, is justified in using a lower discount rate than the market rate of interest on public projects. In the UK, the Treasury will provide a recommended discount rate for public projects.

It is often recommended that **sensitivity analysis**, which considers the effect of changing the discount rate, is undertaken to assess the robustness of the conclusions of the analysis.

Risk and uncertainty

The terms risk and uncertainty are sometimes used interchangeably but they do mean different things and must be tackled in different ways.

Risk

There are several possible outcomes and the probability of each is *known*. When faced with a risky outcome, we can calculate a quantity known as the **expected value**. The expected value is the average that would be obtained if we were treating the situation as an experiment which can be repeated many times. It is calculated by weighting each outcome by the probability of its happening. Thus outcomes which are very probable get high weights; unlikely outcomes get low weights.

For example, given the following table of a range of possible benefits from a project (column 1), together with the probability of each outcome (column 2), we calculate the expected value by first multiplying each outcome by the probability of it happening (column 3) and then adding together these figures (sum of column 3).

Possible benefits	Probability	Benefit × probability
£1000	0.1	£100
£2000	0.3	£600
£5000	0.5	£2500
£10,000	0.08	£800
£20,000	0.02	£400
		Total £4400

The expected value of the benefits is £4,400. Notice that although one of the possible outcomes is very large relative to the others (£20,000), the probability of obtaining it is very small, 0.02, so it contributes only £400 to the expected value.

Two projects may have the same expected value but one may be more risky than another in the sense that the spread of possible outcomes and/or the probabilities attached to lower-valued outcomes is greater. Here measures of variability such as the variance and standard deviation may be useful.

Certainty equivalents

People and societies differ in their attitudes to risk. In many cases people will prefer the certainty of a definite gain of lower value to a risky prospect even though it has a higher expected gain.

Example

Suppose there are two possible outcomes: a gain of £100 with probability 0.4 and a gain of £60 with probability of 0.6. The expected gain is given by:

$$0.4 \times £100 + 0.6 \times £60 = £76$$

Individuals may prefer the certain gain of a smaller sum, say £70, to the gamble (the certainty equivalent). The difference between the expected gain and the certainty equivalent is a measure of risk aversion. Where there is risk and benefits are being valued in money terms, they should be valued at their certainty equivalents.

Uncertainty

There are several possible outcomes but the probabilities are not known. There are other strategies for making choices in this situation. For example, the maximin strategy would involve choosing the decision with the least bad outcome. Sensitivity analysis, where the robustness of the decision is checked by examining the consequences of all possible outcomes, may be carried out. A **risk premium** may be added to the discount rate.

Aggregation and equity

The social aggregate effect is obtained by summing weighted individual benefits, suitably discounted. The weights indicate the importance to be given to the gains or losses of the individuals or groups involved. For example, a utility gain for the poor might be given a higher weighting than that for the rich. There is the problem of deciding on the appropriate weights. It has been proposed that they should be inversely related to marginal rates of taxation or to levels of income.

Using distributional weights allows projects to be evaluated on distributional as well as efficiency criteria. However, there may be problems in actually measuring the gains accruing to different income or social groups. If the distributional weights are determined by those who are carrying out the project, it could be argued (Harburger, 1978) that their objectivity is compromised. According to Jenkins and Harburger (1991) it is more appropriate to document the gains and losses by the different groups and leave it to the ultimate decision-makers to determine how much weight they wish to give to them.

12.4 ■ The stages of economic appraisal

1. Define the alternatives to be examined

> **Example**
>
> A 10-year study of the early detection of cancer of the colon and rectum, carried out by Professor Hardcastle at Nottingham University, produced results which suggested that if all members of the population aged 50 to 75 were screened, the present number of deaths from these cancers of 19,000 per annum would be reduced by some 15%. However, there is not general agreement about the desirability of universal screening. According to some doctors, it would lead to more anxiety for people and many unnecessary investigations; it would be better to screen only those considered to be at increased risk.
>
> If an economic appraisal was carried out, the alternatives might include:
>
> ■ No screening programme.
> ■ Screen only those considered to be at increased risk.
> ■ Screen all people between 50 and 75.

2. List costs and outcomes

At this stage, the range of costs and benefits to be considered is drawn up. For a true economic appraisal, external costs and benefits should be considered.

3. Quantify and value the costs and outcomes

The decision about how to measure the outcomes will depend on the type of analysis. For example, if it is decided to carry out a cost-utility analysis, then the benefits will be measured in QALYs or similar units. A cost-effectiveness analysis would measure benefits in terms of lives saved, or extra years of life gained.

4. Compare the costs and outcomes

Depending on the type of appraisal, costs per life saved, costs per extra year of life gained, or costs per QALY will be compared.

5. Sensitivity analysis

Where assumptions have been made, about outcomes or future costs for example, the results should be examined to see how dependent they are on those assumptions.

6. Distributional issues

Where different groups of the population are likely to lose out, or to benefit to different extents, it is necessary to consider this aspect of the study as well as the overall costs and benefits.

The choice of project

In CEA or CUA a project is technically efficient if it maximizes the benefit available from a given budget or minimizes the cost of attaining a particular objective. An index can be calculated, the cost-effectiveness index (CEI) which measures the cost of obtaining a unit of the relevant benefit, i.e. cost per year of life gained or cost per QALY. In general, the decision rule would be to choose the project with the lowest CEI.

In CBA the decision rules mirror those of financial analysis. All benefits and costs have been measured in monetary terms. If they are spread over a period of time they must be discounted back to the present time using an appropriate discount rate. Having obtained all the appropriate information we can calculate the net present value (NPV), the benefit–cost ratio (BCR), or the internal rate of return (IRR). Where there is a choice of mutually exclusive projects, the one with the highest NPV or BCR or IRR would be chosen. Occasionally the result is not clear-cut because of ambiguities in the specification of costs and benefits or in the solution process. See Drummond (1980) for further explanation and examples.

CBA, CEA and CUA do not make decisions; they help the decision-making process to be rational and systematic and they make the criteria for decision-making explicit.

Case study 12.1 ▇ Cochlear implantation in the UK 1990–4

Cochlear implantation (CI) aims to provide useful hearing for people who are profoundly deaf in both ears and can obtain no benefit from conventional hearing aids. It works by inserting an electrode in the inner ear to stimulate the auditory nerve, directly bypassing the damaged elements of the ear. This electrode is directly connected to a discrete microphone and processor outside the ear.

The procedure is thought to be appropriate for children of 2 years and older where the objective is the acquisition and retention of language. In adults the objective is to improve the capability for understanding speech and being understood when speaking.

In 1990 the UK Department of Health initiated programmes of CI at selected hospitals in England followed by programmes in Scotland (1991), and Ireland (1992). An evaluation was set up with the following objectives:

■ To establish whether CI could be an effective routine treatment for adults.
■ To conduct a broad-brush assessment of the initial benefits of CI to young children.
■ To derive recommendations for the future form and scale of services nationally.

The evaluation took the form of pre- and post-operative questionnaires and tests of adult hearing performance. Data was collected regarding 300 patients pre-implantation, 170 after nine months and 100 after 18 months.

Pre- and post-implantation data was collected for 136 children.

Selected findings

Not surprisingly there was great variability among patients; outcomes were positive, the best were impressive, and only a handful of patients experienced no benefit. Patients receiving multi-channel implants did better than those receiving single-channel implants. These benefits were sustained over 18 months. Wider benefits included objective and subjective improvements in the quality of life, improvements for carers, family and friends, and increased levels of participation outside the home. The authors concluded that these benefits could not have been achieved by existing treatments.

Children who became deaf before they had learned to speak displayed progress measured by the acquisition of pre-verbal communication strategies which was similar to progress made by children with mild hearing loss who wore hearing aids. It was concluded that the evidence was promising but required further investigation.

These outcomes improved as clinical teams gained more experience. There were relatively few complications, although there were some problems of failure with the microphones and processors connected to the implant.

Costing of implants

Costs were measured under the following headings:

1. Direct costs to service provider. This included salaries of professional staff, cost of space,

equipment, consumables, radiology costs, theatre sessions, inpatient hotel charges, implant hardware, repairs and spares, and maintenance contracts.

2. Average cost of managing patient for the first year following implantation. Adult cost was £8,000 (+ implant hardware). Complete cost with most common hardware was £21,000. The equivalent costs for children were £11,500 and £28,500.

3. Estimated cost for managing patient for the next 11 years, making total of 12 years discounted at 6% per annum. Adult cost estimated at £28,500, child cost at £42,500.

It should be noted that over the study period of 33 months costs were falling due to increased standardization of procedures and the cumulative learning effect of teams gaining new experience.

Attempts were also made at cost-effectiveness analysis and cost-utility analysis with the following conclusions:

■ It was estimated that profound deafness in both ears entails an average loss of 40% of the optimal quality of life and that CI permits between 10–30% of that optimal quality of life to be regained. This might be understood as ¼–¾ of the loss. From the age profiles of the adult cohort recipients had an average remaining life expectancy of 26 years.

■ The authors calculated a gain of 1.3 to 3.9 QALYs if future benefits were discounted at the rate of 6%, and between 2.6 and 7.8 QALYs with no discounting.

■ The cost of management over the 26-year average life expectancy was £33,642 with 6% discount per annum.

■ The cost utility of CI for adults was calculated as £8,771–26,313 per QALY with 6% discount or £8,436–13,159 without. This cost was thought to be similar to other commonly used technologies in acute medicine.

(A. Q. Summerfield and D. H. Marshall (1995), *Cochlear Implantation in the UK 1990–1994: Report by the MRC Institute of Hearing Research on the Evaluation of the National Cochlear Implant Programme*, HMSO, London.)

Discussion

This is an example of a cost-utility analysis. The benefits were measured in QALYs. Note the discounting of both costs and benefits. One might ask why an interest rate of 6% was chosen, and also whether QALYs were the most appropriate way to measure benefits in this study since they measure only benefits to the patient and not to relatives, friends and carers. Note also that the costs and outcomes altered during the period of study. Costs fell and outcomes improved. Could more improvement be expected in the future?

Case study 12.2 ■ The heart transplant programme

An interesting insight into some of the problems inherent in economic evaluation can be gained from a study carried out in the early 1980s. In 1981 the DHSS funded a study entitled 'The Costs and Benefits of the Heart Transplant Programmes at Harefield and Papworth Hospitals'. The study was completed in 1984 and the final report, DHSS Research Report No. 12, was published in 1985. A summary of some of the findings, on which this section is based, is given in a chapter by Martin Buxton, one of the authors of the DHSS report, in *Health and Economics* (1987), ed. Alan Williams, Macmillan, London.

In January 1979 Mr Terence English established a heart transplant programme at Papworth Hospital. In January 1980 another programme was begun under Mr Magdi Yacoub at Harefield Hospital. Critics said the programmes were expensive and unproven, offered a poor quality of life and they diverted scarce resources from programmes which provided greater benefits. Supporters of the programmes said they offered patients a greatly improved quality of life.

The DHSS study examined patient benefits in terms of survival and quality of life and examined the costs of the two programmes in detail.

Patient benefits

Survival data was based on aggregate results from both centres. There appeared to be no significant difference between the survival rates for the two centres. One problem in assessing survival rates was that the rates improved during the period under study, partly due to the introduction of a new immunosuppressive drug and partly due to the experience gained over time.

Quality of life

All patients completed the Nottingham Health Profile (NHP) questionnaire. The results showed a marked improvement in quality of life on all dimensions for patients who had had transplants.

Costs

Analysis of the costs showed that there were marked differences between the two centres, much of which could be explained by differences in length of stay. For example, at Harefield the total length of stay in hospital after the operation averaged 13.2 days, whereas at Papworth it was 44.4 days. However, it was noted that during the study period costs at Harefield fell by about 40%.

Discussion

This study highlights a number of problems that arise in economic evaluations. There are the obvious problems, already discussed, of valuing life and the quality of life. Heart transplant programmes were relatively new at the time. It was obvious during the study that survival rates were improving, partly due to new drugs and partly due to other factors such as experience. This means that the costs and benefits were actually altering during the period under study. This will always be a problem when carrying out an economic evaluation of a new treatment.

It was clear that the costs varied between the two hospitals. In general costs will always vary to a certain extent between hospitals. When carrying out a CBA based on results from a small number of hospitals, to what extent can these results be generalized to other hospitals? In addition, the study showed the importance of considering *marginal* costs in an appraisal rather than average costs. During the study, costs were falling. Average costs based on historical data would not be a good guide to the likely level of costs in the future. Similar considerations apply to the estimation of future benefits.

For a heart transplant programme, a true assessment of costs and benefits should be based on long-term survival rates, say after 10 or 15 years. However, when doing an economic evaluation there is a requirement for an immediate decision. The same problem would apply to many other programmes, for example, intensive care for infants.

The implication of these problems is that economic evaluation of new treatments should not be seen as a 'one-off' process. Costs and benefits will alter over time as the technique develops. There is a need for continuous monitoring as new data becomes available.

References

Buxton, M. (1987) 'Costs and Benefits of the Heart Transplant Programme', in Williams, Alan (ed.), *Health and Economics*, Proceedings of Section F (Economics) of the British Association for the Advancement of Science, Bristol, 1986, Macmillan, Basingstoke.

Donaldson, C. and Gerard, K. (1993) *Economics of Health Care Financing: The Visible Hand*, Macmillan, Basingstoke and London.

Drummond, M. (1980) *Principles of Economic Appraisal in Health Care*, Oxford University Press, Oxford.

Harburger, A. C. (1978) 'On the Use of Distributional Weights in Social Cost-Benefit Analysis', *Journal of Political Economy*, 86, pp. 87–120.

Jenkins, G. P. and Harburger, A. C. (1991) 'Examples of Integrated, Economic and Distributive Analysis' (mimeo), Harvard Institute of International Development, Harvard University, Cambridge, MA.

McGuire, A., Henderson, J. and Mooney, G. (1988) *The Economics of Health Care: An Introductory Text*, Routledge and Kegan Paul, London.

Mooney, G. (1994) *Key Issues in Health Economics*, Harvester Wheatsheaf, Hemel Hempstead.

Perkins, F. (1994) *Practical Cost Benefit Analysis*, Macmillan, Basingstoke and London.

Szczepura, A. (1995) 'Finding a Way Through the Cost and Benefit Maze; Standardised Instruments are Needed', *British Medical Journal*, 309 (6965), p. 1314.

Teeling Smith, G. (1990) 'The Economic Impact of Medicines', *Office of Health Economics Briefing*, no. 27, London.

Questions for consideration

Suggest possible methods for carrying out an economic appraisal of the following health programmes:

1. The re-introduction free eye tests on the NHS.
2. Mass vaccination against chicken-pox.
3. An expansion of intensive care facilities for very premature babies (less than 30 weeks gestation).

CHAPTER THIRTEEN

Financing health care

Objectives

- To identify broad patterns in the way health services are funded in different countries.

- To show how these patterns of financing influence answers to the key economic questions.

- To describe the approach taken by recent health care reforms and identify some of the most important likely impacts.

Introduction

In all OECD countries expenditure on health care is made up of a combination of public, private and charitable elements, although the ratios vary considerably as do the conditions attached to the funding. As discussed above the particular qualities of health care services, the nature and perceptions of individuals about social risk, and the uncertainties and costs associated with health care services make it undesirable to leave the consumption of services solely to market mechanisms. Whether the balance of funding points towards centrally managed services or towards market systems with a safety-net, governments are heavily involved in the regulation of health service provision ranging from the accreditation of service providers to the direct provision of services through subsidiary departments. To some extent all markets for health services are managed and this management influences the answers to our key economic questions:

1. What goods and services to produce?
2. How to produce goods and services?
3. Who receives the goods and services?

The pattern of health services in a particular country cannot be accounted for simply in terms of the policies of current governments. While the USA appears to yearn for some aspects of the UK's NHS, the UK government appears to value the incentives for efficiency which it associates with the market. Both governments are constrained by public opinion, political process, views about what is feasible within pluralist economies, the position of opposition parties, professional associations and the media which must be accommodated alongside broad requirements for fiscal and macro-economic management. It follows that changes, while trumpeted as transformations in the interests of patients, tend to be incremental and sometimes questionable in the benefits achieved for patients or communities (Lindblom, 1959).

The purpose of this chapter is threefold:

▓ To provide a broad classification of the main types of health service financing, their advantages and drawbacks.
▓ To examine how the three forms of financing influence particular answers to the three economic questions.
▓ To outline the key components of recent health reforms and to identify some of their likely impacts.

13.1 ▓ Patterns of health service financing

In answer to the question 'Who pays for health care services?', the answer is usually that there are a variety of payers and it depends upon which services are being considered. A simple classification of health services would include:

▓ Public/environmental health.
▓ Ambulatory services.
▓ Hospital services.

While public and environmental health services are normally provided by government or its agents at national or local level, ambulatory and hospital services can be provided by public employees or private sector organizations. Private organizations may pursue profits or be constituted on a not-for-profit or charitable basis.

There are three main sources of funds for health services: public, private and external. *Public* funds include taxation channelled through Ministries of Health, local taxation through regional or local government, and compulsory health insurance through social security agencies. *Private* funds include direct payments by individuals, payments by private health insurers, payments by employers on behalf of their staff (usually, but not always through insurance schemes), local donations and the results of fundraising activities by providers. *External* sources may include grants from official bodies such as the EU, and grants from other sources such as commercial or charitable organizations.

Direct payment by the recipient at the time of consuming the service is unusual for all but the most minor of services or the most wealthy of individuals. Payment usually takes place through one of six mechanisms:

▓ Direct payment by the consumer.
▓ Payment from funds raised by taxation.
▓ Payment from funds collected by a hypothecated tax.
▓ Payment from a national insurance scheme with some sort of actuarial basis.
▓ Payment from a private insurance scheme.
▓ Payment by an employer either directly or through an insurance scheme.

National health services can be categorized on the basis of the primary source of funds or more often on the pattern or balance of funding. It is instructive to look at the proportion of health care expenditure funded from different sources and also the proportion of the population whose health care is funded by different parties and mechanisms. We shall define insurance mechanisms as those processes where there is a link between a payment made by, or on behalf of, a specific individual and an entitlement to receive specified services if required.

In short there are three main types of health finance:

▓ Tax finance.
▓ Private insurance.
▓ Social insurance.

Tax finance has some useful advantages. The cost of raising the funds is comparatively low and shared with the other activities financed from tax. If tax sources are both local and national some of these scale benefits are diminished. This category includes some schemes of national or social insurance in which there is no link between premium and entitlement. It has proved convenient in some countries, including the UK, to maintain the fiction of national insurance for health to disguise the real levels of taxation. This may backfire if large numbers of people believe that they have the right to publicly provided health care which the state finds increasingly difficult to secure to their satisfaction. Tax finance can be used to provide health services directly through state institutions or by contracting for services with private or 'independent' organizations such as NHS Trusts.

The tax finance basis is thought by economists to create *moral hazard* for consumers and providers. The cost to a patient of a treatment is dramatically reduced and so there is no direct financial pressure on consumers to limit their demands as there might be if they had to pay directly for those services. They might adopt unhealthy lifestyles which are more likely to result in subsequent needs for treatment than might be the case if there were no safety net. They might simply overuse the service by attending their GP for trivial conditions which they would ignore or treat themselves in other circumstances. Providers may have little sense of the costs of the treatments and services they provide and may not have a proper sense of economy in their use of public money. They may induce demand in the sense that the receipt of fees for services provides an incentive to provide more of that particular service. They might also be tempted, perversely, to exaggerate the short-comings of their services and facilities as a ploy to obtain higher levels of state funding. Many of the recent reforms might be seen as attempts to reduce the risk of moral hazard.

The tax system depends on GPs to sort out demand, distinguishing relatively serious conditions from trivial conditions and allocating resources appropriately through treatment or referral. The tax system may act as a redistribution system channelling funds from the healthy to the sick, or from those with means to those with needs. This does depend on the characteristics of the tax system which might have progressive elements such as income tax, proportional elements such as national insurance, and regressive elements such as VAT. There is no danger of *adverse selection* since all citizens are covered and payments are not related to risk. A public tax-based system does not imply that service provision will necessarily be undertaken by public enterprises. It is quite common for publicly financed purchasers to contract with private, voluntary or charitable providers.

Private Insurance is actuarially based in that there is a clear link between payment of a premium and entitlement to services. These services are almost always restricted to a defined level of entitlement although in some cases companies might be persuaded by governments or by market opportunities to take on groups of patients some of whom will have pre-existing conditions making them poor risks in actuarial terms. Private insurers may operate to generate profits or on a not-for-profit basis. Private insurance may provide access to a largely separate system of care in private hospitals or it might provide additional facilities or services above those normally available in a state-run institution. Such top-up benefits might include better quality 'hotel services' or compensation for lost income while incapacitated. The limited entitlement may mean that unfortunate, or underinsured, individuals exhaust their entitlement and are then dependent on other sources of funds. In some cases insurance such as medigap insurance will be offered and taken up against co-payments which are not reimbursed by the insurer. This rather destroys the point of co-payments to which we shall return later. Individuals may fail to insure, choose to underinsure because they have other priorities such as buying a house, or be forced by low income to underinsure. This creates problems for individuals and is often regarded as a social problem requiring some form of safety net.

Governments may offer tax relief for payment of insurance premiums as in the case of UK senior citizens or as in the US case of employers who contribute to insurance programmes. This can have a range of intended and unintended economic and social effects. As we saw in Chapter 4, the system of third party payments has the effect of increasing demand, pushing up prices and generating an inefficient allocation of resources.

Social Insurance is where the state acts as the insurer and insists that its citizens take out a minimum level of insurance through a central agency or through a series of insurance companies or sick funds which act as an agent of the state. These companies or funds often have their roots in Trade Unions, occupational, regional, or religious groupings. The government may decree that all members of the population be insured or it may restrict its requirement to low-income or high-risk groups, essentially those who might be unwilling or unable to finance what is thought to be an 'appropriate' level of health care.

13.2 ▓ National patterns of health care

In this section we have identified a series of health care systems from Europe and America chosen to illustrate the basic choices open to countries and their citizens in the financing of health care and to point to some of the implications of their choices.

Tax finance

The National Health Service in the UK provides 100% coverage of the population through a service financed by general taxation and National Insurance contributions. The service is largely free at the point of need and there are few charges apart from prescription charges for pharmaceuticals and appliances and charges for optical services such as sight tests. These charges are not levied on those with low incomes, the elderly, children, pregnant women, or the chronically sick.

Parliament votes a sum of money on an annual basis to the NHS in competition with other government departments. This is then allocated using a capitation system to local health authorities who contract for services from autonomous, but largely public, NHS Trust hospitals and community health services. Access to secondary health care is controlled by gatekeeper general practitioners who practise in groups with a family medicine orientation. There is no direct access to specialist health care apart from the accident and emergency department of the local hospital. Private health insurance is limited to 10% of the population (Fitzhugh, 1989) who often share the costs of premiums with their employers through occupational-based schemes. Private health care is largely limited to elective surgery and provides convenience and a higher standard of hotel facilities than is usually available in the NHS.

General practitioner fundholding schemes now cover more than 50% of the population and are an attempt to increase the range of general practice activity, thus reducing the demands for more expensive secondary care and increasing the number of purchasers in the NHS market and so the incentives for hospitals to increase efficiency and responsiveness. The jury is still out on this bold experiment with early reviews (Glennerster *et al.*, 1994) suggesting positive improvements and later reviews seemingly more critical (Audit Commission, 1996). Undoubtedly the UK spends a comparatively low proportion of its GNP on health care and might be thought to be economic. Questions of efficiency are more complex.

GPs are funded by a combination of a fund for services, a capitation payment based on the list of registered patients, and fees for service payments for special activities.

Compulsory social insurance

The *German system* is perhaps the classic example of social insurance. Insurance premiums are deducted from the payroll and the individual can choose for them to be paid into district, national, or factory insurance funds of which there are about 1,100.

There is a strict separation of inpatient and ambulatory care and hospitals are not permitted to have outpatient departments. Local doctors are largely specialist contrasting with the UK system and they act as gatekeepers to the more expensive hospital services. The insurance funds negotiate with the provider hospitals on a regional basis but the proliferation of funds makes it difficult to exert real purchasing power over the providers.

It might be argued that this is not social insurance at all but a hypothecated payroll tax in which the proceeds are 'ring fenced' for the provision of health care. This permits a greater public influence over the level of expenditure in health care than in the UK system.

However, each fund has to balance its books and so there are significant inequalities in the levels of premiums which relate to the comparative efficiency of funds and also the balance of risk represented by those covered. One fund may have an overrepresentation of the elderly and chronically ill while another may have a high proportion of young and fit members. Also premiums have been rising significantly causing a concern about cost control. Ambulatory care is paid for on a fee-for-service basis which tends to inflate demand for and use of services (supply side moral hazard). Attempts are being made to control hospital costs by the use of global hospital budgets.

Incidentally a lack of central manpower planning has resulted in a serious oversupply of doctors matched by a worrying undersupply of nurses, which suggests something about the limited degree of central planning in this system.

Canada has a highly regarded social insurance system widely seen as a model for its US neighbour. Each province has its own health insurance system and the national government funds 40% of health care costs provided that the insurance system meets a number of key conditions. A provincial health insurance system must provide comprehensive health cover and services to all of its citizens; it must be accessible in the sense that there are no limits on health services or extra charges to patients; it must be portable, enabling all benefits to be received in other provinces; and it must be publicly administered through a public not-for-profit organization. Not surprisingly all 10 provinces have insurance schemes which fit these criteria.

The provincial insurer is the only direct payer for health services, giving it considerable power and also reducing a wide range of administrative costs. There is, for instance, no need to conduct complex tests to check entitlements or eligibility. Hospitals are paid a global budget and do not have to bill separately for services and physicians are paid on a fee-for-service basis. Negotiations take place each year at provincial level to determine a schedule of fees and to agree budgets with providers. Most hospitals are set up on a not-for-profit basis and doctors work in a variety of independent and group settings. Patients are able to choose their doctors and services are free at the point of need. As in the UK the allocation of services depends on the medical definition of relative need and there are a few waiting lists, but this is not a serious problem. A system of provincial technology licensing makes sure that expensive technologies are located in specialist centres and that their diffusion is carefully controlled. This may be seen as having cost control and quality benefits in that patients are not subject to new technologies until they have been tested and doctors have appropriate experience in their use.

The *Netherlands* operates a form of social insurance in which the low and middle incomes (61%) are obliged to pay for health care insurance and the remaining high incomes (39%) choose to pay health care insurance. Both groups receive an employer's contribution and retirement and unemployment funds are required to have a health insurance element to cover those who are not employed. The insurers are obliged to accept all middle- and low-income people regardless of condition or risk, operate as economically as possible, and negotiate the lowest fees and hospital budgets from providers. There are various pool mechanisms for offsetting the potential costs of high-risk patients and a complex system of annual negotiations ensures that there is an agreed set of fees and budgetary rates for all providers.

The GPs act as gatekeepers and there is a minor system of co-payments to try and dampen demand. There is an exceptional medical expenses arrangement operated through the sickness funds and insurers which covers the whole population for long-term care which would go beyond the range of insured entitlements.

The *French* have the most expensive health care system in the EC and their government has been trying to control costs. The cost of ambulatory care is billed direct to the patient who is then reimbursed 75% of the fee in a few days. For the first 30 days in hospital the patient is billed and similarly receives 80% reimbursement, after which the bill is paid direct by the sickness fund. The patient pays a small fee for accommodation while in hospital, charged on a daily basis. Individuals are free to take out supplementary insurance to cover the additional portion of the cost which is not reimbursed.

The social security scheme is largely occupationally based and patients have the right to consult specialists or generalists in the community but must be referred to hospital specialists. The social security fund provides about 74% of funds, mutualist insurance a further 7% and co-payments the remaining 19%.

Private Insurance-based schemes

The *Americans* have the most expensive health care system in the world, if you can call it a system. It is based on the assumption of private insurance taken out by the employed, supported by a vast safety net scheme for the elderly, poor, mentally ill and those who are not insured. The scheme seems to work in that individuals eventually find care, but often this is only after their conditions have deteriorated and care is likely to be more difficult, more expensive, and perhaps less effective.

Approximately 88% are insured through a variety of private and NFP insurers and will have a limited entitlement for health care. This group is likely to experience the best care in the world while their entitlement holds out. Some of this group will prove to be underinsured or will experience health episodes which exhaust their cover, meaning that they have to rely on their own resources, family, or other charitable funds.

The military and veterans have their own high-quality health care system which may make use of military facilities or may contract for care with private hospitals or other health care institutions.

The elderly are covered through a scheme called Medicare in which the costs of their health care are shared between federal and state governments. A similar cost-sharing arrangement applies to the poor, some of whom are covered through the Medicaid scheme. Both of these schemes are designed to enable eligible persons to receive care through the private hospitals rather than being dependent on the local state hospitals or emergency rooms which are frequently underresourced and overcrowded, providing as their name suggests basic health care to those who have no alternative.

The Americans have had the most incentive to try to reduce the cost of care and so many of the cost control mechanisms such as prepayment mechanisms, diagnosis-related groups, global hospital budgets, health maintenance organizations and co-payment mechanisms among others have been attempted and developed in the USA. That none of them have been entirely successful is seen by the very high cost of the US health care system (OECD, 1990, 1995).

13.3 ▓ Financing patterns and the key economic questions

What services should be provided?

The taxation-based system, whether it operates through direct provision or through contracts to purchase services, assumes that the Ministry of Health or its agent will determine the pattern of services on the basis of their view of what the population, and perhaps the economy, needs and the overall level of spending on them. Thus objectives might include to produce a comprehensive health care system or to achieve health gain objectives for a defined population. A social insurance system ensures that earmarked funds are available for the purchase of health care and these are channelled through a variety of independent but regulated sickness funds. In the social insurance scheme there is no direct competition for funds between competing services, e.g. health and education, although government will be concerned about the impact of the level of health premiums on employees and employers since they might be a significant cause of inflationary wage pressure or increasing unit cost of production and potential damage to competitiveness.

The sickness fund will act in a similar fashion to the health authority in the taxation system negotiating with providers in the pursuit of low-cost high-quality services. Social insurance implies some measure of agreement of what constitutes a basic or a comprehensive service and how that can be achieved at minimum premium levels, or in the case of the Netherlands what groups of the population should be obliged to participate in the social insurance scheme. Both taxation-based and social insurance schemes may choose to regulate the introduction of new technologies in an attempt to control costs and to ensure that the public is protected from unproven treatments.

Government regulation may prevent the right of direct access to medical specialists or to hospital treatment by the use of gatekeeping procedures although those who are privately insured are unlikely to be denied. Regulations may also cover the low-income/high-risk groups who may be unable to afford premiums and may be very expensive members.

In private insurance schemes the customer will have a greater influence on the range of services provided, especially if the insurance market is efficient with a large number of providers competing for customers who are able to move from one insurer to another without prohibitive switching costs. It may be that where premium inflation is high, customer pressure will act to reduce the range of services or to increase the significance of co-payments and other mechanisms used to dampen demand and limit the rise in premiums. In the USA it is not uncommon to sign up with an insurer for one year and to review your health insurance on an annual basis.

In all health care systems doctors will have a strong influence on the range of services provided. The combination of technological development, capital diffusion and clinical ambition is a potent driver in the expansion of the range of activities and might be seen as a key source of supplier-induced demand. Linked to this public expectations develop as the media assist in the diffusion of knowledge. The medical profession are seldom backward when it comes to promoting their own activities. The market of insured persons is an important voice which seeks the best available services in return for their premium payment. It might also be argued that these developments often promote the glamorous side of acute medicine at the expense of the less attractive, Cinderella services for the chronically ill and elderly.

How should goods and services be provided?

All countries use legislation and planning mechanisms to control the pattern of health-services provision, the licensing of providers and the development and introduction of new technologies and treatments. Thus legislation may determine whether patients are allowed direct access to specialist or hospital care, or whether they must go through a gatekeeper system such as the local or family doctor. Indeed, governments may decide to treat more patients in primary care settings and fewer in hospital settings, thus moving towards a primary care-led service. The precise powers of different health care professions are circumscribed so that nurses have limited powers to prescribe pharmaceuticals and chiropodists limited powers to undertake surgery. Similarly government may have powers to control the development and diffusion of new technologies as is the case in Canada. Thus in all systems there is a considerable infrastructure of regulation, designed to protect the patient, which limits the possibilities for innovation, and constrains the routes by which providers might seek new sources of operational efficiency.

The tax-based, planned health care system uses the technology of bureaucratic planning and rationing to pursue national goals such as the reduction of inequalities in health while the tax-based market system addresses similar objectives but tries to introduce some of the incentives and efficiencies of the market to increase value for money. In practice, much of the specialist expertise lies with the providers and so services may still be described as supply-led rather than planner or purchaser-driven. None the less, government may choose to change the pattern of mental health services and use a combination of policy documents and financial instruments to move from a hospital-based system to a community-based system.

The social insurance system has a longer history of sick funds negotiating with separate provider institutions to provide the best package of care or the most economic services. In the Dutch system the combination of sick funds together with government support provides more purchasing power than is the case in the more fragmented German system which is trying to assist sick funds to act in regional federations. The Canadian system empowers the province as a monopoly purchaser of health services, thus giving it considerable purchaser power.

Both tax-based and social insurance schemes use a variety of payment methods which influence the pattern of services provided. A fee-for-service mechanism will encourage a hospital to provide more of a particular service whereas a global hospital budget will encourage it to look for new sources of efficiencies within its operations. A contract for services will focus attention on the particular activities in question removing any incentive from doing other activities which are not covered and therefore not financed. Co-payment systems will have the effect of dampening demand to the extent that they are significant and cannot be defrayed elsewhere. Pre-payment systems which use diagnostic or hospital-related groups and pay on the basis of the average price of procedures within that group will have an influence on the pattern of care and will need careful policing, since it is quite possible to exploit the difficulties of defining health care procedures unambiguously within a single category.

Private insurers attempt to influence the patterns of entitlements and services in ways which will be attractive to customers and consumers. This includes short waiting times, consultations with named consultants, increased patient choice over admission and related arrangements, known standards of care and related facilities, privacy and other consumer benefits. Since many customers are interested in the price of their premiums, the insurer will be interested in cost control, and other measures to achieve value for money. They will be happy to use a combination of co-payments if they are attractive to customers and reduce the overall level of premium. They may direct insured persons to low cost services such as those provided by health maintenance organizations in the USA, which provide something between a well-equipped general practice and a polyclinic service referring a patient to external specialist services if required.

The pattern of services provided through private insurance schemes will be driven by what the customer is willing to pay, what risks they are willing to take in terms of possible co-payments, what limits to medical entitlements they are willing to bear, and what quality of service such as reputation of staff and institutions they require.

For the provider the competitive pressures are real and so low-cost or high-value sources of differentiation are important. Some providers will compete on the basis of quality, facilities and excellence, which is sometimes referred to as competing on the basis of amenities, while others will compete on the basis of value for money, offering low cost or tailored solutions to the needs of particular groups of patients.

Who should receive goods and services?

In a tax-based system, whether services are planned or contracted, services are allocated on the basis of medical definitions of need and clinical priority. It is assumed that all citizens are entitled to treatment and so, apart from a few exceptions, entitlement or ability to pay does not have to be established beforehand. As noted above there is no accepted mechanism for deciding between mental health services for adults or paediatric services, although it is possible to set objectives for incremental changes in the pattern of expenditure through new money or marginal redistribution of existing funds. It is generally assumed that services provided will be of proven value and not experimental or subject to evaluation. Government, or its agents, may decide eligibility criteria for the care of the elderly, especially if the population is ageing and this group represents a growing source of demand for long-term care or expensive services.

In a social insurance system it is important to establish entitlement through sick fund membership, although that entitlement may be to a broad range of services and there may be few restrictions or little chance of that entitlement being exhausted. In some schemes all risk categories will be covered, while in others those with known or expensive conditions will be covered by a safety net such as exceptional needs funds.

A private insurance scheme will normally have clear limitations as to individual entitlements and these will need to be established at the beginning of a sickness episode. The provider will need adequate information systems so that charging can reflect the use of services and entitlement can be monitored. The insurer will also require mechanisms to ensure that provider charges are reasonable, services rendered were appropriate and that the services received were the most cost effective for a particular patient. It may also be necessary to take financial guarantees from the patient to cover any uninsured costs which are incurred.

Frequently, private hospitals will provide care for uninsured emergency patients until they are stable and can be moved to a state or charitable hospital. They will not thank the ambulance service which delivers an uninsured person. Thus the uninsured may receive low-cost services while the insured receive more expensive services.

While in some systems we will see evidence of redistribution of resources from rich to poor and from healthy to sick, there are important instances where this is reversed and there is no evidence of redistribution. Julian Tudor Hart argued that there was such a thing as an inverse care law, suggesting that in the UK health care was skewed towards those whose need was least and away from those with most needs. He may have over-stated the case yet the concern is well founded (Tudor Hart, 1971).

13.4 ▓ Key objectives of health care reform

Cost control

Health care services are an expensive commodity in any country regardless of who pays. In 1992 the USA spent 14% of its considerable GNP on health care while the UK spent 7.1% of its much smaller GNP. Most developed countries spend between 6–9% of GNP on health care and in many it is a considerable element of government spending. Inflationary drivers include ageing populations, increased use of expensive technologies, wage pressure in what are labour intensive provider organizations, and increasing costs of pharmaceuticals and other supplies. All developed countries have worked hard to control spending on health care using, copying and modifying a variety of methods which have been developed in private, social insurance and public systems.

In the tax-funded system it is possible to cap the total sum of money spent on health care services, although public pressure might make it necessary to identify supplementary funds to deal with unanticipated demand. A good example of such a 'crisis' is the mental health scares in the UK which accompanied the closure of institutions and the publicity arising from a small number of violent incidents in the community. It is also possible through planning mechanisms and capital charging instruments to control the physical growth of resources. Such instruments can, in practice, result in the failure to achieve efficiencies which might result if investment were more flexible. If health services are provided by public employees, it may be possible to restrain wage increases and through manpower planning limit the number of professionals in any particular category.

Cost control in social insurance systems takes place primarily through a purchaser/provider split which uses the power of the sick funds to agree good payment terms with the independent service providers. In Holland this results in national scales of fees and other prices while in Germany the fragmented purchasing system exercises rather less power. Providers are encouraged to compete for business by pursuing quality and efficiency, although this is never likely to be an efficient market in which new entrants can challenge existing practices and win market share from large established institutions. There is more scope for competition in the ambulatory and general practice areas in which entry costs are lower, there are a larger number of small providers, technology requirements are less and flexibility comparatively greater.

Cost control has been attempted through a number of policy approaches:

1. Increasing customer power in health care markets, making agents more powerful particularly through the role of gatekeeper to more expensive services.
2. Introducing a measure of competition between providers in public health care systems in an attempt to achieve efficiency.
3. Allowing public providers more autonomy to be innovative in their operational processes.
4. Introducing new payment and information systems which change the pattern of incentives for providers, such as

   ▓ Global hospital budgets – focusing on most expensive elements of care.
   ▓ DRG/HRG prospective payment systems.
   ▓ Prospective contracts rather than retrospective reimbursement.

5. Introducing co-payment, co-insurance or deductible systems which attempt to dampen demand for services.

Equity

A second characteristic of health care reforms is the pursuit of equity or the reduction of inequality in the allocation of services or even in health status.

The first objective of this reform is to ensure that there is 100% coverage of the population for a basic package of services. OECD data show that this is largely achieved for its members apart from a worryingly large number of uninsured persons in the USA.

A tax-based system is able to use weighted capitation payments as a means of ensuring that the level of services secured in different localities is not unequal due to a different funding base. For instance, a financial allocation based on the historical location of hospitals might favour wealthy, metropolitan districts as against poorer, rural districts. A social insurance scheme can ensure minimum levels of coverage for the population but fragmented systems of sick funds may imply very significant variations in either premium levels or alternatively levels of service.

The quality of services and therefore geographical equity also depends on the level of capital investment and the efficiency with which capital assets are managed. In some countries there has been pressure to outsource components of services in order to permit more effective management of specialist activities. This has started with hotel and transport services and is beginning to impact on more central activities such as nursing services. In others, attempts have been made to increase the quality of management as a means of improving value for money.

Provider efficiency

A third characteristic is the pursuit of micro-economic efficiency within the provider systems.

Undoubtedly many of the cost control measures indicated above attempt to increase micro-efficiency and hopefully control costs. Unfortunately, it is possible to increase micro-efficiency and to increase costs at the same time since a more efficient supply system may identify more needs and undertake more work. Additional crude attempts to cut costs may penalize the efficient provider along with the less efficient provider, thus removing incentives for efficiency. A global budget irrespective of workload may penalize efficient providers and 'featherbed' inefficient ones.

Perhaps the most important development is the switch from retrospective reimbursement to prospective payment systems using the mechanisms of DRG/HRGs, contracts, pre-payment organizations, global budgets and fixed fund arrangements. This implies that there is a switch in initiative from the provider who undertakes the work and then submits a reasonable bill, to the purchaser who defines what is needed in advance and then pays the agreed charge. The empowerment of purchasers requires a change in the asymmetric nature of knowledge and information systems from the domination of powerful suppliers to the emergence of powerful and informed purchasers.

The use of competition among purchasers and providers is thought to be a way of increasing efficiency, but it is important to take due account of both transitional costs as well as transfer costs which are necessary to make more complex systems work efficiently. For instance, there is a view that the NHS would be more efficient and these costs would be reduced if the requirement that all contracts be negotiated annually were to be removed. It is of course possible that this would reduce many of the incentives for provider efficiency. Purchaser competition may require providers to be more responsive in developing their services but it may also result in significant increases in management costs and other transfer costs.

Both HMOs and GP fundholders attempt to provide incentives for clinicians to manage services using their particular knowledge to provide or buy in services as required. Such clinicians require incentives to take on the administrative chores and the fragmentation of purchasing may limit buying power. It may be that there will be a reluctance to refer to more expensive forms of care since the costs will be readily apparent. It is very hard to disentangle the increase in efficiency of such financial arrangements from the particular characteristics of the practices concerned. Of course HMOs and GP practices may compete as small integrated structures bringing in many of the benefits of small flexible organizations, particularly when they are able to integrate the more common forms of specialist services on an ambulatory basis.

A further form of efficiency is to stop doing things that are not effective and this is seen in the evidence-based medicine developments, the use of limited lists of pharmaceutical products on institutional and national bases, the exclusion of doubtful procedures by purchasers or insurers, and developments such as the Oregon limited list discussed elsewhere. This does involve expenditure in research evaluations and in the dissemination of the results so that practitioners can make sound judgements.

Appendix ▓ Health financing

Levels of health expenditure

Figure 13.1 shows total health expenditure as a percentage of GDP for 1980–1993. The USA with its private health insurance-based system spends a much larger proportion of its GDP on health care than the social insurance-based schemes of Germany, France, the Netherlands and Canada, which in turn spend more of their GDP on health than the UK, with its largely tax-based system.

Increasing health expenditure/cost control comparisons

Figure 13.2 compares the growth in health expenditure per capita in the six countries compared in Figure 13.1. The expenditure is measured at 1990 prices to remove the effects of general price inflation, and since growth is the variable of interest here, the countries have been given a common index of 1980 (the base year). It can be seen that expenditure per capita has grown the most in France, by 70%, compared with about 30% in the USA and 20% in the UK.

Source: OECD Health Data.

Note: The OECD Health Data database contains comprehensive statistics with annual data on many aspects of health systems in the OECD countries.

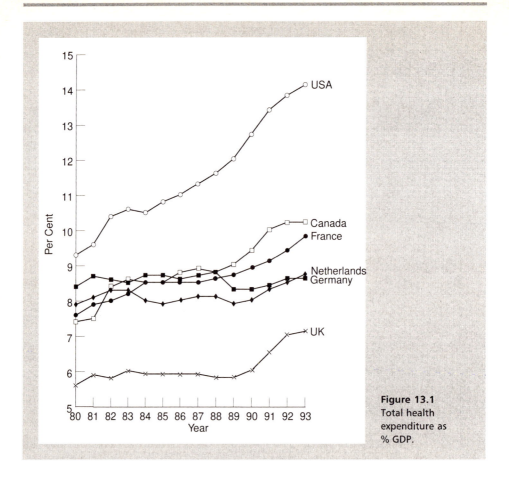

Figure 13.1 Total health expenditure as % GDP.

References

Audit Commission (1996) *What the Doctor Ordered: A Review of GP Fundholding in England and Wales*, HMSO, London.

Donaldson, C. and Gerard, K. (1993) *Economics of Health Care: The Visible Hand*, Macmillan, Basingstoke and London

Eastaugh, S. R. (1987) *Financing Health Care: Efficiency Equity*, Auburn House Publishing Group, Dover, MA.

The Fitzhugh Directory of Independent Hospitals and Provider Associations (1989) Health Care Information Services, London.

Flynn, N. and Strehl, F. (1996) *Public Sector Management in Europe*, Prentice Hall, Hemel Hempstead.

Glennerster, H., Matsaganis, M., Owens, P. and Hancock, S. (1994) 'GP Fundholding: Wild Card or Winning Hand?', in Robinson, R. and LeGrand, J. (eds), *Evaluating the NHS Reforms*, King's Fund Institute, Newbury.

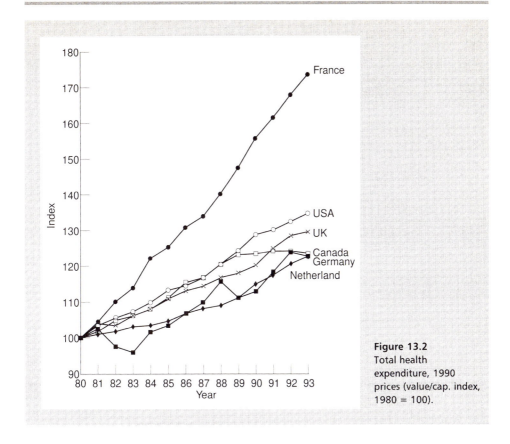

Figure 13.2
Total health
expenditure, 1990
prices (value/cap. index,
1980 = 100).

Lindblom, C. E. (1959) 'The Science of Muddling Through', *Public Administration Review*, 9, pp. 70–88.

Marmor, T. R. (1993) 'Health Care Reform in the United States: Patterns of Fact and Fiction in the Use of the Canadian Experience', *American Review of Canadian Studies*, 23 (1), pp. 47–64.

OECD (1990) *Health Care Systems in Transition: The Search for Efficiency*, OECD, Paris.

OECD (1995) *New Directions in Health Care Policy*, OECD, Paris.

Rackich, J. S., Longest, B. B. and Darr, K. (1992) *Managing Health Services Organizations*, Health Professionals' Press, Baltimore.

Seedhouse, D. (ed.) (1995) *Reforming Health Care: The Philosophy and Practice of International Health Reform*, Wiley, Chichester.

Tudor Hart, J. (1971) 'The Inverse Care Law', *The Lancet*, 1.

Review questions

1. The introduction of the internal market in the NHS created a great deal of controversy. What were the economic arguments underlying these reforms? What criteria could have been used to judge whether or not the reforms were successful?
2. What are the competitive conditions necessary for efficiency amongst producers? Why is it thought that these conditions are absent in the hospital sector? Explain how competitive forces in the hospital sector might lead to excess capacity and increases in costs.
3. How do health economists approach the problem of measuring improvements in the quality of life. What difficulties do they face?
4. What economic techniques can be used to aid health service decision-makers in making difficult choices about priorities?
5. Explain what is meant by the terms:

   (i) merit good
   (ii) externality

   Using examples, explain the relevance of these concepts to decisions about methods of financing and delivering health care services.
6. Discuss the view that the demand for health care can be analysed in the same way as the demand for any other good or service.
7. 'When you get down to it, there are two fundamental health care choices,' said Mr Bush (then the US president). 'We can adopt a system that has been a proven failure all over the world, nationalised health care. Or we can reform the present system, which has its faults, certainly, but which can also provide the highest-quality care on earth.' (*The Times*, 7 February 1992).
   (a) Compare the systems of finance and delivery of health care in the USA and the UK.
   (b) By what criteria might one judge whether a nationalized health care system is a failure?

Index

Activities of daily living, 153
Adams, D., 6
adverse selection, 131, 185
agency relationship, 10, 52, 132, 143, 147–8, 185
allocation of indirect costs, 87
Appleby, J., 35, 129
asset specificity, 135
Audit Commission, 27, 33, 102, 186

Barber–Johnson diagram, 38
Baumol, W.J., 143–4
Beecham, J., Knapp, M. and Fenyo, A., 104
benefit–cost ratio, 252
Bergner, M. *et al.*, 154
bounded rationality, 134
Bowling, A., 21, 162
Brooks, R. G., 160
Brown, M. C., 72
budget lines, 118
BUPA, 59
Buxton, M., 178

Calman, K.C., 161
certainty equivalent, 175
clinical effectiveness initiative, 27
Cochrane Centre, 28
compensating variation, 172
consumers' surplus, 172
contract
    block, 41, 53, 137–9

cost and volume, 137–9
cost per case, 137–9
cost-plus, 136
fixed price, 136
cost, 85–104
    average fixed, 89, 91, 95
    average total, 88–9, 91, 95
    average variable, 89, 91–3, 95, 99
    direct, 87–8, 99
    fixed, 85, 87–90, 95, 98–9, 103
    historical, 103
    incremental, 103
    indirect, 87–8, 99
    long-run average, 100
    marginal, 75, 88–95, 98–9, 107, 110, 114, 123–4, 147, 158, 179
    opportunity, 17, 20–1, 99, 108, 124, 169–71
    semi-variable, 86
    sunk, 103
    total, 88–90, 95
    total fixed, 88. 95
    total variable, 88, 95
    variable, 86–7, 90, 92, 97, 102
cost control in healthcare, 187, 189, 191–5
cost function, 104
cost–benefit analysis, 152, 170, 173
cost-effectiveness analysis, 170
cost-effectiveness index, 177
cost-minimization analysis, 170
cost-utility analysis, 170, 177

cost-weighted activity index, 34
countervailing power, 126, 130
cream-skimming, 131
Cullis, J. G. and West, P. A., 81, 104
Culyer, A. and Posnett, J. W., 140
Cyert, R. M. and March, J. G., 144

Davies, B. P., 29, 30
Davies, B. P. and Knapp, M., 72
Dawson, D., 86–7, 122
Day, C., 37
demand, 42–59
    and income, 45–6
    and population, 49
    and price, 44–5
    and prices of other goods, 47
    and tastes, 49
    complements, 47–8
    derived, 43
    excess, 62–3, 65, 67–9, 127
    for health, 7, 43
    for health care, 7, 43, 52–3
    substitutes, 47
dimensions of transactions, 135
diminishing marginal returns, 74–5, 83,
    112, 158
diminishing marginal utility, 44
discount rate, 167–8, 174, 176–7
discounting, 166–7, 170, 173
diseconomies of scale, 100–1, 159
Donaldson, C. and Gerard, K., 26
Drummond, M., 177

economic appraisal, 10, 18, 21, 166,
    169–71, 176–7
economic evaluation. See economic
    appraisal
economies of scale, 100–2, 104, 130, 148,
    159
economies of scope, 102, 130
economy, 8, 9, 11, 36
effectiveness, 8, 9, 27–8, 34, 36, 53, 150
efficiency, 8, 9, 18, 21, 25–37, 73, 194
    allocative, 29, 37
    and effectiveness, 27
    and externalities, 31
    and marginal analysis, 108
    and quasi-markets, 184, 189

and value for money, 36
cost, 26, 32–3, 37, 170
horizontal target, 46, 47, 57, 58
in health care systems, 32, 34
of contracting, 136
operational, 26, 37
output mix, 30
Pareto, 29, 37
productive, 26–7, 29, 36
social, 29, 37, 171
technical, 26, 29, 34, 36, 170
vertical target, 29, 30, 36–7
elasticity, 53–8
    cross price elasticity of demand, 56
    E_p and revenue, 56
    factors affecting E_p, 55
    income elasticity of demand, 57
    price elasticity of demand, 54–5, 98, 125
    price elasticity of supply, 57–8
Ellis, R. P. and McGuire, T. G., 136, 147
Ellwood, S., 99, 138
Enthoven, A. C., 12
equality, 9
equity, 4, 9, 29, 32, 128, 171, 176, 193–4
    horizontal, 9
    vertical, 9
ethics, 10, 161
Evans, J. R., 26
expected value, 174–5
externalities, 31–2, 37, 44, 108–9, 133,
    151, 161, 170–1, 177

financial analysis, 166–8, 170–1, 177
Frater, A., 8, 28, 150
Friedman, M. and Friedman, R., 4

Glaxo Wellcome, 55
Glynn, J. J. and Perkins, D. A., 16
Glynn, J. J., Perkins, D. A. and Stewart, S., 9,
    28, 151
GP fundholders, 2, 40, 47, 52, 90, 128, 131,
    139
Gray, A. G. and Jenkins, W. I., 16
Grimley Evans, Professor J., 20, 156
Grossman, M., 7

Hamel, G. and Prahalad, C. K., 16
Hanslukwa, H. E., 6

Harris, J. E., 146
health
  and health care, 5
  definitions, 8
health care financing, 182–93
  private insurance, 184–5, 188–92
  social insurance, 184–7, 191, 193
  taxation, 184–6, 189–91
health gain, 8, 19–21, 29, 34, 36, 53, 189,
  195
Health Maintenance Organizations, 131,
  189, 191
health profiles, 154
  Nottingham Health Profile, 154
  Sickness Impact Profile, 154
heart transplant programme, 178
Heather, K., 26
hierarchies, 133–4
Hirschman-Herfindahl Index, 129
Hodgson, K. and Hoile, R. W., 136
hospital objectives, 144–8
human capital, 16, 135
Hunter, D., 19, 156

impact, 28
inferior goods, 46, 57
internal market. 1, 11, 18, 25, 32, 69, 120,
  133, 136–8
  Also see quasi market.
internal rate of return, 168, 177
investment, 43, 166, 194
isoquant, 76–7, 79, 116–18

Knapp, M. and Beecham, J., 104

Lawton, M. P. and Brody, E. M., 153
Lee, M. L., 145
Le Grand, J. and Bartlett, W., 127
Leigh, J. P., 68
length of stay, 33–4, 37–8, 51, 102, 178
Lindblom, C. E., 156, 183
long run, 76, 99, 100, 124

Mahoney, F. I. and Barthel, D. W., 228
March, J. G. and Simon, H. A., 195
marginal analysis, 107–19
  and efficiency, 108
  and employment, 112

  and isoquants, 116
  and optimal combination of inputs, 117
  and output maximization, 114
  and profit maximization, 113
  and revenue maximization, 111
marginal cost. *See* cost, marginal
marginal private benefit, 44, 109
marginal rate of technical substitution, 116
marginal revenue product, 112–13
marginal social benefit, 44, 108, 111
marginal social cost, 108
marginal utility, 44
market
  barriers to entry and exit, 122–5, 127,
    130
  clearing, 61, 63, 65, 99
  equilibrium, 61–2, 65–7
  measures of concentration, 129
market failure, 128–32, 171
market structures, 121–7
  bilateral monopoly, 126
  dimensions of, 122
  monopolistic competition, 125
  monopoly, 124–5
  monopsony, 125
  oligopoly, 127, 143
  perfect competition, 122–3, 170
markup pricing, 98
MacKerrell, D. K. D., 87–8, 99
Marris, R. L., 143–4
Maynard, A., 79, 158
McEwan, J., 154
McGuire, A., Fenn, P. and Mayhew, K, 164
McGuire, A., Henderson, J. and Mooney,
  G., 10, 26, 31, 171
McKeown, T., 7
measures of bed utilization, 33–4, 37–8
measures of health status, 153
  clinical measures, 153
  functional measures, 153
Medicaid, 18–9, 189
Medicare, 18, 189
merit goods, 43
minimum efficient scale, 100
models of hospital behaviour, 144–8
Mooney, G., 4, 6, 7, 9, 10, 152
moral hazard, 132, 184, 187
Morrissey, M., 146

National Audit Office, 9, 36
National Health Service, 1, 11, 63, 69, 186
National Health Service Management
    Executive, 138
net benefit investment ratio, 168
net present value, 144, 167–8, 177
Newhouse, J. P., 144–5
NHS Centre for Reviews and Dissemination,
    28
normative economics, 3

objectives of firms, 142–4
occupancy rate, 33–4, 37–8, 66
opportunism, 135
optimum percentage markup on marginal
    cost, 98
option benefits, 31
Oregon, 18, 56, 159
output
    intermediate, 27, 34, 36, 79, 81
    measurement of in healthcare, 81, 104

partnership, 148
Pauly, M. and Redisch, M., 212
Perkins, F., 169
Pollitt, C., 34
positive economics, 3
present value, 167–8, 173
price
    determination of, 60–9
    effect of restrictions, 62–5
    equilibrium, 61–2, 65–7
    imposition of maximum, 62
    imposition of minimum, 65
    market clearing, 61, 63, 65, 99
    mechanism, 67
    mechanism in healthcare, 68
product
    average, 73, 75, 82–3
    marginal, 73–5, 77, 82–3, 112–13,
        116–17, 119
production, 71–84
production function, 71–3, 76, 80–2
productivity, 72–3
profit, 16, 49, 113–15
Propper, C., 136

QALY, 19, 156–60, 170, 177

quality-adjusted life years. *See* QALY
quasi-market, 1, 120, 122, 127–8, 130–3,
    171

rationing, 11, 18, 21, 62, 158, 161–2, 190
reliability, 150
returns to scale, 80
    constant, 80, 83, 89
    decreasing, 81, 100
    increasing, 80, 100
revenue
    average, 111
    marginal, 111–14, 123–4
    total, 56, 111, 114
Richardson, G. and Maynard, A., 119
risk, 174–6
Roberts, C., 41
Rosser, R. M. and Kind, P., 19, 157

scales of measurement, 151
    cardinal, 152
    ordinal, 152
Scheffler, R. M., 131
Seng, C., Lessof, L. and McKee, M., 35
sensitivity analysis, 174, 176–7
Sheldon, T., Ferguson, B. and Posnett, J. W.,
    40, 101
short run, 73–6, 90–1
short-run cost curves, 89
Siegler, M., 161
sole practitioner, 147–8
substitutability of inputs, 76
skill mix, 78–9
supplier-induced demand, 191
supply, 49–51
    and cost of factors of production, 51
    and price, 50
    and prices o other goods, 50
    excess, 61–2, 65–6, 68
Szczepura, A., 170

Teeling Smith, G., 93, 170
Thorpe, K. E. and Phelps, C. E., 147
throughput, 26, 33, 37–8
transaction cost economics, 134
transaction costs, 134–5, 138
Tudor Hart, J., 192
turnover interval, 33, 37–8

Twaddle, A. C., 6

UK Outcomes Clearing House, 28
uncertainty, 132, 135, 174, 176

validity, 150
value for money, 9, 36, 151
value-judgements, 3, 151, 155, 171

Walsh, K., 32, 136
Wilkin, D., Hallam, L. and Doggett, M. A.,
    153
Williams, A., 178
Williamson, O. E., 135, 143–5
World Health Organization, 24

Zantac, 55
Zechhauser, R. and Eliastam, M., 72